*To Destroy Painting*

# Louis Marin

# *To Destroy Painting*

Translated by *Mette Hjort*

The University of Chicago Press • *Chicago and London*

Louis Marin (1931–1992) was director of studies at the École des Hautes Études en Sciences Sociales in Paris. His books in English include *The Semiotics of the Passion Narratives* (1980), *Portrait of the King* (1988), *Food for Thought* (1989), and *Utopics* (1990).

The University of Chicago Press, Chicago 60637
The University of Chicago Press, Ltd., London
© 1995 by The University of Chicago
All rights reserved. Published 1995
Printed in the United States of America

03 02 01 00 99 98 97 96 95   1 2 3 4 5

ISBN: 0-226-50534-0 (cloth)
          0-226-50535-9 (paper)

Library of Congress Cataloging-in-Publication Data

Marin, Louis, 1931–
    [Détruire la peinture. English]
    To destroy painting / Louis Marin ; translated by Mette Hjort.
        p.    cm.
    Includes bibliographical references and index.
    1. Painting—Philosophy.   2. Semiotics.   3. Poussin, Nicolas,
1594?–1665—Criticism and interpretation.   4. Caravaggio,
Michelangelo Merisi da, 1573–1610—Criticism and interpretation.
I. Title.
ND1140.M3413   1995
750′.1—dc20                                                    94-20786

Originally published as *Détruire la peinture*
© Éditions Galilée, Paris 1977.

*For Anne*

# Contents

# Acknowledgments

In some portions of this text I have revived, at times in substantially modified form, parts of analyses originally published in my *Critique du Discours, Études sur la Logique de Port-Royal et les Pensées de Pascal*, in "La lecture du tableau d'après Poussin," and in "À propos d'un carton de Le Brun: le tableau d'histoire ou la dénégation de l'énonciation."* More generally, the main points made in this study emerged in the course of a series of seminars held in January and March, 1976, in the art history department at the University of Montreal. I would like to express my deepest gratitude to those who participated in these seminars and whose collective efforts helped to develop some of the themes, hypotheses, and terms of this work.

## Translator's Acknowledgments

I am grateful to my research assistant, Brian Lynch, who spent several months painstakingly tracking down bibliographical information that Louis Marin was unable to provide due to a fatal illness. I could not have completed this translation without Brian's help. Grants from the Social Sciences and Humanities Research Council of Canada and the Fonds pour la Formation de Chercheurs et l'Aide à la Recherche made it possible for Brian to work on this project.

*Louis Marin, *Critique du Discourse, Études sur la Logique de Port-Royal et les Pensées de Pascal* (Paris: Minuit, 1975); "La lecture du tableau d'après Poussin," *Cahiers de l'Association Internationale des Études Françaises* 24 (May 1972): 251–66; "À propos d'un carton de Le Brun: le tableau d'histoire ou la dénégation de l'énonciation," *Revue des Sciences Humaines* 157 (1975): 41–64.

# Postscript in the Guise of an Introduction

June 12, 1977

The text that you will read—and that I have just finished writing—traces a trajectory between two paintings, Poussin's *Arcadian Shepherds* (*Et in Arcadia Ego*) and Caravaggio's *Head of Medusa*, between the Louvre and the Uffizi. Mapping this road has taken some ten to fifteen years, and the journey has yet to be completed.

I certainly do not want to suggest that Caravaggio's painting marks the end of an itinerary that somehow starts with Poussin, for I could have invoked the relevant paintings in exactly the opposite order. I could have started somewhere in the middle and gone on to explore first in one direction and then in another, or I could have started near the beginning, with *The Israelites Gathering Manna in the Desert*, and ended near the end, in Rome's Church of San Luigi dei Francesi, with *The Calling of Saint Matthew*.

My text is also a journey through paintings, some of which are referred to by title—sometimes only by title—and some of which are not even explicitly mentioned. It is not only a matter of exploring these paintings through discourse written in the here and now, but of relying on my notes, scribblings, charts, and sketches from visits to museums, galleries, and libraries some time last year, or even ten or fifteen years ago. This text explores painting by opening up a conversation with the image, to use the phrase coined by Hubert Damisch with reference precisely to Caravaggio (and Poussin).

*Transverto*, i, sum, ere, tr., (1) turn toward, change into, transform (Apuleius, *Apologia sive de Magia*); (2) to divert (Arnobius).[1]

This text transforms painting into discourse, diverts images into language. What we are dealing with here is a kind of magic or rhetoric that constantly runs the risk of turning what can be *seen* by all into purely private language, into what a single individual says to himself. At the end of the day, I realize that if this text raises questions even about itself, it does so only about the nature of this transformation, detour, and risk, "enough to annoy the most benevolent reader," as Stendhal wrote in *La vie de Henri Brulard*. This text, if you wish, is autobiographical, but in the sense specified by Benveniste, that is, an enunciation written by *me* and by my *self* or *ego*. I (too) am in Arcadia (itself), even if, in the final analysis and in the depths of the tomb, there is only *this* (*hoc*).

In writing this text I had certain things in mind, but I suspect that the finished product departs quite radically from my initial intentions. I hoped to transcribe the strange murmuring inside my head, inside your head, as you or I look at paintings, the "noise" that conveys a piece of a poem, a fragment of a story, a chunk from an article, an incomplete reference, the echo of a conversation, or a sudden memory. I wanted to capture the noise that exists only to soften the pain that is an integral part of the pleasure (or thrill [*jouissance*]) of mutely seeing forms and colors gathered on a canvas. Put differently, I wanted to articulate the almost retinal, "visual noise" experienced by my eyes when I look at paintings and suddenly fall prey to the murmur of language just described, the murmur that convokes a new image, causing it to penetrate and disturb the one seen here and now. My narrative seeks the phantasms and exploding, starry constellations witnessed when pressure is applied to the eyelids, when the eye, in spite of the darkness, sees its own brilliance.

In order to transcribe this noise and to make it *legible*, it was necessary to make a number of detours, to have recourse to the procedures and instruments of reading and writing: digressions, anacoluthons, parataxes, and asyndetons. An entire arsenal of ruses and tricks is needed if discourse is to explore painting. Or, for that matter, if paintings are to explore discourse, to explore discursive positions and various instances of displaced and partially incoherent knowledge. For my text began its journey long ago. So be it . . .

I have finished. Let us begin.

# Key Texts

Let us consider a statement by André Félibien: "Poussin could not bear Caravaggio and said that he had come into the world in order *to destroy painting.*"[1] This destruction of painting is essentially the sole subject of this book. It will be a matter here of considering the fate of painting through the unrelenting confrontation between two painters, a confrontation fueled by the hatred of Poussin, the great Master, for the painter who preceded him in the history of painting.

> Yet his aversion for Caravaggio is not surprising. For whereas Poussin sought to foreground the nobility of his subjects, Caravaggio allowed himself to be carried away by the truth of nature as it appeared to him. Their approaches were thus diametrically opposed to one another.[2]

Fatal destruction, fatal confrontation. Destiny is played out as Poussin seeks and Caravaggio allows himself to be carried away. The choice is between nobility and truth, between the subject and what is natural. Above all, however, the conflict is between theory and contemplation on the one hand, the gaze and sight on the other.

"However. . . ." Here comes the contradiction. Or perhaps what I take to be a contradiction is in fact merely a momentary hesitation or a passing regret. It may also be linked to the paradox of representation in and through painting. Indeed, what is articulated here may well be the paradox of painting itself: "However, if one focuses in particular on what the Art of painting consists of, it will soon become clear that Michelangelo da Caravaggio mastered this art completely."[3] Poussin, the Master, thus recognizes another Master, a Master, however, who has come into the world in order to destroy the very art that he masters so completely, "the art of imitating what appears before the eyes."

Later, a few months before his death in 1665, Poussin echoes this conception as he provides commentators with an enigmatic definition of a painted work of art: "an imitation made on a surface with lines and colors of everything that one sees under the sun."[4]

Art itself, it appears, is a kind of "echo," for it is essentially the *same* as the thing it depicts, an *imitation.* Yet it is also wholly different from the represented thing. On the one hand, we have the dominating sun that makes visible everything beneath it, what can be seen under the sun and what the sun makes visible. On the other hand, we have the eye that encounters and sees what lies before it: the object. Of interest in this context is Poussin's insistence on the surface where certain lines must be drawn before color can be applied. Giovanni Baglione had drawn attention to this issue a few years earlier:

> Some people consider him [Caravaggio] to have been the very ruination of painting, because many young artists, following his example, simply copy heads from life without studying the fundamentals of drawing and the profundity of art and are satisfied with color values alone. Thus they are incapable of putting two figures together or of composing a story because they do not understand the high value of the noble art of painting.[5]

Once again we notice a kind of textual slippage as certain texts begin to displace or even to repeat others. The surface is crucial, says Poussin, the Master. The critic replies that through drawing and art (which art?) the foundation, the ground, and depth are linked to the story and to history. Following one conception, nobility and excellence involve *knowing* how to tell stories, knowing how to tell the story of the dead through images. A quite different approach finds excellence in the ability to paint from life. The choice is between the nobility of the subject and the vitality of the object, between bringing the dead to life—as a story is told through figures that are carefully interwoven within a scene—and simply seeing what appears in the here and now before one's eyes. And yet Poussin, the Master, did use the word "surface."

> If you were to see the portrait that Caravaggio did of the Grand Master of Malta, which is in the King's chambers, you would admit that nothing more beautiful is possible, because, since he had merely to paint a portrait, he was able to imitate Nature so perfectly that he left nothing to be desired.[6]

I want to propose the following idea, which I know to be based on an interpretive error, for I am intentionally reading the discourse of the Master's representative, Félibien, against the grain. Could it be that in telling a story, in reviving the dead through a series of interconnected figures within a given scene, in allowing the viewer of a painting to see what the sun makes visible beneath it, I leave something to be desired? Two quite different injunctions emerge, depending on whether we follow Caravaggio or Poussin. The former enjoins us to look at what appears before the eye at a particular moment, to look at the vitality of the ob-ject as it is conveyed by color alone. What results is a satiation of desire, or, in other words, pleasure. Poussin, however, would have us focus on a worthwhile subject; we are to read the story of the dead as it is narrated in the painting-tomb, which is itself a monument erected to the solar glory of the deceased. Here it is a matter of an excess or lack of pleasure, of a form of intense delectation [*jouissance*].

The Master says: "[The painting's] end is to please [*la délectation*]."[7] The pleasure that the eye takes in the colors and lines that combine on the surface is thus somehow lacking or excessive. Theory, then involves overwhelming beauty that is at once lacking and excessive.

The alternative is to take complete pleasure in a live object, in an object painted from life. "You would admit that nothing more beautiful is possible . . . [and that] he left nothing to be desired," because he had merely to create a portrait, an object. "One cannot say that this painting is not painted with an admirable use of shadow and light, that a fullness and marvelous power do not pervade its parts."[8]

However, Félibien also says the opposite: "There is nothing that a painter must seek more than to make his works agreeable. But this is what Caravaggio never did."[9] There is no agreeable light: "he chose closed spaces in order to have strong light" that would make the illuminated figures stand out.[10]

And yet Félibien also claims that "he [Caravaggio] painted with as learned an understanding of color and light as any painter. . . . It could be said that nature cannot be better imitated than it is in everything he painted."[11]

The Master explains himself: to contemplate is not to see; theory is not the same as the gaze or sight. "It is hardly a natural operation of the eye. It is a judgment, a function of reason governing the entire painting."

But Caravaggio, it is claimed, "had no ideas of his own."

He made himself a slave to nature and not an imitator of beautiful things. He represented only what appeared before his eyes and did so with so little judgment that he neither sought out what was beautiful nor fled what was ugly. Instead he painted both the one and the other.[12]

Karl Van Mander said in 1603:

[Caravaggio] will not do a single brushstroke without close study from life which he copies and paints. Surely this is no wrong way to achieve a good end. For to paint after drawings, even though they be done after life, is in no wise as reliable as facing life and to follow Nature with all her different colors. Yet one should first have reached a degree of insight that would enable one to select and distinguish from the beauty of life that which is most beautiful.[13]

According to the discourse of the Master, theory is not sight and cannot be reduced to *aspects*. Rather, it is a judgment involving a *prospect*. The fundamental condition of possibility of such judgments, then, is the *prospective* governing the entire surface of the canvas, the network or frame that, by constructing depth in and through the surface, builds the story itself, that is, the monument of representation, the noble tomb of the dead.

We realize, then, that notions such as theory, contemplation, *jouissance,* judgment, and the function of reason were merely "prospettiva," that is, technical rules and mechanical procedures—a ruler and compass, or a string stretched from one point to another, a map detailing points of construction, an optical box, or Dürer's device for immobilizing the chin and eyes.

Yet one of the Master's statements gives us pause. It is a strange statement, almost as if he had murmured it to himself on the eve of his death. "Judgment" and its condition of possibility, "prospective," is not a procedure that the painter can learn. "It is the Golden Bough of Virgil, which no one can find or pluck unless he be led to it by Fate."[14]

Fate, then, leads Poussin to pluck Virgil's Golden Bough, just as fate leads Caravaggio to destroy painting. In one case the issue is the fate of theory and of the painting-tomb of history; in the other it is the fate of the eye and its encounter with what is before it. The *dead* are revived in and through representation, producing the *jouissance* associated with an overwhelming beauty. The thing itself, however, is quite simply there, fascinating, *stupefying.*

# Allegory: The Golden Bough
# or the Theory of Mimesis

How does one go about discovering a way into a painting? And why does one even need to comment on a painting if the end envisaged by the painter's action can be achieved simply by experiencing pleasure or *jouissance*? And in commenting on a painting, does one not somehow kill both it and the pleasure or *jouissance* its lines and colors on a surface provoke? This would seem to be the case unless we imagine a substitution of desires, such that what the painting leaves to be desired and the pleasure the painting offers, are replaced by that other kind of desire and pleasure. I am thinking of the desire to know the enigma that opens up the space of desire only to withhold all gratification; the desire to decipher the secret, to identify the letters (or letter) that constitute(s) the formula providing access to the painting; the desire finally to make explicit the discourse whose origin this formula conceals, the longing to transform the pleasure of painting or its *jouissance* into a pleasure or *jouissance* of language.

It is quite possible that this desire to know and decipher the enigma is the only reason or justification for this study. What is sought, perhaps, is the young, golden-leafed branch that conceals the path toward a discourse *of* painting, the ancient bough once plucked by Poussin. It is not a matter of explaining or interpreting a given work, but of indicating the arduous path leading to the sacred portal that was opened for Aeneas by the Sibyl.

> But the god-fearing Aeneas made for the shrine where
> . . . Apollo
> Sits throned on high, and that vasty cave—the deeply-recessed
> Crypt of the awe-inspiring Sibyl, to whom the god gives
> The power to see deep and prophesy what's to come.
> Now they passed into Diana's grove and the gold-roofed temple.[1]

But at what price? Have we reflected adequately on the fact that Poussin, at the moment of death, linked delectation to the fatal Golden Bough described in book 6 of Virgil's *Aeneid*? As Poussin's body was being defeated, so also was his painting, his trembling hands allowing only for an uncertain manipulation of the brush. Have we considered that at that point Poussin was suggesting that theory—because it is overwhelming—has something to do with death?

What is the price of plucking the Golden Bough from the tree? What conditions does Fate place on the bough's being found and plucked? The answer is a double death of representation:

> The story is that Daedalus, when he escaped from Minos,
> Boldly trusting himself to the air on urgent wings,
> An unprecedented mode of travel, went floating northwards
> Until he was lightly hovering above the Cumaean hilltop.
> Here he came first to earth, hung up his apparatus
> Of flight as a thanks-offering to Phoebus, and built a great temple.[2]

In his temple Daedalus then carves out a long theory of figures from the past, thereby weaving together his personal history and his life's horrors; the figures all return, appeased and silenced, harmonious, surrendering themselves readily to his chisel:

> On its door was depicted the death of Androgeos; also the legend
> Of how the Athenians, poor souls, were forced to pay yearly tribute
> With seven of their sons—the scene when the lots had just been drawn.
> Facing this, there's a bas-relief; with Crete rising out of the waves;
> Pasiphae, cruelly fated to lust after a bull,
> And privily covered; the hybrid fruit of that monstrous union—
> The Minotaur, a memento of her unnatural love;
> Here's the insoluble maze constructed by Daedalus;
> Yet, sympathising with Ariadne in her great passion,
> He gives her himself the clue to the maze's deceptive windings,
> And guides with a thread the blind steps of Theseus.[3]

But an impossible representation interrupts the artistic act in a moment of weakness that leaves the painting unfinished. The fall that forever postpones the gratification of desire is traceable to the impotence of the Father of the painting, who cannot represent the death of the Son:

> . . . In the artifact
> Icarus too would have had a prominent place, if his father's
> Grief had allowed: but twice, trying to work the boy's fall
> In gold, did Daedalus' hands fail him.[4]

If, as was suggested above, the viewer is somehow thrown off course while responding to a painting, it is because of this death of representation, which creates a blind spot and obliterates the central moment in the Story. The call back to law and order, the signal for a ritual act, interrupts the contemplation of the represented story.

> . . . They'd have perused
> The sculptured tale right through, but that Achates, who had
> Been sent ahead, turned up with the priestess of Phoebus and Trivia,
> Deiphobe, daughter of Glaucus. She now addressed Aeneas:—
>    This is no time for poring over those works of art.
> Just now you would do best to sacrifice seven bullocks
> That have not been yoked, and as many properly chosen sheep.
>    She addressed Aeneas; and he promptly performing the rites she
> Requested, the priestess summoned them into the lofty temple.[5]

Such is the price of admission to the temple where the Voice may be heard.

> Thus from her sanctum spoke the Cumaean Sibyl, pronouncing
> Riddles that awed them; her voice came booming out of the cavern,
> Wrapping truth in enigma: she was possessed; Apollo
> Controlled her, shaking the reins and twisting the goad in her bosom.[6]

The Hero simply addresses a prayer to her, which, if answered, will allow him to fill in the absent yet central moment of the representation or Story created by Daedalus at the gates of the Temple. The Father of the painting could not possibly have *represented* the dead Son; the request now is that the living Son be allowed to *contemplate* the face of the dead Father, his *double* living in Hell, without dying as a result.

> . . . Maiden, there's nothing
> New or unexpected to me in such trials you prophesy.
> All of them I have forecast, worked out in my mind already.
> I have one request: since here is reputed to be the gateway
> Of the Underworld and the dusky marsh from Acheron's overflow,
> May it befall me to go into my dear father's
> Presence—open the hallowed gates and show me the way!
> Him through the flames, through a thousand pursuing missiles I rescued
> Out of the enemy's midst and bore him away on these shoulders:
> He voyaged with me, enduring sea after sea, enduring
> All menace of sea and storm, weak as he was—great ordeals
> Beyond his strength, exceeding the normal lot of old age.
> Yes, and he himself most earnestly bade me, more than once,
> To come to you here and make this appeal. I pray you, kind one,
> Take pity on father and son. You have the power: it was not

For nothing that Hecate put you in charge of the grove of Avernus.
Orpheus, with only the tuneful strings of a Thracian lyre
To aid him, could conjure forth the ghost of his wife; Pollux,
Who, turn about, shares life and death with his mortal brother,
Constantly comes and goes this way; I need not mention
Theseus or Hercules; I too am descended from great Jove.[7]

At this point the most extraordinary response is proffered: it is easy
to descend into the realms of the dead. What is difficult is to retrace
one's steps, to rise to the light above, beneath the sun:

But if so great your love is, so great your passion to cross
The Stygian waters twice and twice behold black Tartarus,
If your heart is set on this fantastic project,
Here's what you must do first. Concealed in a tree's thick shade
There is a golden bough—gold the leaves and the tough stem—
Held sacred to Proserpine: the whole wood hides this bough
And a dell walls it round as it were in a vault of shadow.
Yet none is allowed to enter the land which earth conceals
Save and until he has plucked that gold-foil bough from the tree.
Fair Proserpine ordains that it should be brought to her
As tribute. When a bough is torn away, another
Gold one grows in its place with leaves of the same metal.
So keep your eyes roving above you, and when you have found the bough
Just pull it out: that branch will come away quite easily
If destiny means you to go; otherwise no amount of
Brute force will get it, nor hard steel avail to hew it away.[8]

The fateful and somber gesture of plucking a bough is then presented as necessarily connected to the erection of a tomb:

Also—and this you know not—the lifeless corpse of a friend
Is lying unburied, a dead thing polluting your whole expedition,
While you are lingering here to inquire about fate's decrees.
Before anything else, you must give it proper burial and make
Sacrifice of black sheep: only when you are thus
Purified, shall you see the Stygian groves and the regions
Not viable to the living.[9]

Virgil's Golden Bough, it turns out, is a form of judgment dispersed
throughout the entire painting:

[The subject matter] should be nobly conceived: not fashioned by man, in order to give the painter free scope for his genius and industry. The subject matter must be chosen so as to be capable to receive treatment of the most excellent form; one should consider first the disposition, then the ornament, the decoration, beauty, grace, vivacity, costume, verisimilitude, and above all, good judgment. These last things depend on the painter and cannot be learned. It is the Golden Bough of Virgil, which no one can find or pluck unless he be led to it by Fate.[10]

The Golden Bough, one might argue, is judgment's very condition of possibility, its foundation in mimesis, the theory whose end is pleasure [délectation]. Theory is not vision but a function of reason. According to Félibien's citation of Poussin, judgment is an entire system of anticipations that generates the law of the story and encompasses everything represented in the painting:

the function of reason depends on three things, that is, on the eye, on the visual ray, and on the distance between the eye and the object; and it is to be hoped that those who wish to pronounce their judgment [on painting] be well informed.[11]

The goal is a perspective that will reveal the depths of another world on the surface of the canvas, the depths of a world which, although other, is the same as this one: a painting, a representation.

But our detour with Aeneas to the shores of Euboean Cumae has taught us this much: in order to achieve its end—delectation—the theory of mimesis has to make room for an enigmatic exchange, for a strange chiasmus between an interdiction and its transgression. This chiasmus-exchange is effected by a sign, a monument in which contraries are enclosed.

Indeed, the creator and the viewer are burdened by a double interdiction: the former may not *represent* the story's central moment—the paternity of creation in the image of the dead son—in the center of the work; the latter must turn away from the spectacle that he contemplates in order to return to life and its demands.

But Icarus, who is absent from the representation that his father Daedalus produces in this world, returns as Aeneas, the son who contemplates Anchises, the lost father, here and now in the depths of the next world.

Yet the transgression and return implicit in the plucking of the

Golden Bough and in the opening of the sacred gates are conditional on the monumental construction of a sign, a sememe, a tomb:

> Aeneas the true now raised over his friend a massive
> Tomb, laying on it the man's own arms, his oar and his trumpet,
> Beneath that high headland which takes its name from him,
> Misenus, and preserves his fame unto all ages.[12]

# Part I

The ancients can hardly be said to have had places of burial more pleasant than our country cemeteries, where the simple images of meadows, fields, waters, forests, and lovely views blended harmoniously with the tombs of the farmers. . . . In these places one heard only the song of the robin and the sound of sheep grazing on the tomb of their former shepherd. . . .

The epitaph said no more than this: *William* or *Paul, born in such and such a year, died in such and such a year.* Some tombs were even without name. The farmer lies forgotten in death, much like the useful plants among which he lived; nature does not inscribe the name of oaks on their fallen trunks in the forests.

—François Auguste René Chateaubriand,
*Génie du christianisme, ou Beautés
de la religion chrétienne*

# Questions, Hypotheses, Discourse

I, too, would like to erect Poussin's tomb, to lift the interdiction on a discourse of painting, and to open up to language a way into the space of theoretical desire and the *jouissance* of painting. I have in mind the painting of the tomb that Poussin situates at the heart of a space of happiness: Et in Arcadia ego. If I cannot decipher it, I would like at least to spell out the letters of the enigma governing the painting in question.

What is the relation between language and painting if in speaking of a painting we undermine the *délectation* or *jouissance* that is its end, the deadly beauty of theory, death through representation?

Now it turns out that *The Arcadian Shepherds* contains several words, words painted not in the margins or on the frame, not in some corner of the representation, but in its central space. In this instance, Daedalus's chisel was not used to attempt to sculpt an image of Icarus but to inscribe four words in the center of the representation. What is more, these words are not only visible but legible: "Et in Arcadia ego" we read on the tomb as the painting begins to speak. What does it say?

## Questions

Is a discourse on painting possible? More precisely, is a discourse *on* painting possible that would be different from the discourse *of* a given painting? Can there be a verbal metalanguage for the language of painting? Are all systems of signification to be interpreted through language?

## Hypotheses

Poussin's *Arcadian Shepherds* raises pictorially the very question of a discourse on/of painting, and does so in its composition, in the disposition of its figures, in its subject matter, and in the economy of its properly painterly methods. In voicing the question that Poussin's painting asks, I cease to develop a discourse about (this) painting. Instead I simply lend my voice and my pen to a painting that makes pictorially explicit the relation between linguistic signs—words and

15

sentences(?)—and icons—images and paintings. *The Arcadian Shepherds* is self-interpreting, for it represents the very process whereby the story is represented. It is self-interpreting because it represents the process of representation by means of the representation of four words placed in the middle of the canvas, on the wall of the tomb that is situated in the story's center.

## Discourse of Knowledge

Yet another digression is called for at this point as I define in the most general way the type and network of problems in which I am interested: the semantics and metasemantics of systems of representation. I allude here to the program of research outlined by Benveniste at the end of his important article "Sémiologie de la lanque (2)."[1] I shall refer only to the main points made in the conclusion, which are based on a fundamental distinction between semiotics and semantics. "Strictly speaking, every semiotic study consists in identifying certain units and in describing their distinctive traits." Taken by itself, a sign exists when it is recognized as meaningful.

> In turning to semantics, however, we engage with the specific mode of meaning that is engendered by discourse. The problems raised here are a function of language seen as producing messages . . . and as governing a set of referents. . . . The semantic order is linked closely to the world of enunciation and the universe of discourse.[2]

This second-generation semiology aims at getting beyond a Saussurian semiotics of the sign and seeks to grasp the production of meaning through discourse. Attention is given to semantics and to the development of a metasemantics of works, texts, and paintings, "a metasemantics based on the semantics of enunciation."[3]

The field of research evoked above is vast, and I shall thus limit myself to the more specific domain of systems of representation. These systems may be characterized generally by three closely related features of discourse, whether iconic or textual, that allows them to function.

1. Autorepresentativity: the discourse of representation has a specific dimension enabling it to reflect itself as representation. As it represents the world and encompasses a set of referents, this discourse

represents itself performing these very operations. That is, it consti-tutes a subject of representation that is an effect of the system and not its origin, although it does posit this subject as its transcendental foun-dation.

2. Self-referentiality: the discourse of representation refers to the world by referring to itself in the course of the referential process. As a result of this operation, being and discourse are exchanged in a sup-posedly perfect equivalence involving neither a surplus nor a lack.

3. The third characteristic is the most striking, but is in the final analysis only a consequence of the first two: systems of representation are centered and closed; they are centered on account of their auto-representativity and closed on account of their self-referentiality.

## Theoretical Digression 1: On the *Smallest* Unit of Discourse: The Sentence and the Verb in the Classical System of Representation

Consider the following process: I *represent* some thing to *myself* by means of an *idea*. What is noteworthy is that we here have the three poles supporting the very notion of representation: the I who functions as the *res cogitans* or subject of representation; the process of represen-tation itself, which involves a "specular" *relation* to the thing; and the idea by means of which the thing is made present to thought. Now, according to the grammarians and logicians of Port-Royal, a judgment is a form or manner of thinking that does not in itself depend on a pro-cess of representation but only on the existence of an I engaged in an act of pure assertion. On this view, there is absolutely nothing in the sphere of being that corresponds to judgment. Indeed, references to instances of being are effected by means of representations that are united in a synthetic act of judgment. Yet it is important to note that representations would also be pure forms of thought were it not for the intervention of some judgment. Although judgment is itself a pure form of thought, it posits representations as representing some thing in the realm of being. To represent oneself is simply to cast a glance at the things that present themselves to our mind, but in so doing we "form no explicit judgment about the thing":[4] through representation, the thing as presence becomes accessible to the mind in the form of an idea. Judgment construes this mental form not as the thing itself but as legitimately standing in for it, as having the *right* to represent it. The act of judgment, then, is concerned with the well-foundedness of representations.

Insofar as it is the specific function or very nature of representations to represent, an "explicit" judgment is hardly called for: "We have no knowledge of what is *outside* us except by the mediation of the ideas *within* us."[5] But it is nonetheless crucial that a given representation properly make contact with the thing itself, that the idea in us *be* the thing outside us. Given that this equivalence cannot be fully achieved since the idea remains a *cosa mentale,* the juridical status of the thing *must* be bestowed on the idea. "Truth" is the term used to identify the status in question. If representation, for a thinking subject, is the manifestation of a doubling of being, then the legitimacy of an act of judgment hinges on the substitution that is effected by the thinking subject. Substitution is what enables a given representation to efface itself before some instance of being and thereby to underscore its own validity and truth.

But if this line of reasoning is correct, then the act of judgment is not simply a matter of predicating relations between representations: it also posits representations that are so linked, and these links are understood to be ontologically real. Judgment must be both the act of predication and a real relation if it is to avoid being engulfed entirely by the system of representation. Were it to be so engulfed, the correspondence between $x$ and $y$ that defines objectivity and constitutes judgment as an element of the system of science would be ruled out. But is it not the case that the notion of representation, both as a process and as a general economy, already contains this ontological implication? Is not the doubling that being effects, through representation and for a thinking subject, the very site of a substitution by which the subject gains access to being in a primitive yet fundamental operation of the mind? Does not representation always imply a judgment? One could argue that our everyday mode of seeing and appropriating the things that present themselves to us already constitutes a kind of primitive judgment. This may not be an *explicit* judgment *articulated in logical form,* but it is arguably a judgment nonetheless. I have in mind the ways in which the immediately round earth, brilliant sun, and blue sky are grasped by the subject in all the complexity of their representations.

## The Subject's Right of Appropriation

A judgment is the explicit *expression*, in the form of a predicate, of the operation of representation; it is a reproduction of this operation at the level of a grammatical and logical metalanguage. If we consider the discourse of science, we realize that it, too, is nothing but the *expression* of what the subject always already knows as a thinking and rational being. In the discourse of logic, which emphasizes clarity of expression, this knowledge takes the form of an "explicit" judgment. Ordinary language, on the other hand, allows such knowledge to remain implicit. A new twist would be to think of the judgment implied in representation as taking the explicit form of predication. As a result, representation acquires the juridical status that it lacked. This status not only allows the thinking subject to appropriate a given being in the form of an ideal substitute, but also accords this subject the *right* to possess that being. The legitimacy surrounding the relevant act of appropriation may be traced to the true judgment that establishes the substitutive value between the mental form of a representation and the being that it represents. Could one claim that the thinking subject, as the subject of representation, engages in a project of self-definition through this juridical act? Does this act somehow ground the subject and define his status? The act seems to allow the subject to define himself as having the right to being because he represents being to himself.

We now understand better the crucial importance of the sentence's central kernel, which is also the smallest unit of discourse: the verb. In the verb, grammar and logic meet in a common term that has the double characteristic of not being an *end point* and of being *unique*: grammar and logic become identical, for at issue is nothing less than the organization of thought itself into a discourse of being. A representation, a sign, and a thing are linked in one and the same form of thought in order to constitute the indivisible and most basic starting point for a coherent discourse: "The verb is nothing else but a word whose principal function is to indicate assertion—that is to say, to indicate not only that a man conceives certain things but rather that he judges concerning these things and makes an assertion."[6] The characteristic of the verb "to be" is to manifest in all simplicity this link (in the field of representation), positing (in the sphere of being) what the representation represents. It is for this reason that the act of judgment, the principal *mode* of thought, is called "being" (from the verb "to be"). Similarly, that is why the verb "to be" is called a substantive. "To be" is the point where the act of assertion, the process of synthesis, becomes a substantive, where the act counts as a substance and the mode as the thing itself.

It is now possible to understand the enigmatic remark in *The Art of Thinking* according to which verbs share with pronouns the privilege of taking the place of nouns, "but in a peculiar way."[7] Verbs have this privilege because the basic kernel of all verbs is the verb "to be." This substantive verb—a pure mode of thought in the way it links representations—designates the being that all nouns signify, Being as the totality of beings. As both mode and substance—that is, as the mode of a subject and as a process of substantification—the verb effects the meeting of representation and being, of the subject and the thing. The verb thus stands in for nouns, but in a manner different from pronouns. It is not only a matter of "removing the displeasure caused by repetition . . . [by representing] a noun in a confused manner,"[8] but of taking control and tipping the nominal designation into the sphere of what it designates, of construing what is designated as a determined thing among things. In the judgment "the sky is blue," the verb takes the place of a noun as a mode (like "blue"), but it is the mode of an asserting subject. It also takes the place of a noun as a substantive (like "sky"), but in this case it is this subject's process of being that is in question. The problem, then, is the eclipsed presence of the subject. In *affirming* certain representations by using the appropriate nouns, the subject of representation leaves behind the field of representation in order to let the things that he thus designates be, in their very being. He bestows on himself the right to all things while letting these things be; he grants himself the right to possess these things through their representational equivalents. The subject, it is true, is always operative in the field of representation, where he is engaged in an interminable discursive process of combining and disjoining; but each utterance of the substantive verb renders him transparent, even if this verb is what allows him to construct and appropriate his own discourse. It is through this transparence that the things this discourse names, designates, and links together are themselves determined in being.

## The Reductionist Analysis of Verbs: The Present Tense
## and the Third-Person Pronoun

We have seen that in the logico-grammatical discourse of the Port-
Royal logicians the basic function of verbs is predication. It is also
noteworthy that, according to the logicians, all verbs are reducible to
the present indicative of the verb "to be" and to the third person of this
tense and mood. If the indicative mood positively expresses actions or
states of affairs, the present tense points to the temporal dimensions of
enunciation; this tense presupposes the presence of a locutor and of an
auditor, for "what is said is governed by the category of the person."
Discourse is constructed with reference to an "I," and the present tense
grammatically marks the presence of the "I" at the moment of the
enunciation of his discourse. The use of the present indicative in "the
sky is blue" imbues this phrase with the following meaning: "I, who
speak to you, affirm that the sky is blue"; *my* discourse exists in the
"here and now" and shares the temporal frame of the sky's blueness.
Insofar as language is assumed to have a purely designative function—
reference to objects and representation of objects through words—the
present tense depends on "an individual and subjective instance of discourse in that it is always and necessarily realized by the act of discourse and as a result of this act." Verbs in the present tense and indicative mood function as important markers of self-reference; that is, they
anchor in an agent the process of representation through which words
and concepts replace things.

If it is true that all verbs are reducible to the present indicative of the
verb "to be," it follows that all verbs, and even the entire field of discourse, are centered around a space that is occupied by what may be
called the "ego of enunciation," the I thinking in the mode appropriate
to his desire. This desire is not simply to put things into words, but also
to articulate these things, along with all their striking similarities and
differences, *to and for himself.* From the desire to speak, to signify, theoretical desire finally arises, the desire to appropriate and to identify; it is
this desire that constitutes beings as subjects of truth and knowledge.

There is, however, another aspect of the reduction of the verb "to
be" as the logicians of Port-Royal understood it. This aspect effaces the
first discursive order based on the tense and mood of the enunciation,

and on the presence and mode of the subject of the enunciation, in favor of a quite different order related to the *person*. Consider the following statement: "Only the verb 'to be' has retained this simplicity, and strictly speaking this is really only so in certain instances of the third person, present tense." Why, one might ask, is the third person viewed as the privileged *prosopon* for the assertions of human beings? Why is this role not instead assumed by the *ego cogitans*, who occupies such a central place in the discursive order based on tense and mood? Unlike the first and second person, the third person concerns "someone absent," a nonperson. Used in an impersonal construction, "it" designates either an infinity of subjects or nobody. It is no doubt true that "it" posits a grammatical subject. Yet this pronoun does not introduce a philosophical subject, nor does it situate the act of enunciation in relation to a speaking subject. As a result, linguistics is able to analyze the grammatical subject as providing a genuine contrast to a kind of neuter or absence that is the real subject of the verb.

This point is crucial, even if the Port-Royal logicians only partially grasped its implications. What is revealed in this line of argumentation is the other side of the philosophical ideology that first became apparent in the emphasis on the present indicative. For the act of reducing the verb to the third person, by effacing all personal subjects of enunciation, effectively authorizes the ontological emergence of representations from the realm of things. Judgments such as "the sky is blue" or "the earth is round" can thus be rewritten as follows: "it is, blue the sky" or "it is, round the earth." In such utterances "it," the subject of the verb "to be," functions as a purely neutral marker of the indescribable emergence of a given thing's being. As a result, "it" excludes all reference to a subject of representation and discourse. In opposition to this (personal) subject, "in excess" as it were, a determinate representation is formulated in order to produce an utterance that makes sense and has meaning. In other words, the impersonal subject "it" is formulated to "signify" the representation. But then, within the neutral realm of being's emergence into discourse, this subject is posited *in being* as what determines the representation.

We discover at this point the thrust of the double reduction of the verb: in both processes, it is a matter of effecting a chiasmus between a mode and a substance, between a subject and a thing. What is more, this dual chiasmus between the subject and being must take place entirely within the field of representation as circumscribed by the system of language. Predication, as we have seen, is an activity intimately connected to the subject's characteristic mode of thinking and desiring. It comes about through the verbal substantive. In representation, it is by means of this substantive that the attribute determines the subject to which it is attributed either conjunctively or disjunctively. In so doing, the attribute makes the subject a knowable object in the predicate clause. But the act of predication also concerns the subject to whom the present indicative of the verb "to be" constantly refers, even as this very subject is effaced through the effects of a neuter third-person pronoun. This pronoun makes possible the kind of pure predication that apparently involves no subject and instead pertains only to a determinate object. What is striking, however, is that predication is traceable to both a subject and an object. If we focus on predication as an act of enunciation, we are led in the direction of a speaking subject; if we instead focus on the utterance generated by predicative acts, we are led to foreground the object to which the utterance refers. One might say that "is" always refers to a speaking subject. Yet, since "is" may be unpacked as "it is," the term is also a site where a neutral emergence of being occurs without reference to this speaking subject. We thus note that the act of predication serves a dual purpose: it legitimates the representation in which the subject acquires the right to represent things while grounding the subject's right to possess the thing itself through its representational equivalents.

Moreover, to be fully effective from an ideological point of view, judgment must rely on the instrument of language. That is, language is what makes possible the chiasmus between mode and substance, attribute and subject, between a thinking I and a determinate object. Operating at the limits of the field of representation, language establishes the juridical status of the subject.

In conclusion, and by way of introducing my next theoretical excursis, let me propose the following paraphrase of the four words inscribed within the spatial and representational center of Poussin's *Arcadian Shepherds:* "Et in Arcadia" (a sentence, a proposition, a judgment *without a verb*), but "Ego." In this phrase the subject identifies himself using the self's proper name: "Ego." The tomb speaks, as does the painting. What do they say? Who exactly is doing the speaking?

## Summary

In an attempt to define the distinctive traits of systems of representation, I have been drawing heavily on the theory of sentences and verbs articulated in the *Grammar* and *Logic* of Port-Royal, sources that clearly indicate the historical dimension of my discourse: so-called "classical" thought. To speak of representation in general is thus to rely on a number of theoretical and historical assumptions concerning discourse and signs as well as on knowledge relevant to science and to the subject and its relation to being—in short, on what Foucault has called an episteme. It is a matter of drawing on what essentially amounts to a historical cross section of my theoretical problems in which representation and its discourse are articulated not only in a dictionary, in syntax, and in grammar, but also in an encyclopedia that, as a comprehensive representation, recapitulates the issue of representation in a global but discontinuous manner.

Another theoretical and historical cross section follows directly from those above: the study of the enunciative modality of stories, which is the starting point for any semantics. Thus, I shall start with the distinction made by Benveniste between narrative (history) [*histoire*] and discourse [*discours*] in order subsequently to explore its peculiarities. A narrative (history), then, is characterized by a specific mode of enunciation that consists in effacing or excluding all signs of the enunciative process from the resulting utterances: in a narrative (history), the act of enunciation is not itself enunciated. A story [*récit*], in short, is a discourse without a narrator, a discourse whose narrator is absent. The events of the narrative (history) *seem* to narrate themselves without referring to the act that produces the story. A first peculiarity of stories is that they are discourses bearing no sign of discourse. The historical enunciation, which occurs only in *written* language, is used to narrate past events. This form of enunciation represents events of the past in such a way as to efface the role played by the locutor. "In order for them to be recorded as having occurred, these events must belong to the past." Strangely enough, Benveniste then shifts his approach: "No doubt it would be better to say that they are characterized as past from the time they have been recorded and uttered in a historical temporal expression."[9] This lack of intervention by any locutor, *which is characteristic of writing*, designates the events as past. This line of reasoning may be pushed one step further: unlike speech, which exists only in the present, writing could be said to exist only in the past. This idea is paradoxical indeed, for I could easily make exactly the opposite claim: the fleeting nature of speech entails a perpetual vacillation between "already" and "no longer"; this helps to explain why verbal exchanges often depend on unstable and successive efforts at memorization, which are marked by gaps and lacunae. Writing, on the other hand, is always present in its traces.

Et in Arcadia ego. What do these words tell us? Who utters them? By whom were they written? What we have here is an enigmatic "fusion" between the past and the subject of speech: writing is the silence of the act of saying in what is said.

Although historical stories were written by someone, when I read, the effect of reading leads me to overlook the fact that the text was written. Indeed, the text articulates a paradoxical injunction: "Remember to forget." The implicit command may be seen as the effect of the power of the enunciative agency. Yet one of the features of this kind of power is precisely to remain hidden.

Historical stories are governed by the signs and power of negation, of denegation, the simultaneous positing and suppressing of the act of enunciation itself. It is as though the writing subject of (historical) narratives were saying: "I am not saying what I am saying: it is written [ça s'écrit]." Indeed, in a sense, since he is writing, he must say as much, for that is what writing amounts to: "It is written; therefore, I speak." The present is a splitting of the present: the enunciative modality of a story consists in the writer's expulsion of his product and in the return of what is thus expelled as an object that is real, but of the past. Writing essentially performs the operation of splitting the present in its representation of reality, of making the past present through representation. Thus, in elaborating a (hi)story, I make the dead speak: as I fall silent, ça s'écrit. But in so doing, I silence the dead. At that point it is indeed I who speak, but what is written is not what I say. In narrating a (hi)story, I do indeed speak to you about something, but what you read is quite different from what I tell you.

At this point we encounter a theoretical and historical surprise: the theory of the sentence and the verb articulated by the Port-Royal grammarians and logicians as that of the smallest unit of discourse is no different from the theory of stories (of history) elaborated by Benveniste.

This striking similarity can mean one of two things, depending on whether knowledge and truth are made to underscore the importance of history or of theory. In historical terms, we would have to conclude that the "science" of linguistics, including the semantic theory of Benveniste and others, remains trapped within the "closure" of representation. If we instead focus on theory, we conclude that there are always only narratives and stories. Speakers constitute themselves as subjects of discourse, as locutors and addressees, only in order to possess and appropriate these stories, to transform them into discourse. The choice is yours.

## Return to Arcadia

Drawing on aspects of Freud's theory, I would like to propose the following reading of *The Arcadian Shepherds:* the painting in the Louvre is a representation of the process of narrative representation associated with history. It *reveals* to the attentive viewer the kind of denegation of enunciation that is characteristic of (historical) enunciations. What we have here is a metarepresentation of a (hi)story, a meta(hi)story in the painting of a (hi)story.

My theoretical concerns come together in Poussin's painting, for this work exemplifies the semantics and metasemantics of systems of representation. On my reading, *The Arcadian Shepherds* is a representation that represents representation and its relation to some referent, to a (hi)story. The question is: which one? The painting, I have been arguing, is autorepresentative and self-referential. In *The Arcadian Shepherds,* it is less a matter of telling a (hi)story than of recounting the representation of (hi)story in its dual relation to writing and death. The (hi)story it recounts, its singular narrative, is the representation of (hi)story; it is the (hi)story of representation.

*The Arcadian Shepherds* is an unusual narrative in that its surface seems to suggest the point made by Freud toward the end of his article on denegation, where he locates the roots of the act of judgment—so *central* to the classical episteme and to its systems of representation—in the duality of Eros and destruction. The passage from Freud reads as follows:

> The study of judgment affords us, perhaps for the first time, an insight into the origin of an intellectual function from the interplay of the pri-

mary instinctual impulses. Judging is a continuation, along lines of expediency, of the original process by which the ego took things into itself or expelled them from itself, according to the pleasure principle. The polarity of judgement appears to correspond to the opposition of the two groups of instincts which we have supposed to exist. Affirmation—as a substitute uniting—belongs to Eros; negation—the successor to expulsion—belongs to the instinct of destruction.[10]

Poussin's painting, I have argued, recounts a (hi)story in which the primary agenda is to represent the processes by which such (hi)stories are represented. As a result, the painting may well lay bare the process whereby the subject of the enunciation is denied or suppressed, the denegation in question being a feature, as we have seen, of narrative (history). On my reading the painting represents, in the *erotic* image of Arcadia, the death that lies at the heart of representation, a death made present by the tomb and its epitaph. In the very affirmation of happiness, we discover denegation.

## Pastoral Interlude

For some time, and in a kind of religious silence, the young shepherds and shepherdesses contemplated the Tomb on which these words were engraved; "And I, I too lived in Arcadia." The young lovers, side by side, who had been sadly preoccupied by the sight of this monument, then turned away from it, both moved and pensive. Some had their eyes cast down, others seemed in their tender looks to be expressing the movements of their soul; some of the lovers held hands, seeming to say to each other: if death is where it all ends, let us at least love each other until then.

Their minds were still preoccupied with such melancholic thoughts as they emerged from the copse surrounding the Tomb and caught sight of a solitary shepherd's hut at the edge of the small valley. Sitting next to the door was an old man lost in the depths of sadness. His body was bent and his head bald except for a sprinkling of white hair. His head rested heavily on a gnarled stick clutched between his hands, and he did not notice the young shepherds and shepherdesses approaching; only when he heard their voices did he raise his head and heavy eyelids. They were all struck by his venerable air: an unhappy King could not have exhibited greater majesty. . . .

The sight of the old man filled the shepherds with respect, and they kept a certain distance from the hut before which he was seated; however, one of them approached him and asked him to tell them whose Tomb they had seen in the copse. That Tomb, replied the old man, holds all the charms of youth, all the wealth of life: beauty, glory, love, happy love. Buried there, with my only daugher, are all of my hopes and my joy: it is the Tomb of Lycoris. Having uttered these words, Palemon slowly directed his sad gaze at the copse, letting his head fall into his hands once more.[11]

Poussin's painting, then, is a pastoral allegory and simulacrum in which the system of representation deconstructs itself by representing its own processes. At the center of the representation is a tomb, and in the center of this center an inscription engraved in marble. What we have here is a tomb bearing the inscription of the subject's proper name: ego.

## Return

Let us recall a passage cited earlier:

Poussin could not bear Caravaggio and said that he had come into the - world in order to destroy painting. Yet his aversion for Caravaggio is not surprising. For whereas Poussin sought to foreground the nobility of his subjects, Caravaggio allowed himself to be carried away by the truth of nature as it appeared to him. Their approaches were thus diametrically opposed to one another.[12]

If Caravaggio can be said to have destroyed painting, can we not claim that Poussin deconstructed representation? In painting the truth of nature as it appears to our eyes, in giving pleasure to the point of pain, to the point of fascination, Caravaggio effectively destroys painting *as representation* in a prodigious and stupefying process. What is instigated is the violence of the effect of representation.

Poussin, on the other hand, emphasizes what is beautiful in nature, just as he hopes to bring to the painterly process what is noble and great about himself. He construes the painting as a kind of "theoretical" paradigm while representing representation as contemplation. Yet his conception deconstructs the painting in the very instant its end is achieved, the moment it provokes the delectation or *jouissance* that is the effect of representation itself.

We somehow need to envisage, rising from the tomb situated at the heart of Arcadia, from the tomb of the story and of history, the terrifying face of the Uffizi's *Medusa*.

What we discover in Poussin is a deconstruction of historical painting through metarepresentation, a theory of the denegation of the subject of representation that characterizes such paintings.

In Caravaggio we find the destruction of historical representation through a display of the eye that sees and stupefies itself. The crucial image here is, of course, that of Narcissus fascinated by his fetish.

# Readings

Let us consider a statement made in 1639 by the great master, Poussin, in a letter sent to Chantelou that accompanied *The Israelites Gathering Manna in the Desert:* "study [read] the story and the picture in order to see whether each thing is appropriate to the subject."[1] The Master has spoken, and he has articulated an injunction to read. On Poussin's view an appropriate response to the painting cannot be simply a matter of seeing it or attentively looking at it. Instead, the viewer must read or decipher the painting, or simply scan the canvas as if it were a large printed page. The viewer must engage in an ongoing process of making meaning, must grasp what the painter intended to say. Yet what exactly does the expression "read the painting" mean when the painting is the representation of a story? How can the painting represent a story?

The injunction also embodies a certain hierarchy: the viewer must first read the story or historical narrative; only then should he read the picture or painting. Poussin instructs Chantelou to begin with the (historical) narrative that is known to him before he even glances at the painting. The narrative is clearly identified by name, even summarized, in the title of the painting: *The Israelites Gathering Manna in the Desert.* The viewer should begin with the (historical) narrative and proceed from there to the painterly story. The latter must be read through the optic of the former. Poussin accepts the legitimacy of the rules, conventions, and norms associated with the classical period: the painting, he suggests, represents the manna story in its entirety, just as it respects the proper sequence of narrative moments. The representation's appropriation of the story is as complete, precise, and legitimate as the constraints imposed on the representation by the story. The appropriation is such that one can speak neither of a remainder nor of a lack. It is a matter of going back and forth between the painting and the (historical) narrative in a manner that recognizes the two as perfectly identical, precisely analogous, and rigorously proportionate. Read the story, that is, the painting, or its twin. It turns out that the injunction specifying that the (historical) narrative be read before the painting serves no other function than to challenge the viewer/reader to put the painting to a certain test. Poussin confidently dares Chantelou to look for an illegitimate element in the painter's appropriation of the narrative.

The same point can be made in a more learned manner: the painting legitimately is (or should be) the text of a (historical) narrative whose "characters" and "writing" are at once formal and expressive signs. Whereas formal signs are a matter of the disposition or distribution of certain figures within the space established by the representation, expressive signs involve the kind of "expressions," gestures, looks, movements, and attitudes that exactly mirror the passions of the soul. I am not inventing anything new here, for Poussin, in conversation with Félibien, expressed the same idea: "Just as the twenty-four letters of the alphabet are used to form our words and to express our thoughts, so the forms of the human body are used to express the various passions of the soul and to make visible what is in the mind."[2] If the formal and expressive signs distributed throughout the painting constitute a legible text, then they must be subject to certain syntactical rules. Given that these rules are properly figurative, they cannot be reduced to the narrative syntax governing the story represented in the painting. What is needed, then, is an elucidation of the rules constitutive of this syntax. Curiously, we already know that however different the narrative and painterly syntaxes may be, they generate identical results: the representation appropriates its (historical) narrative while the narrative rigorously puts certain constraints on its own representation. Poussin's injunction may thus be rephrased as follows: read the painting as the text of a story told by painterly means, but also as the representation of the story's text. It is in the simultaneous *difference* and *substitutability* of text and representation that the mastery of the most learned of painters is revealed.

Even when put briefly, the point remains the same: a historical painting is a vast sentence, a major proposition or judgment spread across the entire surface of the painting. If this is so, then where or what is the verb? The verb, we recall, is the central element that holds everything together. It provides the means by which a purely theoretical desire constitutes the subject of representation at the center of any given representation. The verb is what makes the story visible to a *given subject;* it makes possible the *illusion* of events or narrative utterances telling themselves. And this illusion marks a secret fissure, a minute scission, even a denegation.

Poussin's injunction to "read the story and the picture" thus gives rise to a question and a related suspicion. Why does the Master feel the need to dictate an order of reading to Chantelou, or to you and me for that matter? It is because Poussin's injunction is not self-evident, because it is not clear why we *must* read. The alternative would simply be to see and take pleasure in the forms and colors brought into play in a certain order on the canvas. The suspicion generated by the injunction is a masochistic one: we need constraints, a kind of supplementary contract. So be it. Let us now read.

## Reading 1

I have before me a painting: *The Arcadian Shepherds*. I see it. I look at it attentively. Now, nothing in the painting, other than its existence and my looking at it, marks or unmarks the painter or viewer, the theoretical subject. Indeed, the painting accords with an ancient method discussed by Alberti in his *Trattato della Pittura*: none of the figures looks beyond the painting at *me*, not even to "position" me in the place of the painter as a seeing eye or theoretical subject and thereby to designate and constitute a space of contemplation, the enchanted circuit involving what might be called the painting's gaze and the viewer's eye.

The painter effaces himself and by the same token he effaces me. What we are dealing with here is a kind of purifying ascesis: I do not become part of the illusion. The latter does not reach out to me in order to capture or seduce me. The singular event represented in the painting is but a distant scene existing in and for itself, in a space of pure contemplation. This extraordinary self-sufficiency accounts for the "spectacularity" of historical painting, just as it explains the painter's decision to dictate a mode of behavior to *his* viewer: "Read." I order you to take up a position that will allow you to read freely and to ascertain through contemplation whether each and every detail is appropriate to the chosen subject matter.

"Read the story and the painting." But what exactly is the story? Do you know it? These are questions posed by the spirit of Leonardo da Vinci to the spirit of Poussin in the kingdom of the dead as they contemplate in absentia another of the great Master's paintings: *Landscape with a Man Killed by a Snake*.

Pouss.— . . . Is it not true that these various levels of fear and surprise [the formal and expressive signs, the characters of the representational alphabet distributed with precision throughout the space of the painting] create a kind of play that is both touching and pleasing?

Leon.—I agree. But what exactly does this painting depict? Is it a story? I don't know it. It's more like a caprice.

Pouss.—It's a caprice. That kind of work suits us well, as long as the caprice is rule-governed and in no way departs from real nature.[3]

Is *The Arcadian Shepherds* merely a caprice? Does Poussin's injunction itself encourage capricious behavior? Could the injunction be restated as follows: read the painting and tell yourself a story that satisfies your whim? After all, this is essentially what Marmontel does in the pastoral tale of Palemon published in the *Mercure de France*. Perhaps this is what my own text and theory of figurative painting does. If *The Arcadian Shepherds* may be characterized as a theoretical caprice on the part of Poussin, then my theoretical tale is perhaps itself a caprice, the representation of the story's representation.

## Theoretical Digression 2: On the Creation of the Space of Representation

Poussin's letter to Chantelou reveals one of the conditions of possibility of reading the painting:

When you receive yours, I beg of you, if you like it, to provide it with a small frame; it needs one so that, in considering it in all its parts, the eye shall remain concentrated, and not dispersed beyond the limits of the picture by receiving impressions of objects which, seen pell-mell with the painted objects, confuse the light.[4]

Although this passage seems primarily to provide technical or practical advice, it in fact describes a complex theoretical operation whereby a painting is constituted as an object to be contemplated and read. Indeed, if all aspects of the painting are to be properly considered, then a frame must effectively separate the pictorial space from the space that surrounds it. Although the frame occupies only a fragment of space, it plays a crucial role. Being part of neither the viewer's nor the painting's space, the frame can neutralize the surrounding world. This neutralization directs the eye's rays toward the painting, locking them into its space. From that moment on, the optical pyramid consists only of the painting. It is not hard to understand, then, why Poussin, some three years later, toward the end of his stay in Paris, establishes a contrast between the mere sight of objects and their contemplation (in his "Mémoire à Sublet des Noyers"). The eye's natural grasp of the object's form and appearance is thus opposed to the search, through the act of seeing itself, for the means of properly knowing the object. Poussin contrasts aspects to prospects, thereby emphasizing the prospective element that is the formal structure of enunciation/representation.

The frame thus marks a rupture in the perceptual continuum. This rupture constitutes a new space, the unique function of which is to manifest a range of shapes and colors before the gaze of the attentive viewer. What is constituted is the space of representation, a space where the object as figure can be known and read. The frame thus marks the condition of the viewer's gaze and of the object's readability.

This account of the limiting function of the frame can be supported by two pieces of evidence. First, the relation between the frame's limiting function and the geometrical optical structure of the gaze is clearly evident in Poussin's careful analysis of plans to decorate the Louvre's "Grande Galerie":

> The intention is that one should take in at a glance, from the same point and distance, half the arch of each vault above the panelling, and it must be understood that everything I have set out in this vault should be considered as laid on to its surface. *Nothing should break through this skin, figures should not be allowed to jut out beyond or be embedded deep into it. Instead everything on the surface should reinforce the form and structure of the vault.*[5]

The second piece of evidence can be found in what Poussin's critics and contemporaries saw as his penchant for painting medium-size canvases: "He found in medium-size paintings a field large enough to reveal his learning."[6] Referring to *The Plague of Ashdod*, Félibien makes the following claim: "It gave him the opportunity to keep his brushstrokes within rather narrow limits, limits that nonetheless allowed him to reveal his noble conceptions and *to display large and learned dispositions in small spaces.*[7]

The point is that in the case of a painting or a decor the space of representation must occupy the gaze in a manner differing significantly from that of the perceived world. And if the construction of representational space depends entirely on prospective, the formal structure of enunciation/representation connecting three fundamental terms ("the eye," "the visual ray," and "the distance between the eye and the object"),[8] then the frame makes manifest the strange play of enunciative denegation. We saw that the frame *encloses* the eye's rays within the space of the painting, thereby enabling a *disinvestment* of the gaze from the perceived world. Yet, in enveloping "his brushstrokes within rather narrow limits," the frame also *releases* the gaze from the represented space.

The very condition of reading a painting and its story—its prospect, the function of reason—may be articulated in an injunction to gaze attentively at the painting and the painting only. Yet it must be remembered that what is thus contemplated is only a painting, a representation, and not even a "trompe l'oeil." On the contrary, for the eye is ultimately released and given theoretical access to real knowledge. It is in that moment that I may be said to *contemplate* the Arcadian scene.

## Reading 2

If we consider once again that the viewer may be unfamiliar with the story represented in the painting, it turns out that this neutralizing of the eye and gaze, of the relation between painter and painting, and painting and viewer, is itself the story expressed in the representational scene and its "frieze" of figures. In *The Arcadian Shepherds*, three figures—a "shepherdess" to the right and two "shepherds" to the left—exchange looks and gestures in connection with a fourth figure who has one knee on the ground. What we have here is a kind of silent dialogue or mute poetry: painting. There are no words mouthed or heard by ears. Instead it is a matter of making a pointing gesture and three gazes visible, of constituting them as the minimal alphabet of a painterly language. Even before expressing the passions of the soul through the "contours" of the body in order to display what is on one's mind, pointing and looking are part of what I want to call "movements-toward-the-other," passions of the other, affects of exteriority. These signs of ostension refer to the structure of enunciation while underscoring the superfluous nature of the words that accompany them: "this," "see." What is indicated as present is the instantaneous presence of a message exchanged prior to speech, a minimal and most primitive discourse. The message concerns the kneeling figure, who is thus the referent. And in this mix of gestures and gazes, I discover that the shepherd on the left, who is leaning his elbow against the tomb, is connected to the two figures on the right by nothing more than the figure who is the object of his gaze. It is this gaze that makes the kneeling figure visible or noteworthy: the shepherd on the right points at his fellow herdsman and proposes that the "shepherdess" look at him. The shepherdess welcomes this herdsman into her own range of vision; in contemplating him, she receives him. What is striking is that the shepherd standing to the right points at the kneeling figure while directing his gaze elsewhere, at the shepherdess. In so doing he articulates a question that is generated by the double play of his gesture and look, by their separate directions. The shepherd seems to be saying, "I am showing *him* to *you*, for I look at *you* in pointing to *him* instead of looking at *him*." The question, then, would run as follows: "Do you know what the person I am pointing out to you [this is the question in the gesture] is doing [the question in the gaze], the person whom you see in much the same way that the other one on the other side of the scene sees him?" In this case the question surfaces in the distance separating the shepherd's pointing gesture from his gaze. As a result one might claim that it is based on the negativity of the gaze, itself a very strange characteristic that becomes apparent only when the gaze is contrasted with a gesture of pointing. Put differently, the question is only "visible" between a positing and a negating-for-the-other. In pointing to the kneeling shepherd, I posit him as an object-to-be-seen by you. Yet, in looking at you and thereby causing him to disappear qua object seen by me, in excluding him from the field of my gaze, I anticipate a response from you. The question is the space wherein this expectation that the other posit something is made manifest. What is extraordinary is that this complex process occurs in a speechless moment. I know that you are not looking at me. Do you nonetheless hear my mute question? Without seeing me, you gaze at the man I point out to you. Yet is the kneeling figure really what I point out to you? As this play of diverging looks and gestures unfolds, so, too, does something like *primal time*. Once the kneeling man is identified in a pointing gesture, he is destined to become the object of the shepherdess's gaze at some future moment. Once the shepherd directs his gaze at the woman beside him, he ceases to see the kneeling figure. Yet his pointing gesture clearly indicates that he saw this figure at some point in the past. The future, the past in the present, presence, the present instant in the gesture of pointing thus only appear at the limits of a failure to see. I am no longer looking at him. You are not yet looking at me. You are looking at him. I am pointing him out to you.

This analysis can be repeated with regard to the shepherd leaning against the tomb. As mentioned above, this individual looks at the kneeling figure much as the woman on the right does. The figure has their undivided visual attention, for neither sees the man engaged in the activity of pointing. One might say paradoxically that they do not yet see him *and* that they no longer see him. Time, duration, is suspended and captured in an instant that is once liminal and englobing, the instant of a communicative exchange in process.

This, then, is my claim: the representation of the story is elaborated in the space of the representational scene following the general functions of enunciation—utterance, message, reception, reference, code. The "shepherd" on the left offers something to be seen; the "shepherdess" receives his gift; in performing a pointing gesture, the "shepherd" on the right engages in a referential act while making his gaze the vehicle of a question; the kneeling "shepherd" is the message. When we reduce the represented story to this basic schema, we realize that it recounts the most basic "(hi)story" of the exchange, the origin of communication.

The schema in question is none other than the model that Jakobson proposed of the fundamental structure and conditions of possibility of enunciation. Let us consider two related diagrams:

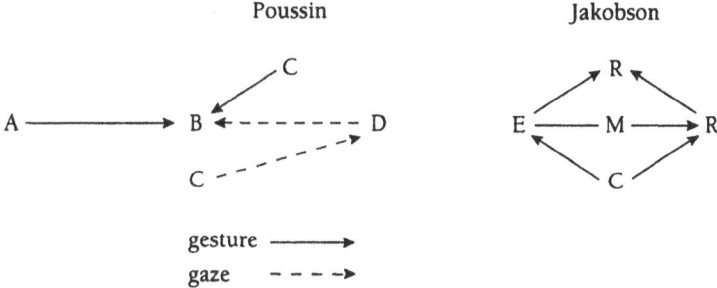

## Theoretical Remarks

1. It is as though Poussin, in his painting, enunciates the basic model of enunciation or represents the elementary structure of representation. As a painter, he thus seems to occupy the "metalinguistic" and theoretical position of the linguist who constructs and makes known his basic model of communication.

2. The schema or communicative flow is directed from *A*, the speaker, to *D*, the receiver. There are properly pictorial reasons for this, including the painting's balance and composition, a point to which I shall return. Other reasons might also be mentioned, such as the typical direction of reading from left to right, which, in the case of this particular painting, has the effect of underscoring the importance of the sentence inscribed on the tomb.

3. Yet the gaze that *D* directs at *B* lends itself to two interpretations. It can be seen as an operation of closure, completing a model that is theoretical, atemporal, achronic, logical, and metalinguistic. It can also be construed as a response in the "dialogue" taking place between the various figures. In this dialogue, it should be noted, time is at once a process of change and a form of exchange, a duration marked by alternating enunciative positions.

4. Finally, a single represented figure can serve a number of semantic functions. For example, *C* embodies both reference and the code needed to decipher the representation. Several functions may be semantically condensed in a single figure that may be said to be overdetermined. This feature provokes a key question, one already raised with regard to *C* and the gap between the gesture and gaze: is the space that opens within the representational scene as the site where a question is anticipated not also a space to be filled by my discourse, by the discourse of the viewer or painter? Does not the opening somewhat surreptitiously become the empty space of enunciation and representation *within the story*?

## Reading 3

I would now like to develop further my insights about the figure whom I designated as the vehicle of the painting's message, the kneeling shepherd about whom the others are "speaking," be it in the form of a steady gaze or a pointing gesture. We are dealing here with a man who performs three actions simultaneously: he *looks at* a written line, he *points to* it with his finger, and he *reads,* or at least he tries to read it. Actually, he almost seems to be spelling aloud the relevant signs. Better yet, insofar as "Et in Arcadia," the first three words of the inscription, can be read off the shepherd's opened mouth, a silent voice arises within the representation, a voice that *says* "Et in Arcadia/Ego." The figure sees, points out, and reads a written fragment. The shepherd is the medium through which the "id speaks" [*ça dit*] its message; the gestures and tense body of the kneeling figure effectively construe him as an attentive recipient of the message in question. Through a kind of "mise en abysme" the shepherd incorporates all the functions of communication: his pointing behavior bears directly on the issue of reference; his reading and deciphering of the inscription presupposes a code; and his steady gaze implies a moment of reception. What is it exactly that he receives? A message for which he himself is the mouthpiece and of which he is a silent repetition at the heart of the painting. It or id writes and speaks through him, through the opened mouth represented in profile.

Who writes? Who speaks in the here and now, through a remobilization of the signs inscribed on the wall of marble? Ego? Who is there? I am. Who are you? It is impossible to proceed. My reading comes to a halt. Much like the kneeling shepherd, I reiterate "I." And yet he and I, we and you, know full well that it is not I, not you, not we who have inscribed "I" at the center of the tomb's wall. Not I, not you, not we, but Ego or nobody; Ego, or the traces left on the opaque and smooth surface of the tomb by the chisel of a writer/sculptor. It is written, id has spoken: the tomb silently speaks.

*Reminder:* "Just as the twenty-four letters of the alphabet are used to form our words and to express our thoughts, so the forms of the human body are used to express the various passions of the soul and to make visible what is in the mind."[9] In the same way, the fourteen letters of the inscription, the four words, make visible on the outside—on the surface—what is in the "sememe."

## Reading 4

What follows is essentially a rereading of the previous readings. As I contemplate the painting I note two absences, one in the opening moments of my theory, another in its conclusion. The absences, then, exist precisely where an eye or voice should have been present. The role of the *eye* in the painting would have been to denote, designate, and constitute the space in which a creative/contemplative gaze might operate. Instead, however, the painter effaces himself. The painter effaces *me* as he effaces *himself*. Further, *a word* emerging from the center of the stone would have provided the proper name of the writer/author who inscribed the signs on the marble slab, a name that everybody and nobody can appropriate. This double absence nonetheless serves to establish a connection between the gaze and the name—because they are both missing—between the subject of the enunciation with his point of view and its opposite, the signifier with its vanishing point in the center. The painting, we know, enunciates or states a story through the harmonious frieze comprising four figures whose attention, in one way or another, centers on four written words. What is noteworthy in this case is that the representation represents an absence at its origin and in its moment of completion. More specifically, it posits the subject of representation as absent at the beginning and this subject's "other", an utterance that is at once highly unstable and forever fixed, as absent at the end. The instability can be explained by the fact that the utterance belongs to everyone and no one. Its stable nature, on the other hand, derives from its inscription on the marble slab. Either way, we are dealing with an absence, since the utterance has no enunciator. We touch here on the enigma of autobiography, the inscription of a living self, "zoographos"—which in Greek means "painter." "Zoographos" then, is perhaps nothing more than the relation established through absence between an autobiographical subject and an autothanatographic subject. It is also possible, however, that the two subjects are one and the same, that the autobiographical subject must assume a certain form in order to become present through representation. The form in question is "insignificant": without meaning, but giving rise to meaning. I am thinking of a dead sign, a sememe, of four signs, of the beginnings of a story that is told by everyone and no one, a story that the ego must grasp hold of if it is to constitute itself as an "I" in what is essentially a violent process.

The very fact of articulating a theoretical question concerning a dual absence (at the painting's origin and at its end) has rather extraordinary consequences. In posing the question, I bring about this violent self-constitution: I find myself, finally, inscribed within the painting, where I discover my double in the figure of the kneeling shepherd. Within the represented scene, this double has already achieved what I achieve once I begin to write and to contemplate. He sees as I see, reads as I read, and points as I point. In his case, it is a matter of seeing, reading, and identifying the inscription on the wall of the tomb; in my case, these activities concern the painting in which both he and the inscription are inscribed. The kneeling shepherd of Arcadia is a repetition of me, just as I am a repetition of him, in an endless interlacing: he represents me in the painting just as I imitate him beyond its frame; at once included and excluded, the shepherd and I hover around a double absence, between two absent terms. The painting is to me what the tomb is to him: the tomb is his painting; the tomb is my painting. It is not impossible that the intense thrill of theory is precisely this kind of violence.

What exactly does it mean to represent something? How, in the case of painting, is the *process* of representation articulated and constructed in and by the product we refer to as a "painting"? How can the depths of another world be revealed on the painting's smooth, geometrically circumscribed, and framed surface? How can the painting make legible the indecipherable secret of this other world?

## Theoretical Digression 3: On Theory or the Readerly Gaze

Let us consider Charles Le Brun's 1667 reading of *The Israelites Gathering Manna in the Desert*. The analysis is of great theoretical interest not only because it presents a well-reasoned description of Poussin's painting, but also because it stages the scene of representation. Le Brun studies the painting in two psychologically linked stages. He first scans the painting in order to grasp it in its totality, to contemplate it as a whole, and then focuses attentively on its individual parts. These two stages are carefully identified in Félibien's "Entretien VIII": "This painting was exhibited in the Academy, not only so that it could be seen by the entire assembly, but also so that each of its parts could be scrutinized."[10] Now it turns out that these two moments in the process of reading echo two logically connected moments in the process of creation, those of invention and arrangement. "Invention" refers to the choice of subject matter and to the general conception of the composition. "Arrangement," on the other hand, concerns the painter's distribution of forms and of light, his organization of the space and of the figures.

As he scans the painting more generally, Le Brun first takes in the landscape, the scenic space or backdrop. He then turns his gaze to the foreground, where he perceives the group on the left, then the group on the right, and then the empty space between the two. Next the critic's eye explores the painting's center, registering Moses and Aaron "accompanied by the people's Elders displayed in various postures."[11] Finally, Le Brun's gaze returns to the landscape and morning sky that serve as the backdrop of the representation.

The analysis of the painting's specific elements and use of figurative space takes place within this general framework. The problem to be resolved concerns the connection between the figures and the sites they occupy. Put differently, it is a matter of clarifying how space can be represented. Le Brun makes a remarkable theoretical comment along these lines: the gaze must in fact be free—"the eye must be able to move about" the expanse of this desert—but it cannot simply "wander."[12] The gaze must be brought to a halt, but may not become fixed. Through representation, the viewer's gaze must somehow articulate a connected and integrated representational space that adequately accounts for the specificity of the various figures. In so doing, the viewer transforms a perceptual continuum, the site of a wandering gaze, into a figurative discontinuum, the site of reading. And this transformation is itself a condition of possibility of meaning. The viewer's eyes should not constantly be caught up in scanning such a vast countryside. Thus attention is focused on "groups of figures that in no way detract from the main subject, but serve to bring it together and make it more readily understandable."[13] A beautiful and harmonious painting is an integrated whole made up of oppositions and differences, an ordering of diversity through the completion of a series of visual trajectories.

Le Brun fully understands that in *this* painting the principle of articulation governing the distribution of figures is the central and empty space in the foreground, a space that frees the gaze from the peripeteia, including the groups on the left and right, thereby orienting it instead toward the two crucial figures in the middle. It is in this central area that the painting's subject matter is constructed by means of a spatialized architecture. This is where the subject matter's meaning is articulated and grasped: "The two parts of this painting, the one on the right, the other on the left, form two groups of figures, thereby leaving the center open for the gaze freely and better to discover Moses and Aaron, who are farther away."[14]

Félibien proposes something like a definition of "peripeteia":

> One notices that these groups made up of different figures performing various actions are much like episodes serving the function of what is called a "peripeteia." That is, they provide the means of conveying the shift that occurred in the plight of the Israelites, who went from a state of extreme hardship to happier times.[15]

Father d'Aubignac also provides a useful definition of the term in chapter 5 of his *Pratique du théâtre*: "a transformation and stabilization of theatrical matters, in the course of which the hero goes from a state of prosperity to one of adversity, or vice versa."[16] If we were to aim at a more precise analysis, it would be a matter of accounting for the interpretive displacement of the viewer's vision of the painting, a displacement that takes place in all "readings." Indeed, we would have to explain the way in which Le Brun's reading distorts Poussin's painting. Le Brun suggests that the groups are distributed symmetrically to the right and left, around the central empty space in the foreground and around Moses and Aaron in the middle ground. In fact, however, the figures are organized according to a subtle play of oblique lines running from left to right in the foreground and from right to left in the middle ground. These lines generate the zigzag movement that is so characteristic of Poussin's landscapes painted toward the end of the decade, that is, after the studies dating from 1643–44 that are currently housed in the National Gallery in London. There is, however, a fundamental difference between *The Israelites Gathering Manna* and these landscapes: in *The Israelites Gathering Manna* it is the arrangement of the figures that imbues the space with movement; in the later paintings, the representation of space does not depend on the figures, except at key points.

It would be possible to run through essentially the same analysis with regard to the distribution of light, expressions, and proportions. "Seeing" and "reading" are articulated as follows in and by the painting: (1) as a result of the figures' arrangement in a figurative locus, a space emerges that can be explored by the viewer's gaze; (2) at the same time, the arrangement in question is the formal condition of possibility of interpretation and meaning; it is the space in which the gaze becomes discursive. The operative principle governing this articulation is the creation of a series of oppositions that is contained not only by the frame, but by the law that condenses a story from history into a subject matter appropriate to painting. Yet stories are not governed by laws deriving from their external referents, but by an internal law determining the organization of differences. The question is, how?

# Denegation

*Hypothesis 1:* Perspective and prospective together make up the formal structure of enunciation and representation.

*Hypothesis 2:* In order to be effective, the "iconic" story must *inscribe itself* within the apparatus of enunciation and representation; it must transform and *neutralize* this apparatus in what amounts to (de)negation.

*Goal 1:* I would like to uncover the transformational rules governing the apparatus of enunciation and representation in a case of narrative painting.

*Goal 2:* I would like to prove that the painting *The Arcadian Shepherds* is unique because (1) it is governed by these transformational rules, and (2) it reveals these rules in an iconic and narrative process.

## Brunellesco's Optical Box or the Paradigm of Hypothesis 1

Let me begin by citing a lengthy passage from Antonio Manetti's *Vita di Filippo di Ser Brunellesco:*

> As for perspective, the first work in which he showed it was a small panel about half a *braccio* square on which he made a picture of the church of S. Giovanni of Florence. He painted the outside of the church and as much as can be seen at one glance. It seems that to draw this picture he went some three *braccia* inside the central door of S. Maria del Fiore. The panel was made with much care and delicacy and so precisely, in the colors of the black and white marble, that there is not a miniaturist who could have done better. He pictured in the center the part of the piazza directly in front of him, and thus, on one side, that which extends toward the Misericordia as far as the arch and the Canto de' Pecori; and on the other that from the column commemorating the miracle of St. Zenobius all the way to the Canto alla Paglia. For the distance, and the part representing the sky, where the boundaries of the painting merge into the air, Filippo placed burnished silver so that the actual air and the sky might be reflected in it, and so the clouds that one sees reflected in the silver, are moved by the wind when it blows.
>
> The painter of such a picture assumes that it has to be seen from a

single point, which is fixed in reference to the height and the width of the picture, and that it has to be seen from the right distance. Seen from any other point, the effect of the perspective would be distorted. Thus, to prevent the spectator from falling into error in choosing his view point, Filippo made a hole in the picture at that point in the view of the church of S. Giovanni which is directly opposite to the eye of the spectator, who might be standing in the central portal of S. Maria del Fiore in order to paint the scene. This hole was small as a lentil on the painted side, and on the back of the panel it opened out in a conical form to the size of a ducat or a little more, like the crown of a woman's straw hat. Filippo had the beholder put his eye against the reverse side where the hole was large, and while he shaded his eye with his one hand, with the other he was told to hold a flat mirror on the far side in such a way that the painting was reflected in it. The distance from the mirror to the hand near the eye had to be in a given proportion to the distance between the point where Filippo stood in painting his picture and the church of S. Giovanni. When one looked at it thus, the burnished silver already mentioned, the perspective of the piazza, and the fixing of the point of vision made the scene absolutely real. I have had the painting in my hand and have seen it many times in those days, so I can testify to it.[1]

## Claims

Brunellesco's optical box establishes the structural equivalence, within the system, between the point of view and the vanishing point in the pro-duction (*Vor-stellung*), in paint, of certain appearances, and/or in their reception by a contemplating eye (*Darstellung*). The box makes the gaze and the eye equivalent in the sense that it submits the gaze to the eye, to its geometrical and optical law. This equation, which is also a subjugation of the gaze and the eye, is the means by which the eye-subject is constituted. Yet the equation is only made evident in the effects produced by a mirror placed before the painting; the viewer looks at the painting in the mirror through (*per-spectiva*) the support, and his eye thus receives from the mirror (*pro-spectiva*) the projection of objects represented on the surface of the canvas: the reflection of what the painting "represents."

Representation, we note, is at once a matter of what might be called "spectacularity" and specularity, for the window onto the world is also a mirror. In its capacity as realized abstraction, Brunellesco's experimental apparatus identifies what is brought together in the realization or actual production of a painting or representation.

The referent's clear visibility through specularity coincides with its absence: the world in all of its scientific exactitude is actually present in the appearances perceived by the viewer. Thanks to the laws of what is called "new painting," there is no world other than that of immanence, identity, and sameness. Yet the painting's surface is the vehicle for nothing other than the image or reflection of this world. The representational screen is a window through which the viewer contemplates the scene represented in the painting *as though* he were seeing a scene in the real world. It is important to keep in mind that insofar as this screen is a plane, a surface, and a material support, it is also the reflexive/reflecting apparatus on which real objects are drawn and painted.

My first claim, then, is that if a painting is a surface or material support, then it does not exist: in coming to terms with the natural world, the human gaze is in no way bound by interpretive grids or filters. My second claim is that if the natural world is to be represented at all, then the kind of surface or material support referred to as a "painting" must exist; paintings make possible an exact mirroring of reality. It follows that the human eye registers only the world's double.

These claims explain why the material "canvas" and "real" surface must be posited and neutralized in what is essentially a technical, theoretical, and ideological assumption of transparency: the invisibility of the painting's surface or material support is itself the condition of the represented world's visibility. Translucence is the technical/theoretical definition of the plastic screen of representation.

## Hypothesis 1 Revisited

Perspective and prospective do in fact constitute the formal structure of enunciation and representation. Rephrased in Poussin's terms, the structure consists in the reduction of aspects to prospects, of vision to theory, and of the perceiving gaze to the rational eye. But if perspective and prospective make up the structure, they do so only as a result of a systematic (de)negation of the reflexive/reflecting apparatus: the painting. Thus, representation as mimesis is made possible only by (de)negation. I argued above that historical paintings negate the sub-

ject of enunciation and representation. We now learn that a prior negation occurs at the level of the representational apparatus itself.

It is important to remember at this point that Brunellesco's optical
cube has no ceiling. In this respect it resembles the scenographic cube
that representational painting makes accessible to the theoretical eye,
which has only three walls. The sun's natural light and the play of its
rays in the clouds light up the reflection in the mirror of the representation of the Church of San Giovanni in Florence. While the (absent)
fourth wall of the scenographic cube is illumined by the same source,
the represented scene is not. What we confront here is the problem of
representing light, the problem of what I want to call a "gaze-light" or
an "eye-source-of-light." These terms are meant to capture the idea of a
source of light that does not fall within the scope of a given point of
view. What needs to be pondered, then, is the exact site of this source.
Caravaggio may well help in this regard. Let us consider some of the
claims made by Giulio Mancini in his manuscript entitled *Considerazioni sulla Pittura* (1619–21):

> The salient feature of the school of Caravaggio is the use of a constant
> source of light that illuminates from above without reflections, just as this
> might occur in a room with only one window and with walls painted
> black; the light is so bright and the shadows so dark as to create a certain
> sense of depth in the painting. . . . In my mind these procedures are not
> appropriate to the composition of the story and the expression of emo-
> tion . . . for it is impossible to arrange within a single room illuminated
> by only one window a large number of figures who enact the story, who
> laugh, cry, and walk, and who at the same time stand still in order to be
> painted.[2]

## Theoretical Digression 4: On the Mirror-Window as Mirrored Representation of the Window in the Representational Scene, or the Representation of the Reflexive/Reflecting Apparatus

I want to focus on a tapestry by Le Brun that is part of the "History of
the King" series. The tapestry in question tells of a meeting that took
place between Louis XIV and Phillip IV of Spain on the Île des Faisants
in 1660. If we construct the perspectival network of the "painting"—
an easy task thanks to the traces of construction on the "ground" of the
represented scene—we note that the vanishing point of the perspec-

tival framework is situated in the lower left-hand corner of what would appear, at first sight, to be an open window at the back of the room, but which "in reality" is a mirror reflecting a window. Thus, the window must necessarily be situated outside the "painting" and its scenography, in the very site occupied by the viewer, which is identical to his point of view. Light enters and illuminates the "painting" through this invisible window: thanks to the mirror, which itself illuminates nothing, the eye is at once a source of light and its receptacle.

As a result of this mirror and the window it reflects, the point of view is shown in the representation as the vanishing point. The point of view, which in one sense is absent from the "painting," is also present as the vanishing point generated by the mirror's reflection. The absent origin of the painted objects is at the same time their present represented end. What we have here, at the level of representation, is the structural equivalence of two points. One might be tempted to assume that the represented reflection of the painting, which is also a reflection, somehow captures the world as it naturally and historically unfolds, in an operation that is the exact opposite of the first one performed. This is anything but the case, for the reflection in question in fact multiplies the mimetic aspects of the painting by representing the operation that constitutes it. In short, the representation represents the operation of which it is a product. The reflection's reflection is what I want to call a mimeme "to the second degree." Its function is simultaneously to posit and to efface the structure of representation while representing the effacement in question. The mirror bears the mark, through absence, of the ultimate denegation. This mirror, we recall, visibly reflects the window that is *absent* from the painting precisely because the painting itself is a *window-mirror* that makes visible the absence of real things. I have been suggesting that the point of view is situated in the lower left-hand corner of the window reflected in the mirror, the site where the viewer's eye necessarily is located. Yet this eye is not itself made manifest. Indeed, it is not reflected in its virtual image, unless, of course, we construe the mirror reflecting the window as the gaze by which the painting conveys to the viewer the image of his own eye.

We have seen that the perspectival syntax of Le Brun's historical "painting" defines the structure of representation/enunciation only in order to (de)negate it. It is this structure, however, that allows the exact site of the point of view to be determined, both geometrically and optically. The "painting" is thus seen, produced, or emitted from the point of view of an "I" existing in the here and now. At the same time, the equivalence established by the mirror's reflection identifies this point of view as absent, even as it is made manifest in the vanishing point of the "painting." The reflection posits the subject of representation/enunciation as absent. What we have here is the iconic equivalent of the grammatical "it" characterizing the texts of historical narratives.

Support for this analysis can be found in the folds of the sumptuous, raised curtain in the upper part of the painting. Much like the two tapestries on the left and right, this curtain is an element of the represented scene. We need only consult the *Memoirs* of Mademoiselle de Montpensier to know that the curtain played an important role in the actual meeting. By lowering or raising it, the scene of the ceremony could be transformed, that is, it could be divided up or enlarged according to the exact rules of diplomatic etiquette. Certain political exigencies could thus be taken into account as the historical event unfolded. As far as the scene of the meeting is concerned, it makes sense to assume that the curtain normally covered the length of the wall, including the one window that was the room's only source of light. The curtain, then, we may further assume, was raised for the occasion in question. Yet, on closer analysis, the wall and window seem to disappear from the "painting" in order to make the representation possible. More precisely, the wall becomes the painting's transparent window through which we, as viewers/painters, contemplate the spectacle of the meeting.

Le Brun's tapestry brings to light a certain ambiguity that is quite typical of historical painting from the French classical period. The raised curtain is *part of the represented scene* that picks out a given object as its referent; it is part of the historical event described by the painting's story. However, the curtain is also necessarily an *element of the representation* that transforms the scene into a form of theater or spectacle. The curtain is no longer an instrument of the scenography of the event but of the scenography of the painting. In short, it is a means by which the frame encompasses and posits the painting as representation. The curtain is thus both an element of the utterance and a feature of the enunciation. The ambiguity in question here is part and parcel of the operation of the denegation of the enunciation discussed above.

What is noteworthy is that this first ambiguity is accompanied by a second one. Indeed, we note that the curtain's most ample and solemn folds are deployed in the center of the painting, above the heads of the two kings. By virtue of its centrality, the curtain is a *plastic and decorative element of the composition*. By virtue of its position above the two royal heads, it becomes a *coded sign of their importance* relative to the other figures, a symbol of their supreme political and religious power, the ultimate avatar of the triumphal arch or the imperial baldachin. The part of the painting that may be called the "raised curtain" turns out to involve many facets: (1) a representation of a curtain referring to a real aspect of the event and its topographical environment; (2) a curtain in the theatrical sense of the term, that is, a means of marking the staged nature of the event and the process of enunciation itself; (3) a represented curtain whose lavish folds underscore the "aesthetic" nature of the composition of the "painting": this aspect of the representation reinforces the symmetry of the scene, which is traceable to the central point identified in the mirror/window and to the balanced movements that animate the two groups of figures and culminate in the meeting of the royals; (4) a curtain/baldachin that is the symbolic sign of the kind of royal and religious power that is invested in these two figures. In enumerating these meanings through a study of the polysemic nature of one element of the painting, we engage in a reciprocal process involving the mobilization and application of semantics and grammar. The specific function of this process is to give rise to a perpetual oscillation between the enumerated meanings, thereby bringing about an unending positing and negating of the operation of enunciation and representation: the viewer only occupies the plane of enunciation in order to abandon it immediately and regain the plane of utterances, and vice versa. In this way the denegation of representation that gives the painting its historical/narrative dimension is *represented in the painting*. Enunciation is posited and identified only in order to be dissimulated and negated.

## *The Arcadian Shepherds* Revisited

We have seen that the mirror in the background of Le Brun's tapestry *reflects* the translucent and invisible window through which the eye contemplates the historic royal scene and thereby highlights its glory.

For the sake of argument, I now want to suggest that the mirror is to this royal scene what the opaque and visible wall of the tomb is to the Arcadian or utopian scene of Poussin's *Arcadian Shepherds*. Inscribed on the surface of this wall, we recall, are four written signs that are legible and that are indeed read. These signs are the epitaph of a (hi)story as well as the *shadow* of the person—I, you, all of you, all of us—who contemplates the scene and attempts a reading of it.

## Some Important Citations

### On the Origin of Painting

Shall we follow the example of those painters whose sole aim is to be able to copy pictures by using the ruler and the measuring rod? It is a positive disgrace to be content to owe all our achievement to imitation. For what, I ask again, would have been the result if no one had done more than his predecessors? . . . We should still be sailing on rafts, and the art of painting would be restricted to tracing a line round a shadow thrown in the sunlight.[3]

### Who discovered painting? The Egyptians, the Chaldeans, the Greeks?

But it is my opinion that design, which is the foundation of both arts, and the very soul which conceives and nourishes in itself every part of the intelligence, came into full existence at the time of the origin of all things, when the Most High, after creating the world and adorning the heavens with shining lights, descended through the limpid air to the solid earth, and by shaping man, disclosed the first form of sculpture and painting in the charming invention of things. Who will deny that from this man, as from a living example, the ideas of statues and sculpture, and the questions of pose and of outline, first took form; and from the first pictures, whatever they may have been, arose the first ideas of grace, unity, and the discordant concords made by the play of lights and shadows? . . . But according to Pliny this art was introduced into Egypt by Gyges of Lydia, who, on seeing his shadow cast by the fire, at once drew an outline of himself on the wall with a piece of coal.[4]

### From the Reflection in the Mirror to the Shadow on the Wall

It is scarcely possible to find any superior art which is not concerned with painting, so that whatever beauty is found can be said to be born of painting. *Moreover, painting was given the highest honour by our ancestors. For, although almost all other artists were called craftsmen, the painter alone was not considered in that category.* For this reason, I say among my friends that Narcissus who was changed into a flower, according to the poets, was the inventor of painting. Since painting is already the flower of every art, the story of Narcissus is most to the point. What else can you call a painting but a similar embracing with art of what is presented on the surface of the water in the fountain?

Quintilian said that the ancient painters used to circumscribe shadows cast by the sun, and from this our art has grown.[5]

## The Distribution of Bodies/Figures or the Paradigmatic Example of Hypothesis 2

Pymandre said to me: Can it be that in such a large group there was no one who could find anything to criticize in this great work? Your question, I replied, makes me think of the member of the Academy who, after having praised Poussin's painting, raised an objection in order to captivate his audience. He said that it seemed to him that although Poussin had been scrupulous in wishing to exclude none of the necessary incidents from the story's composition, he nonetheless had failed to produce an image that sufficiently resembled what happened in the desert when the manna fell from God. Poussin, he said, represented the manna as snow falling during the day and for all the Israelites to see; which is contrary to the text of the Bible, where they are said to have discovered it, spread around the camp, in the morning like dew that they might then gather up. What is more, the great need and extreme suffering that he has underscored is inappropriate to the time of the action that he depicts: for when the people of Israel received the manna, they had already been saved by the quails, which had been sufficiently numerous to still the most acute hunger; thus it was unnecessary to paint people in a state of such languor, and even less to have this miraculous meat fall from Heaven in the manner of snow.

To this someone replied that Painting is different from History: a Historian makes himself understood by means of an arrangement of words and a series of discourses that form an image of things and successively represent the desired action; but since the Painter has only a single moment in which to grasp the thing that he wishes to depict on the canvas, it is sometimes necessary for him to conjoin many preceding events in order to make the subject that he exposes comprehensible. In the absence of this fusion, those who would see his work would be no better informed of the action that he represents than if a Historian, instead of reporting the entire subject of his story, was satisfied merely to report its conclusion.

It is for this reason, he continued, that Poussin, who wished to show how the manna was sent to the Israelites, thought that it was inadequate merely to spread it on the ground, and to represent the men and women as they were gathering it up. Poussin, he said, believed that, in order to mark the greatness of this miracle, he had simultaneously to show their previous condition. In order to do so he represented them in a desertlike site; some in a state of languor, others busy gathering the food, and still others thanking God for his mercy: these different states and these diverse actions took the place of words and discourse, allowing him to make himself understood. And since the Painter hardly has at his disposal a language or characters other than these kinds of impressions, he was obliged to show the manna as falling from Heaven; he has no other way of making its origin known. And if the manna were not shown as falling from on high but as being gathered off the ground by men and women, then the viewer might easily mistake it for grain or some kind of fruit. It is true, he continued, that the Israelites had already received nourishment from the quails that had fallen within the camp: but since this happened only one night, it makes sense to assume that the quails could not fully have restored the vigor of the starving. Even so, it is true that, on the preceding day, God had promised, through his prophet, to provide his people with meat that evening, and with bread every morning: however, given the number of people involved, many of whom were spread out over a large area, it is not impossible that some had not yet heard the promise that had been made to them, or if they had, that they did not believe the words of Moses, since they were naturally incredulous. To all these reasons someone else added that if the rules of theater allow Poets to conjoin into a single action a number of events that occurred at different times, as long as no contradiction results, and as long as the issue of verisimilitude is taken carefully into account, it is only fair that Painters also be allowed to take this license, since their works otherwise would be deprived of what makes the composition all the more admirable, and the beauty of the Author's genius all the more apparent. He added that one could not accuse Poussin, in bringing these elements together, of having included anything that hinders the unity of action, or anything that is contrary to verisimilitude, there being nothing in the painting that does not converge in a single subject. Although he did not entirely follow the Holy Scriptures, one cannot say that he departed from the truth of the story.[6]

## Claims

An iconic story is the representation of a narrative moment or instant in the form of an achronic model of intelligibility. By arranging certain bodies/figures on a plane that is schematically parallel to that of the plastic screen, the painter employs the basic means by which this narrative model may be constructed. This use of space is also what makes possible an articulation of the timeless present of the moment of representation (the only moment the classical painter is allowed to represent) and its topographical circumstances. What is thus created is a potential story capable of converting the description of the painting's spatial and logical relations into an ongoing reading governed by the order in which the reader actively registers the elements. We discover here a new way of approaching the (de)negation of enunciation and representation. More specifically, it is a matter of analyzing the way in which bodies and figures are arranged in a painting, the order in which the narrative utterances are received by the viewer. The "iconic" story is thus clearly inscribed within the apparatus of enunciation and representation.

But, as we have seen, this apparatus is far from static: the structural equivalence of the vanishing point and point of view implies that the movement leading from one to the other is reversible with regard to what is represented. The network underwriting the painting is vectorial and comprises lines of directed force. Yet the general orientation or direction of this network can be reversed by foregrounding the logical features of the "temporal" process of enunciation and reception. Insofar as the construction of a "model" involves spatializing the relations governing the represented elements distributed throughout this two-way network, these elements are necessarily affected. Without even being aware of doing so, we thus shift our attention from the emitting of the iconic "message" in the here and now, from the temporal and spatial situation in which the message is produced, to the structure of the emission, to the model articulating its mode of production, from the utterance as it is apprehended in the process of enunciation to the grammar governing its production, grammar being the only appropriate object of any analytic study. But why, one might ask, are we unaware of this shift in focus? Because the discourse that enunciates this grammar and *produces* its syntax is itself a verbal message, a process of enunciation and production that retemporalizes the model. This retemporalization essentially follows the semantic and lexical imperatives of the propositional contents that are made accessible, through the painting, to the viewer's visual and cognitive capacities. These contents, it should be noted, are accompanied by what we might call a "referential temporality," for they refer to the historical actions that are incorporated into the painting's story. For the curious viewer whose eye registers what is represented in the painting, there has to be a story. That is, it has to be possible to bring together coherently the past and future moments that are posited as coming either before or after the central moment in the representation. Yet, in so doing, the viewer will merely enunciate in the temporal forms proper to stories, the grammatical and syntactical relations underwriting the model known as narrative painting.

*This raises the problem of the link between the arrangement of bodies/figures and the structure of represented space, and also provides the solution.* Poussin's painting seems to effect a transformation, in the geometric sense of the term, consisting in *lateralizing* the depth structure of the represented space—a deep structure that perspective (and its various geometric and aerial modalities) regulates and organizes—by arranging the figures of the story or *istoria* in a frieze that parallels the plane of the painting or *tavola*. This point is crucial and has been made repeatedly, especially in comparisons of the two versions of the painting, that of the Louvre and that of the Chatsworth Settlement in Derbyshire. Yet my suspicion is that the significance of the transformation in question has yet to be properly grasped; the same can be said of the specific nature of the operations involved. The transformative process essentially involves two key operations. It is first of all a matter of *displacing* the vanishing point from both the perspective's *visible* depth structure and from the *horizon* of the represented space at the central point of the lateral structure. This also entails displacing the vanishing point from the legible surface of the iconically told tale. The second operation effects something like a ninety-degree rotation of the bundle of optical rays whose vertices coincide with the painting's perspectival point of view and with its vanishing point. These rays are then situated on a plane that parallels that of the painting and that is marked by figures arranged as groups facing each other in a frieze. It is in this parallel plane that the inverted equivalence of the network's two points is established.

As the first transformative operation (T1) is effected, the point of view and vanishing point, which are structurally equivalent, together become the central event in the narrated tale, its focal moment. This focal point, which is also the "site of the speaking subject," is where the tale is concentrated. The event seems to describe itself in much the same way that it engineered its own production. That is, the telling takes place not on the horizon of the painting, but on that of the story. There is nobody speaking here, for there is no longer a narrator.

The second operation (T2) transforms the point of view (Pv) of the perspectival apparatus or formal structure of enunciation/representation into a point of origin (0), just as it makes the vanishing point (Vp) of the apparatus the final moment (F) in the painting's represented story. We recall that the gaze of the "shepherd" on the left (A) is directed at the figure kneeling by the tomb (B). This gaze is essentially directed back at the shepherd via the "shepherdess" on the right (D), whose own gaze marks the end of a silent dialogue with her companion (C), the last mute "word" in an exchange of gestures and looks.

The second transformative operation has implications for the point of view/vanishing point that together produce and absorb the appearances painted in the depth of the (illusory) space of representation. This point, largely hidden by the central tomb, is displaced with great precision onto the center of the tomb's wall, where it becomes at once the place and the time of the story's unfolding. Between the right-hand index fingers of the two shepherds facing each other, we discover the place and time of the event—its inscription, decipherment, and designation. What we have here is precisely the site of a letter in the event's epitaph, the site of a fissure in the surface of its wall.

It should be clear by now that the transformational operations identified above are crucial. They essentially free the representation in question from its own process of production, a process on which it nonetheless depends. As a result, this representation is posited as objectively autonomous. Yet its autonomy is based purely on satisfying the kind of theoretical desire that allows the subject to constitute and efface itself.

The following diagrams constitute useful tools for visualizing the two transformational processes:

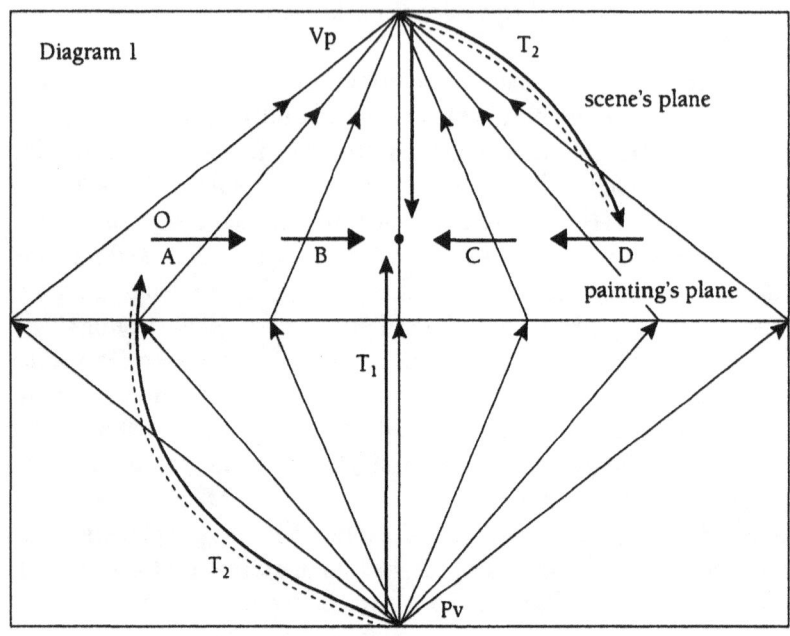

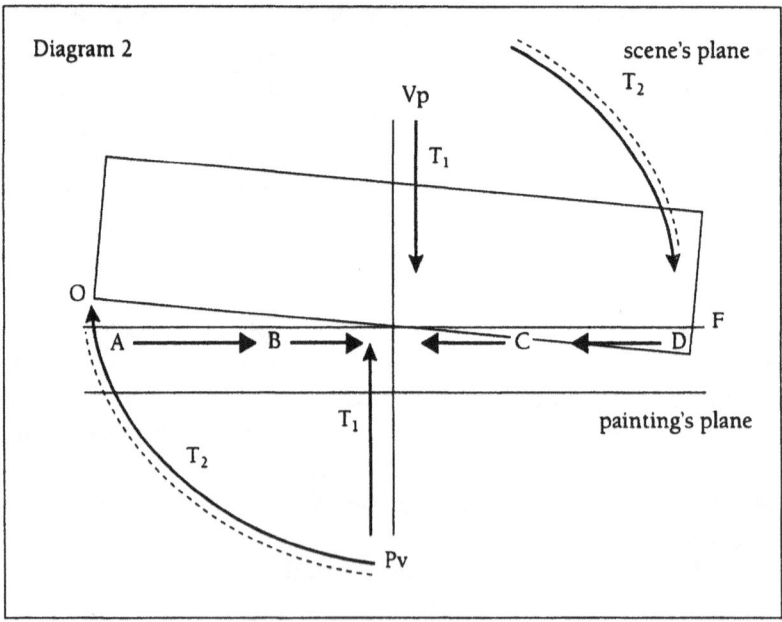

It is as if there were a second eye somewhere in the wings to the left of the scene, near the plane of the painting. From its hidden site, this eye seems to perceive the dimension of *depth* that is opened up within the painting's plane by the relation between the representation's point of view and its vanishing point. What is curious, however, is that the eye perceives this depth as *breadth*. Moreover, this relation could never be grasped by the eye of the viewer/painter, as it coincides entirely with his line of vision. It is as if the iconic story, displayed by the bodies arranged within the plane of the scene paralleling the plane of the painting, somehow makes it possible for the theoretical eye to see itself. Yet this eye does not in fact see itself but a story. In the center of this story, the eye flattens itself against the tomb's marble wall and leaves a trace. The eye thus sees itself in a series of visible and legible substitutes, in the bodies, gestures, looks, and fingers that point to four signs, the last of which is "Ego," a sign that stands out from the rest.

Yet there is a trace throughout the painting of the second, hidden, enigmatic, and anamorphotic eye, a trace that inscribes the hidden eye within the represented figures. Indeed, it is this sunlike eye that illumines the scene from the wings on the left, thereby casting onto the wall of the tomb the *shadow* of the reading and deciphering shepherd who functions as our representative within the representation. What is striking is that the shadow falls exactly on the key event in the painting's narrative. This is surely the most remarkable of points, for it is where a represented finger, its shadow, and one of the written signs from the epitaph *come together.* Existing on the *surface* of the tomb, this point cannot be reduced to the end of a finger, the tip of its shadow, or the trace of a sign, for it is all these things at once. The point is blind, neutral, and neutralizing; it resembles the tip of the blind man's cane that Descartes described in his *Dioptrics* as evoking precisely, the instantaneity of a ray of light.

According to Poussin, a painting is "an imitation made on a surface with lines and colors of everything that one sees *under the sun.*"[7] In my analysis I have been focusing on what I have referred to as the "iconic story," that is, the story that the viewer/reader tells herself as she contemplates a serene and immobile representation enshrined within the optical pyramid of her eye. Perhaps the iconic story always presents this Apollonian presence that will generate time, order, and change in an ongoing discursive murmuring. There seems to be evidence sug-

gesting that every story that is ineluctably produced in the timeless matrix of painting can be traced to the *hidden presence* of a second eye
lurking in the wings. Drawing on the solar light that emanates from it,
this eye-fiction shapes the bodies and figures beyond the smooth and
invisible surface of the painting's mirror/window. The dimension of
depth is invisible since it cannot be discerned within perceptual space
or within the illusion realized on the canvas. This is so because depth is
generated by the gaze of a perceiving subject in an imaginary projection extending all the way to the vanishing point on the horizon, where
it is negated. The dimension of depth is what is seen by the illuminat-
ing and fictional eye that is virtually hidden from the plane of the specular screen. It is also what is cast back to the eye of the viewer/reader in
the rhythmic movements of figures and bodies. What we have here is a
story that tells itself.

## Some Important Citations

The operations constitutive of representation in general, and of narrative and iconic representations in particular, consist precisely in denying the existential character of depth in order to lateralize, reflect, or
represent it as breadth.

> Traditional ideas of perception are at one in denying that depth is visible.
> Berkeley shows that it could not be given to sight in the absence of any
> means of recording it, since our retinas receive only a manifestly flat pro-
> jection of the spectacle. If one retorted that after the criticism of the
> 'constancy hypothesis' we cannot judge what we see by what is pictured
> on our retinas, Berkeley would probably reply that, whatever may be true
> of the retinal image, depth cannot be seen because it is not spread out
> before our eyes, but appears to them only in foreshortened form. In ana-
> lytical reflection, it is for theoretical reasons that depth is to be judged
> invisible: even if it could be registered by our eyes, the sensory impression
> would present only a multiplicity in itself, which would have to be ranged
> over, so that distance, like all other spatial relations, exists only for a sub-
> ject who synthesizes it and embraces it in thought. Though diametrically
> opposed to each other, the two doctrines presuppose the same repression
> of our affective experience. In both cases depth is tacitly equated with
> *breadth seen from the side,* and this is what makes it invisible. Berkeley's ar-
> gument, made quite explicit, runs roughly like this. What I call depth is in
> reality a juxtaposition of points, making it comparable to breadth. I am

simply badly placed to see it. I should see it if I were in the position of a spectator looking on from the side, who can take in at a glance the series of objects spread out in front of me, whereas for me they conceal each other—or see the distance from my body to the first object, whereas for me this distance is compressed into a point. What makes depth invisible for me is precisely what makes it visible for the spectator as breadth; the juxtaposition of simultaneous points in one direction which is that of my gaze. The depth which is declared invisible is, therefore, a depth already identified with breadth and, this being the case, the argument would lack even a semblance of consistency. In the same way, intellectualism can bring to light, in the experience of depth, a thinking subject who synthesizes that experience, only because it reflects on the basis of a depth already in existence, on a juxtaposition of simultaneous points which is not depth as it is presented to me, but as it is presented to a spectator standing at the side, in short as breadth. By assimilating one to the other from the very outset, the two philosophies take for granted the result of a constitutive process the stages of which we must, in fact, trace back. In order to treat depth as breadth viewed in profile, in order to arrive at a uniform space, the subject must leave his place, abandon his point of view on the world, and think himself into a sort of ubiquity. For God, who is everywhere, breadth is immediately equivalent to depth. Intellectualism and empiricism do not give us any account of the human experience of the world; they tell us what God might think about it. And indeed it is the world itself which suggests to us that we substitute one dimension for another and conceive it from no point of view. All men accept without any speculation the equivalence of depth and breadth; this equivalence is part and parcel of the self-evidence of an intersubjective world, which is what makes philosophers as forgetful as anyone else of the originality of depth.[8]

As the subject becomes God, a theoretical eye, it ceases to be a perceiving body in the world, flesh that is both open and folded back on itself, a gaze that can both see and be seen. The embodied subject is instead neutralized as it divests itself of its worldly situation in order to constitute itself as the viewer of a painting.

More directly than the other dimensions of space, depth forces us to reject the preconceived notion of the world and rediscover the primordial experience from which it springs: it is, so to speak, the most 'existential' of all dimensions, because (and here Berkeley's argument is right) it is not impressed upon the object itself, it quite clearly belongs to the perspective and not to things. Therefore it cannot either be extracted from, or even put into that perspective by consciousness. It announces a certain indissoluble link between things and myself by which I am placed in front of them, whereas breadth can, at first sight, be taken as a relationship between things themselves, in which the perceiving subject is not implied.[9]

Merleau-Ponty can thus conclude his phenomenological description of depth by evoking a dual and reciprocal relation between time and space. This relation is itself the deep structure that will be neutralized by the narrative iconic representation. And this neutralization facilitates a surreptitious reproduction of the relation at the level of the imaginary.

One cannot, therefore, speak of a synthesis of depth, since a synthesis presupposes, or at least, like the Kantian synthesis, posits discrete terms, and since depth does not posit the multiplicity of perspective appearances to be made explicit by analysis, but sees that multiplicity only against the background of the stable thing. This quasi-synthesis is elucidated if we understand it as temporal. When I say that I see an object at a distance, I mean that I already hold it, or that I still hold it, it is in the future or in the past as well as being in space. It will perhaps be said that it is there only for me: in itself the lamp which I perceive exists at the same time as I do, that distance is between simultaneous objects, and that this simultaneity is contained in the very meaning of perception. No doubt. But co-existence, which in fact defines space, is not alien to time, but is the fact of two phenomena belonging to the same temporal wave. As for the relationship of the perceived object to my perception, it does not unite them in space and outside time: they are *contemporary*. The 'order of coexistents' is inseparable from the 'order of sequences', or rather time is not only the consciousness of a sequence. Perception provides me with a 'field of presence' in the broad sense, extending in two dimensions: the here-there dimension and the past-present-future dimension. The second elucidates the first. I 'hold', I 'have' the distant object without any explicit positing of the spatial perspective (apparent size and shape) as I still 'have in hand' the immediate past without any distortion and without any interposed 'recollection'. If we want to talk about synthesis, it will be, as Husserl says, a 'transitional synthesis', which does not link disparate perspectives, but brings about the 'passage' from one to the other. Psychology has involved itself in endless difficulties by trying to base memory on the possession of certain contents or recollections, the present traces (in the body or the unconscious) of the abolished past, for from these traces we can never come to understand the recognition of the past as past. In the same way we shall never come to understand the perception of distance if we start from contents presented, so to speak, all equidistant, a flat projection of the world, as recollections are a projection of the past in the present. And just as memory can be understood only as a direct possession of the past with no interposed contents, so the perception of distance can be understood only as a *being in the distance* which links up with being where it appears. Memory is built out of the progressive and continuous passing of one instant into another, and the interlocking of each one, with its whole horizon, in the thickness of its successor. The same continuous transition implies the object as it is out there, with, in short, its 'real' size as I should see it if I were beside it, in the perception that I have of it from here. Just as there is no possibility of engaging in any discussion of the 'conservation of recollections', but only of a certain way of seeing time which brings out the past as an inalienable dimension of consciousness, there is no problem of distance, distance being immediately visible provided that we can find the living present in which it is constituted.[10]

We have seen that in the case of *The Arcadian Shepherds* the spatio-temporal quasi-synthesis is brought about *between* two pointing index fingers, between two *bodily* hands and a *shadow,* between figures and signs, on the surface of the tomb that is the very sign of death itself. We are thus led quite naturally to reflect on the *Living Present* of the phenomenological monad, a Present that is made manifest only through the emergence of a scission or gap. A claim made by Aristotle comes to mind here: "Time, then, also is both made continuous by the 'now' and divided at it."[11]

## Goal 2 Revisited

As a painting, *this* painting, *The Arcadian Shepherds*, remains unique in its very generality. This is so because its center harbors a sememe or tomb, and because the center of this center itself reveals four written signs, the last of which is an empty signifer waiting to be filled by a living voice. The fact that this central site is identified in an indexical gesture that is also the tip of a shadow projected onto a wall by a solar light makes this painting a representation of representation itself, a representation of the relevant scenes, surfaces, supports, and bodies/figures. The painting clarifies the nature of all representation, which is essentially the (de)negation of the process of enunciation and representation. Poussin's work may be seen as a staging of this (de)negation. It represents the theoretical eye to itself by examining it from the blind center (blinding and blinded) where the body is nothing but a shadow and the painting nothing more than an opaque surface, the marble support where a silent word is pronounced: writing.

# The Arcadian Landscape

Let us temporarily forget about the bodies/figures and the tomb in order to describe the scene's Arcadian landscape. In passing, in this passage, we may well ask why I refer to the scene as "Arcadia": my act of forgetting, in order to read and to see, persists as the recollection of a title external to the canvas and its painted illusion, as the memory of a name that is bestowed on the painting by the knowledge, texts, stories, and history that bring together successive acts of contemplation. This memory, however, is preceded, at the "origin" of the History of knowledge, texts, and stories, by a memory that is far more ancient, since it is already inscribed in the center of the painting, on the wall of the tomb: Et in *Arcadia* Ego.

Yet my act of forgetting is literally impossible, for the name and the four bodies/figures surrounding it are all I see and read. It is a matter, then, of a kind of rhetorical forgetting that allows me to articulate what I see beneath, above, and to the left and right of the bodies/figures arranged around the tomb.

A wild and uncultivated landscape surrounds the figures, a "desert" as one said in the seventeenth century. I am thinking here of the discussion of the Sinai "desert" that took place at the Royal Academy of Painting when *The Israelites Gathering Manna in the Desert* was first exhibited, "not only so that it could be seen by the entire assembly, but also so that each of its parts could be scrutinized."

> First the members considered the spatial arrangement that perfectly represents a barren desert and uncultivated earth.
> For although the landscape is composed in a learned and agreeable manner, the figures are represented against a background consisting only of boulders. The trees are entirely leafless: there are neither plants nor grass; and one perceives neither the roads nor the paths that would lead one to assume that the land in question has been traveled.[1]

A desert, Arcadia, the Sinai . . . I refer to the untamed nature in question as "Arcadia" because of the commemorative sign in the middle of the painting: the tomb, "Et in Arcadia" . . .

> Poussin painted a shepherd who, with one knee on the ground, points to the following words engraved on a tomb, *Et in Arcadia ego.* Arcadia is a

land that has been described by poets as delightful: but this inscription is intended to indicate that the person in the tomb lived in Arcadia and that death may be found even where there is great happiness.[2]

The written name, and memory of it, transform the desert landscape into the original delights of nature.

Suffice it to say at this point that the landscape is an open curve extending all the way to the horizon. It provides a kind of natural casket for the sign, one whose massive geometry and quasi-abstract masonry annuls the learned art of making topographical and aerial transitions between the foreground and background.

Poussin's representation of space in *The Arcadian Shepherds* has been called "divergent" because of the dynamic it generates by means of a spatial rotation. More specifically, as the ground recedes on the left and right, it comes to the fore in a manner reminiscent of an animated circular scene; the ground stands out on the right and recedes on the left, creating a dynamic that evolves in stages around a straight vertical line at the painting's center. These stages are marked by the variously inclined axes of the shepherds' staffs, just as the line is created by the fissure that cuts across the tomb's wall. The dynamic is itself represented by the distance between the two hands and the curve of the shadow that is cast by the kneeling shepherd's arm, a distance that is traced at the center of the canvas, along the central axis of its depth of field.

Consider the following framework:

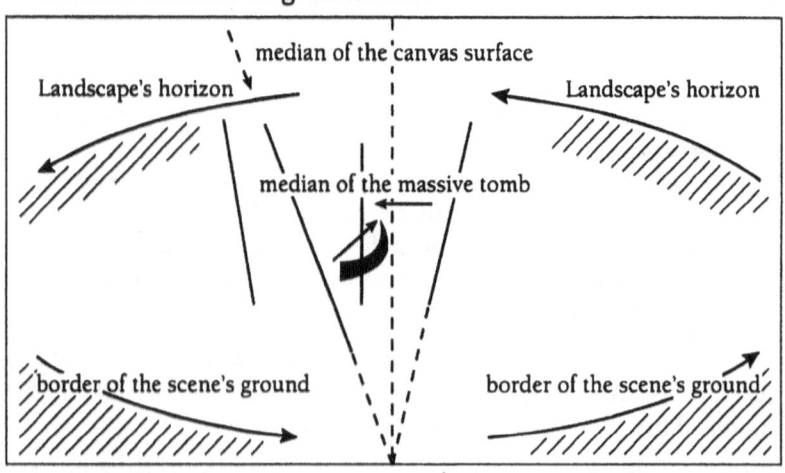

The diagram illustrates a divergence and convergence created by the circular movements of the painting's overall spatial organization and figures. The resulting rhythm reverberates in the spatial distribution of the figures at the center of the canvas and at the heart of the "story." The ground and figures making up the scene's theatrical dimension make visible a certain music, calling for a return to Arcadia and its landscape.

## A Digression on Music

Since the Arcadian nation on the whole has a very high reputation for virtue among the Greeks, due not only to their humane and hospitable character and usages, but especially to their piety to the gods, it is worth while to give a moment's consideration to the question of the savagery of the Cynaetheans, and ask ourselves why, though unquestionably of Arcadian stock, they so far surpassed all other Greeks at this period in cruelty and wickedness. I think the reason was that they were the first and indeed only people in Arcadia to abandon an admirable institution, introduced by their forefathers with a nice regard for the natural conditions under which all the inhabitants of that country live. For the practice of music, I mean real music, is beneficial to all men, but to Arcadians it is a necessity. . . . For it is a well-known fact, familiar to all, . . . that in the first place the boys from their earliest childhood are trained to sing in measure the hymns and paeans in which by traditional usage they celebrate the heroes and gods of each particular place: later they learn the measures of Philoxenus and Timotheus, and every year in the theatre they compete keenly in choral singing to the accompaniment of professional flute-players, the boys in the contest proper to them and the young men in what is called the men's contest. And not only this, but through their whole life they entertain themselves at banquets not by listening to hired musicians but by their own efforts, calling for a song from each in turn. Whereas they are not ashamed of denying acquaintance with other studies, in the case of singing it is neither possible for them to deny a knowledge of it because they all are compelled to learn it, nor, if they confess to such knowledge can they excuse themselves, so great a disgrace is this considered in that country. Besides this the young men practice military parades to the music of the flute and perfect themselves in dances and give annual performances in the theatres, all under state supervision and at the public expense. Now all these practices I believe to have been introduced by the men of old time, not as luxuries and superfluities but

because they had before their eyes the universal practice of personal man-
ual labour in Arcadia, and in general the toilsomeness and hardship of the
men's lives, as well as the harshness of character resulting from the cold
and gloomy atmospheric conditions usually prevailing in these parts—
conditions to which all men by their very nature must perforce assimilate
themselves. . . . The primitive Arcadians, therefore, with the view of soft-
ening and tempering the stubborness and harshness of nature, introduced
all the practices I mentioned, and in addition accustomed the people,
both men and women, to frequent festivals and general sacrifices, and
dances of young men and maidens, and in fact resorted to every contriv-
ance to render more gentle and mild, by the influence of the customs they
instituted, the extreme hardness of the national character. The Cynaetheans, by entirely neglecting these institutions, though in special
need of such influences, as their country is the most rugged and their
climate the most inclement in Arcadia, and by devoting themselves ex-
clusively to their local affairs and political rivalries, finally became so
savage that in no city of Greece were greater and more constant crimes
committed.[3]

The nature made legible by *The Arcadian Shepherds* is of the untamed variety, for it hardly reminds us, for example, of the Sicilian
charms in Poussin's *Landscape with Polyphemus* (Hermitage Museum,
St. Petersburg). The represented horizon is broken by mountains, in
the center and on the right, that function as slight plastic reminders of
the central tomb. The trees, rocks, and bushes surrounding the sep-
ulcher similarly evoke a wilderness, as do the hollows that break up the
scene's ground. Now, we note that Polybius is careful to oppose the hu-
manity, austerity, hospitality, and simplicity of the Arcadians' life in a
rough, mournful, and cold country to that of the Arcadian tribe called
the "Cynaetheans," who had regressed to brutality and savagery. The
cause of their regression was their failure to remember the wisdom of
their compatriots, who had surmounted the hardship of nature
through the collective practice of music, particularly song, that is,
through the *art of voice*.

In my theoretical musings the formal articulation of the scene's
space becomes meaningful in the Arcadia of Polybius the Arcadian, in
what may be called the "natural origin" of man. The formal features are
based on a radical and dynamic opposition between the open desert
space and the sheer volume of the massive tomb. They point to the
historically unidentifiable moment when the natural/cultural har-

mony resulting from the taming of savagery by song is disturbed, giving way once more to dissonance; suddenly the song of the origin is silent. What the shepherd encounters—indeed, what you, I, and all of us encounter—are the indecipherable signs on the tomb's wall, signs that he recognizes as signs yet cannot read, traces of the past engraved on what is itself a sememe. *The Arcadian Shepherds* recounts, in what is at once a musical and plastic manner, the moment when the song of the origin is interrupted, the silent moment when history intrudes upon the scene. The painting appears to sing of an encounter with the signs that are themselves the mark of historical civilization in the story, an encounter, that is, with death. And if I were to read the three shepherd figures from left to right as symbolizing ignorance (the Arcadians "are not ashamed of denying acquaintance with other studies"), effort, and labor—as the suffering of knowledge (the deciphering of the signs) and the rational investigation of the signs' hidden meaning—then the tall and noble female figure on the right may well represent the response of Wisdom, a response that is at once a warning and a kind of resignation to the inevitable. This two-fold response may be articulated as follows: "Do not concern yourself with signs or writing; turn away from knowledge and power, from the power and knowledge of signs"; and "Now that you have encountered the signs of mortality, you can no longer escape them; you have encountered death and are thus condemned to the sphere of memory and history."

Poussin's *Arcadian Shepherds*, I have been arguing, is also the Arcadians' writing lesson. In this painting the intrusion of history is captured at the very *moment* when the rupture marking the temporality of presence occurs, that is, when the capitalization of duration in traces and letters is discovered. This intrusion, which is also a discovery, has always already taken place, here and now, in the utopia of present immediacy, where there is a direct communication of meaning through sense impressions. In this utopian nowhere, voice and song are always present as they construct an architecture of rhythm and melody without ever being locked into any given site.

"This is a tree, and it is now night." "That is a prairie, and it is now day." These are phrases characteristic of the language of sense certainty. The personal perspective accompanying this kind of certainty is broken and fragmented by a negation, even as it is preserved from the very beginning. And since truth loses nothing in writing, let us write "it is now day." The moment we do so, the light of sense certainty is invaded and effaced by dusk and the approaching night. There is a parallel, it would seem, between Poussin's conception of Arcadia and Hegel's understanding of sense certainty in *The Phenomenology of Spirit*.

There is an echo of Virgil at this point in my theoretical revery. If we assume, with Panofsky, that the tomb makes its first Arcadian appearance in Virgil's "Eclogue V," then I believe, somewhere in the depths of my memory, that Daphnis's tomb and its *written* epitaph evoke the fragility of the art of voice and song. The point is striking, and I am probably not the first to have noticed it. Indeed, although Daphnis loves song and is worthy of being sung about, he is not himself a singer. What is more, the only verses he ever composes are those *written verses* that are inscribed in the middle of the poem as an epitaph on a tomb. These verses are framed by two songs: whereas Mopsus' song describes how the cultivated countryside becomes savage once again after the death of Daphnis the leader, Menalcas' song evokes a universe mysteriously reconciled with itself beyond death through Daphnis's apotheosis.

In the foreground we have the semicircle outlined by the ground of the scene and its hollows; in the background we have the convex space traced by the crags, mountains, and bushes; in the center, finally, is the tomb, which turns almost imperceptibly on its axis, thereby placing itself somewhat obliquely in relation to the representational screen even as it organizes and divides the scene.

## The Tomb's Figures

This slight and almost unnoticeable rotation to the right in the foreground and to the left in the background has the effect of situating the two standing and immobile figures. As corner figures, the shepherd behind to the left and woman in front to the right are both sufficiently still to stand out from the couples of which they in other respects are a part. These figures are the guardians of the tomb, its virtues.

The story, I have claimed, originates in, and completes itself through, these two outer figures, for it is their mediating and dual gaze that allows the narrative to return to its central moment. The story's action begins and ends there, in two postures of rest, even as it underscores its own culminating moment. By virtue of their position at the tomb's left and right corners, the two statuesque figures are linked to the origin and end of the story conveyed by the painted scene. Their position, then, has the effect not only of creating a certain distance between them and the rest of the group, but of making them somehow transcend the story of which they are a part. These figures are symbolic, if not allegorical, and they give rise to an experience of *delectatio*, the kind produced by the philosophical beauty of allegory. What we have here is the assumption of allegory into the heaven of symbols.

> These examples clearly convey the intelligence, clarity of mind, and nobility of expression with which our illustrious painter was able to treat all manner of subjects. He did so with ease, without obscurity, and without making use of those empty thoughts and worn, vulgar, and disagreeable incidents with which many painters, anxious to make use of allegories, have filled their works, due to ignorance and a lack of formal learning.[4]

As a result of an almost indiscernable integration into the story, allegory is transformed into symbols. This process is so complete that my act of contemplation, my reading, theory, and discourse cannot but open up a space of *jouissance,* a space of unspeakable happiness between story and allegory. The delectation that thus arises is ineffable and can be neither shown nor proved.

> Now I say the beautiful is the symbol of the morally good, and that it is only in this respect (a reference which is natural to every man and which every man postulates in others as a duty) that it gives pleasure with a claim for the agreement of everyone else. By this the mind is made conscious of a certain ennoblement and elevation above the mere sensibility to pleasure received through sense, and the worth of others is estimated in accordance with a like maxim of their judgment. That is the *intelligible* to which . . . taste looks, with which our higher cognitive faculties are in accord, and without which a downright contradiction would arise between their nature and the claims made by taste. In this faculty the judgment does not see itself, as in empirical judging, subjected to a heteronomy of empirical laws; it gives the law to itself in respect of the objects of so pure a satisfaction, just as the reason does in respect of the faculty of desire. Hence, both on account of this inner possibility in the subject and of the external possibility of a nature that agrees with it, it finds itself to be referred to something within the subject as well as without him, something which is neither nature nor freedom, but which is yet connected with the supersensible ground of the latter. In this supersensible ground, therefore, the theoretical faculty is bound together in unity with the practical in a way which, though common, is yet unknown.[5]

In this passage from Kant's *Critique of Judgment,* Beauty is, as it were, the symbol for Morality. What comes to mind is a kind of delectation and *jouissance* associated with the utopia of "theoretical" happiness. In the philosophical beauty of the allegory, it is *as if* the freedom of the imagination is in harmony with the law of understanding and with the law of freedom. This harmony is simultaneously withdrawn from and proffered to the gaze and language by the symbol.

Let us give free rein to our imagination: I want to draw a connection between the laurel-wreathed head of the shepherd on the left and the figure of Apollo in *The Inspiration of the Poet* (Louvre, Paris). Their similarity allows me to *glimpse* in the figure of the shepherd, who is the tomb's guardian and the "origin" of the iconic story, an epic poem in prose. But whereas in *The Inspiration of the Poet* the poet prepares to write what Apollo is about to dictate, the person contemplated by the shepherd limits himself to trying to read something that is already written.

The woman on the right serves as the interlocutor of the shepherd whom she touches lightly with her hand, although she seems oblivious to his mute question. With an air of peaceful detachment, she contemplates the shepherd attempting to decipher the inscription, and in so doing she makes me *dream* of a figure of Mnemosyne, Memory, through her relation to an oblivion that is even more originary than she is. Her monumental stature, her profile, the position of her right hand, her unseeing and "statufied" gaze—these are all so many traits evoking the passion of admiration that Descartes analyzes in his *Traité.* This originary passion of knowledge, without bodily effects, is a passion for difference and alterity. Inasmuch as admiration is the Memory of forgetting, it is a passion for the traces of what has been forgotten. This line of reasoning allows us to articulate the question that might be put to the statuesque figure by the shepherd on the right: "What is the name of the person who created the written traces before us, the traces that the kneeling figure/reader now tries to read?" We are also in a position at this point to understand the meaning of the female figure's response, which might run as follows: "You, the reader, are condemned to try to decipher the message, yet you are destined to understand nothing; you will remember only one thing, and that is that you have always already forgotten."

Although this response initially may seem troubling, it is in fact no cause for concern. The very destiny of deciphering and interpretation lies in their interminability and undecidability, the very means available to the living for neutralizing their fear of loss. We must now consider the narrative scene itself (of which the two outermost figures are and are not a part). This scene, we know, comprises two sites that are occupied by the figures facing each other on the left and right, by the two figures who can be said really to "act." These two figures are arranged in a symmetrical manner involving an inverse complementarity in relation to a central axis. Whereas the one on the left has his foot on the ground, the other has his foot on a slab of stone. While the former spells out the inscription by means of an intense gaze and pointing gesture, the latter points to the tomb and to his reading companion, even as he interrogates the woman, Memory, his Memory, with a gaze. What we have here is a mirror structure, the plane of the mirror being perpendicular in this case to that of the painting; we can detect the mirror's almost invisible plane between the index fingers of the two figures. This is the plane of the tomb, and it is an inversion of the painting's plane. What is more, the only trace of this inversion is the fissure in the tomb's wall.

An analysis of the scene calls attention to a kind of contrapuntal music, to a play of differences, spacings, echoes, and displaced repetitions taking place between the two all-too-perfectly-symmetrical pairs of figures. The "shepherds" on the left and the "shepherd" and "sheperdess" on the right crisscross in something like a chiasmus. However, the movement dominating this figural "architectonic" runs from left to right, as is evident from the manner in which we read the painting and the epitaph on the tomb as well as from the flow of light. This movement is underscored by the detail of the backward-looking gaze that the shepherd directs at the Arcadian female. We also notice the scherzo of a broken diagonal line, running from the left foot of the reading shepherd to the head of the dignified woman via the vigorous accents of opposing arms and hands. The syncopation of this scherzo occurs in the middle of the canvas, between the figures, at the focal point of history, at the center of the chiasmus between the right and left hands, and in the circular movement generated by their index fingers.

The figures and their staffs are grouped in such a way as to form the letter M, a consonant that stands for the French word *mort*, death. The figures thus reinforce the message of the tomb, which is itself the sememe of death. I am following the example here of Anthony Blunt's account of Poussin's last painting, *Apollo and Daphne*.[6] In his analysis of this work, Blunt focuses on the manner in which a Heraclitean lyre and bow establish a harmonic tension based on contraries. The lyre, we know, is held by Apollo, while the bow is drawn taut by Cupid.

Finally, by virtue of their positions, the two shepherds facing each other are in a sense emanations of the outermost figures standing at the corners of the tomb. It is as though the shepherds are the products of these other figures, even if their positions are reversed from back to front. It is this very inversion that allows a certain spatial and "semantic" depth to emerge in an otherwise narrow scene. Apollo, then, who inspires and contemplates, pro-duces (sets forth) the figure reading or uttering the inscription. The shepherd who asks Memory to explain the meaning of "deciphering," and to provide the name of the deceased, in turn refers back to the female figure who knows the response and what has been forgotten. At this point the iconographic argument rests on the poorly squared block of stone on which members of the group lean. The block functions as a plastic metonym for the tomb, and it turns out that artists from Raphael to Ripa have used such stones to signal Memory and History, the Memory of History. Hence there is a movement from back to front, with the two poles in question inverting themselves at the level of the inscription. The scene's spatial dimensions unfold as we move from History to deciphering and from the question of meaning to Memory. This process is mediated by the figures discussed above and hinges on a rotation that occurs in the central area of the painting. At that moment, the story, or, rather, the discourse in which it is enunciated, is produced.

It is clear, then, that the basic articulation of the entire scene and its figures takes place in the central area that is also a spacing between two pairs of figures. In the context of a discussion of Poussin's *The Israelites Gathering Manna in the Desert*, I focused on the importance of its empty center, which is the place/time of a narrative transformation. We have now seen that the center of *The Arcadian Shepherds* functions similarly, although it is not empty but the site of an inscription.

## Poussinian Music Revisited: On *The Israelites Gathering Manna in the Desert*

Inasmuch as this painting constitutes a properly pictural text representing the "symbolic" in the story it tells, it points to the problem of writing and syntax. Let us recall Félibien's claim: the painter's language, or, more precisely, "the characters" he uses are the kind of impressions to which "the different states and diverse actions" give rise in the viewer. The painter represents and distributes the movements on the canvas by means of grouped figures, for they provide "the discourse and words allowing him to make himself understood."[7] These figures represent the text of the story.

The characters employed in pictural writing are thus the bodily signs or traces of emotion left by movements of the mind. Although Poussin and Le Brun may embrace a Cartesian theory of emotion, in practice their representation of affect owes much to Giotto.

> The *istoria* will move the soul of the beholder when each man painted there clearly shows the movement of his own soul. . . . These movements of the soul are made known by movements of the body. . . .
>
> Thus all the movements of the body should be closely observed by the painter. These he may well learn from nature, even though it is difficult to imitate the many movements of the soul.[8]

How can this writing be constitutive of the painter's discourse in the painting? In our effort to get at the inexpressible unity that is the basis of theory and practice (to use Kant's terms), that is, the space of delectation and *jouissance* opened up by the work of painting, we must consider two competing models, the one theatrical, the other musical. We know from Sandrart's *Journal* and Le Blond de la Tour's *Letter* that Poussin imbued the stage and theatrical representation with great technical value. Indeed, as a prelude to his painterly creations, Poussin constructed real dramatic models, including figurines, which he would arrange in elaborate scenographic patterns. If Poussin employed a theatrical model for practical purposes, Le Brun and Félibien mobilized it to theoretical ends. The playwright's rule-governed license aimed at achieving unity of action justifies the liberty taken by the painter as he constructs the spatial unity underlying a succession of narrative events.

The musical model is embedded within the theory of modes that Poussin explains to Chantelou in his letter of November 24, 1647. The interpretive difficulties surrounding this letter are well known and have to do with the fact that Poussin relies heavily on Gioseffo Zarlino's *Institutioni Harmoniche* (circa 1573), generating a number of contradictory applications of the theory in the process. In spite of these problems, we can retain the idea of the mode defined as *ratio,* or as a manner or determinate order of organization. Poussin writes that "the Modes of the ancients were a combination of several things put together." As an internal law of organization, the mode makes apparent

> a certain difference of Mode whereby one was able to understand that each one of them retained in itself a subtle variation; particularly when all the things which entered into combination were put together in such a proportion that it was made possible to arouse the soul of the spectator to various passions.[9]

As a specific scale, the mode is defined at once by the initial chord and by the system of intervals between the notes. It allows a certain causality of the pictural object to appear, a system based on the play of differences between parts. The mode is thus instrumental in inducing an overall effect, particularly within the viewer, as Poussin clearly underscores in this text.

Le Brun and Félibien ask themselves how to signal narrative change in painting. The response is by inducing a modal difference consisting in a spacing, not of notes or letters, but of expressive signs and affects in the figures and their figurative site. The mode is a certain type of interval in which the articulation or spacing of the parts of the painting is a function of a play of oppositions or a "judicious contrast," as Le Brun puts it. The interval between expressions, figures, and grouped figures is at once temporal and spatial to the extent that it engenders the space of representation through an ordered or "modalized" representation of the figures.

In music, a mode is defined by a system of intervals and by a chord characteristic of the tonic, of the dominant and the mediant to the third of the tonic. Why not try to find, along with Poussin and despite the eight-year gap, equivalents in *The Israelites Gathering Manna*? Might it not be possible to use the musical model to reconstitute the constitution of the pictural text insofar as it represents the literary text? I am interested, more specifically, in retracing the process through which the space of representation is engendered. The task at hand can be taken up either in a thematic manner, which is what Le Brun chooses to do, or in a more formal manner, which is my own preference.

The foreground of the painting is a site of change, for it is here that a contrast is established between a prior and a subsequent moment. The first moment pertains to the group on the left, the second to the group on the right, while the contrast between the two is marked by the empty space at the center.

The moment of representation identified by Le Brun occurs in the painting's middle ground. It is centered around the dual figure of Moses/Aaron, marking the link between the two groups characterized by contrasting postures. Whereas members of the group on the left are represented as standing with their arms raised, the figures on the right kneel and have their arms lowered toward the vessels.

Space and a landscape are what appear in the painting's background, where a contrast exists between the boulder and arc of light on the left and the dark cluster of trees on the right. Once again the contrast is marked by an empty central space, in this case, that of the sky.

I have been describing what I want to call the pure syntax of Poussin's painting. What interests me about this syntax is that it effects the *transformation of History, as change, into Space, in the form of a landscape, by means of a representational moment.* This abstract schema can be invested with meaning and interpreted along the lines suggested in Poussin's letter to Jacques Stella. In the foreground, which is that of history, we thus discover the suffering and hunger that comes *before* the avid desire to be nourished, which is represented as arising *afterwards.* What is striking is that the actual transformation of History, which is not *figurable,* is *represented* by the empty space whose sole function is to space the two groups of figures. Yet this historical dimension, which cannot be expressed by means of figures, is in fact figured in the middle ground, where, in the very *instant* of representation, the moral and religious lesson of history is made clear. Attention is thus drawn to the dual figure of the prophets, which serves as the mediating instrument of the miraculous transformation depicted in the painting. The motif of the miracle is further amplified by the contrast established between the people's elders, who give thanks to God, and the individuals who contravene divine decree by hoarding the manna. We note that the greedy figures in the middle ground correspond to the avid figures in the foreground, just as the individuals giving thanks correspond to those who are visibly suffering. It is this vertical "semantic" arrangement that allows us to find meaning in the space/landscape of Poussin's *Israelites Gathering Manna.* The boulder/arc, a recurrent feature in seventeenth-century landscape painting, underscores the glory of God by means of a contrast with the dark forest. (Another example of this feature may be found in the work by Claude that draws on an ancient fresco in the Barberini Palace.) Space thus has symbolic value in *this* painting, but only as a result of the way in which it is integrated into the whole. What is more, this symbolic value is quite different from the allegorical meaning that Le Brun, for example, seeks in Poussin's *Ecstasy of Saint Paul*. If we bring together the two ways in which the painting's representational space is constructed, a certain perceptual depth emerges, allowing us to grasp the syntax and order of the discursive and visual trajectory embodied within the system of spacing the figures.

But a mode is defined not only by its system of intervals but also by its characteristic chord. Poussin himself indicates in his letter to Chantelou what the determining chord of his painting is. In Poussin's mind, the group on the left provides the starting point for an exploration of, and discourse about, the figures:

> Furthermore, if you can remember the first letter I wrote you concerning the movements of the figures which I promised to depict, and if you consider the picture at the same time, I think you will be able to recognize with ease which figures languish, which ones are astonished, which are filled with pity, perform deeds of charity, are in great need, seek consolation, etc. The first seven figures on the left side will tell you everything that is written here, and all the rest is much the same effect: study [read] the story and the picture in order to see whether each thing is appropriate to the subject.[10]

Poussin provides a list of seven affects, each of which finds multiple embodiments in the painting's figures. It is important to note, however, that these affects also find expression in the first seven figures on the left. Indeed, why would these figures be situated as they are if not to provide the painting's *modal tone* by being seen, and hence read, first? Thus, the seven figures on the left may be said to represent all other figures in the painting. I do not, of course, mean to suggest that the remaining figures merely reproduce the first seven. Rather, the set of expressive signs the viewer encounters on the left establishes the modal difference of all the figures in the painting.

# On Nominal Sentences, Fragments, Epitaphs, and Epigraphs

In its own manner and particular *mode*, Poussin's music sings an interrupted Arcadian tune. The specificity of Poussin's song resides in a systematic spacing of figures, that is, in a series of intervals between the expressive signs of the painting. The system in question, we know, generates the characteristic chord through which the painting's modal tone is established. I now want to take the musical analogy one step further by proposing a reading of the inscription "Et in Arcadia ego" as an Arcadian aria. This aria, which is syncopated as a result of the inscription's arrested words, finds its notes in the figures and their expressive signs, in the landscape, and so on. Is it up to me, then, to bring song to life through memory? And if so, then which song? The answer, I believe, is the song of the painting.

But can I even produce the libretto or at least the song's refrain? The epitaph must be read. But *can* this epitaph be read? These are the very questions the two shepherds facing each other in the painting ask. As the one attempts to read the inscription, the other asks Mnemosyne for a response to the question "What do these four words mean?" These two figures call attention to the inscription, as their intense gaze and various gestures mobilize within the scene the emotions that fascinate our theoretical eye and our reading and viewing eye all at once. How, then, should I "translate" or properly understand "Et in Arcadia ego"?

## A Study by Erwin Panofsky

Panofsky's admirable study of Poussin's *Arcadian Shepherds* may be usefully evoked at this stage in the argument.[1] Panofsky raises the key question of the meaning of the enigmatic inscription. Does the inscription mean "Even in Arcadia, me" or "In Arcadia, me too"? If we unpack these phrases we are left with a choice between "Even in Arcadia, me (I am)" or "I too (I was) in Arcadia." Taking into consideration the fact that *Et* pertains to the words immediately following it, the inscription may be read as follows: "Even in Arcadia, me, I died." The first interpretation —"Even in Arcadia, me"—has *Death* itself inscribe its epigraph on the tomb and in the painting. In the second interpretation—"In Arcadia, me too"—it is the *Deceased* who inscribes his epitaph.

It may be helpful to preface the ensuing remarks about grammar and meaning with a brief consideration of the literary references that echo throughout the space of the painted scene, thereby animating the various figures and signs that it conveys. More specifically, it is a matter of bringing the historical painting into the space of history and culture, of effecting this transition in Poussin's work itself.

Panofsky's thesis hinges on an opposition between the "hard" and "soft" primitivism discussed in G. Boas and A. O. Lovejoy's important study, *Primitivism and Related Ideas in Antiquity.*[2] His thesis also relies heavily on the two contradictory characterizations of Arcadia that may be found in classical texts. On the one hand we have the Arcadia of Ovid and Polybius the Arcadian. This Arcadia is the land of precivilized origins, of the origin construed as a wilderness. On the other hand we have the conception of Arcadia described in Virgil's *Eclogues,* a conception resulting from a transference, that is, a renaming of the Sicily of Theocritus's *Idylls.*[3] In Virgil's text Arcadia is the land of blissful origins evoking the happiness of a golden age. Yet Panofsky quite rightly points out that in the course of this transference, Virgil maintains one of the characteristics of Theocritus's *Idylls,* that is, the discordance between the supernatural perfection of an imaginary space and the natural limits of human life, namely, between desperate love and death. What is more, he projects this tragic dissonance into time, into the future, or rather the past. This dissonance, then, is refracted by memory and softened by a sense of time. The ultimate Arcadian avatar can be found in Jacopo Sannazaro's *Arcadia,* a text that, in Panofsky's opinion, emphasizes the salient features of Virgil's conception. Sannazaro, more specifically, imagines Arcadia as a utopia of happiness and beauty, as an object of nostalgia and loss. Arcadia, on this view, is a lost kingdom of happiness perceived through the veil of melancholy and memory.

> It was through him [Sannazaro] that the elegiac feeling—present but, as it were, peripheral in Virgil's *Eclogues*—became the central quality of the Arcadian sphere. One more step and this nostalgic but as yet impersonal longing for the unbroken peace and innocence of an ideal past was sharpened into a bitter, personal accusation against a real present.[4]

These different views of Arcadia together provide the guiding thread of Panofsky's analysis of the two versions of Poussin's *Arcadian Shep-*

*herds.* In the first version, referred to as the Chatsworth work, the Arcadians suddenly discover the mortal destiny of their human condition, their inexorable future, death allegorized in the tomb's death head. In the second version, however, they gently muse over a beautiful past.

> They seem to think less of themselves than of the human being buried in the tomb—a human being that once enjoyed the pleasures which they now enjoy, and whose monument "bids them remember their end" only in so far as it evokes the memory of one who had been what they are.[5]

The divergent conceptions of Arcadia help to explain the hesitation experienced by anyone who tries to interpret the inscription "Et in Arcadia ego," who must ponder two quite different interpretations or translations: "Even in Arcadia, me (I am)" belies the elegiac and nostalgic meditation that gives the Louvre version its particular "atmosphere" as compared to the more dramatic Chatsworth work. "Even in Arcadia, me (I died)" supports the meditation in question, but only at the price of a grammatical error. In this intersection of iconic and linguistic meaning, we recognize, with Panofsky, art history at work. Indeed, art history unfolds in the very articulation of motifs and themes, forms and legends, where the perceptual and iconographic overlap. It is this intersection that constitutes the iconological level of cultural symbols. These remarks only too briefly summarize the very rich discussion that has evolved over a number of years among Panofsky, Werner Weisbach, Anthony Blunt, and Jerome Klein.[6] As Panofsky himself points out, this discussion, however rich, merely reiterates the divergent seventeenth-century interpretations, elaborated by Bellori and Félibien, of the inscription "Et in Arcadia ego."

Once again, then, it is a matter of reading and understanding the inscription, for this reading is precisely what is at stake in the painting. Let us follow Panofsky in his grammatical analysis of the phrase:

> The phrase *Et in Arcadia ego* is one of those elliptical sentences like *Summum jus summa iniuria, E pluribus unum, Nequid nimis* or *Sic semper tyrannis,* in which the verb has to be supplied by the reader. This unexpressed verb must therefore be unequivocally suggested by the words given, and this means that it can never be a preterite.[7]

The missing word, then, cannot be a verb in the historic past tense, which is a narrative tense. The only immediately imaginable verb and tense is the verb "to be" in the first person of the present indicative: "sum," "I am." Panofsky adds that "it is also possible, though fairly unusual, to suggest a future as in Neptune's famous *Quos ego* ("These I [shall deal with]")."[8] Although the same motto, "Et in Arcadia ego" is central to both the Chatsworth version and that of the Louvre, Poussin significantly transforms the "meaning" of the scene that is represented and narrated. Indeed, it is almost as though Poussin somehow misread his own reading at a syntactical and semantic level. While the Louvre version of *The Arcadian Shepherds* makes Poussin's classical mastery of the painterly medium apparent, it also reveals the Master of great and learned painting to be a bad student of Latin grammar.

The suspicion might arise at this point that such remarks are meaningful only within the context of a futile debate between scholars. Yet there is something important at stake in this exchange of arguments, for it raises the questions of truth in painting, of the subject of representation/enunciation, and of the "autonomy" of narrative utterances.

### The "Cartesian" Theory of Judgment Revisited

> A verb is nothing else but a word whose principal function is to indicate assertion—that is to say, to indicate not only that a man conceives certain things but rather that he judges concerning these things and makes an assertion.[9]

This definition of the verb as the core, or smallest unit, of human discourse explains why every verb can be understood, at least at the level of *usage,* in terms of the present indicative of the verb "to be," that is, the verb "to be" at the moment of enunciation. "Ego affirmo, ego sum affirmans . . ." The entire discursive field can thus be shown to gravitate around a central site occupied by the *ego* of enunciation, by a desire to say and to mean manifesting a desire for theory. It is in this central site, involving appropriation and identification, that the subject of truth and knowledge constitutes itself.

But at the same time, another movement runs exactly contrary to the one just described. The subject's positing in enunciation/representation is negated by the reduction, at the level of *usage,* of all verbs to the third-person singular. This "it" may refer either to an infinite number of subjects or to none at all; as a result, it constitutes a *neuter.* This "it" is where being in truth comes into language; it is the representation of the subject, the being that is presented. The desire for theory oscillates in an unending manner between the subject of enunciation and the utterance, between judgment and history, between discourse and story. The abyss between these poles is uninhabitable, or, more precisely yet, is inhabited only to be immediately abandoned, deserted. Thus, we have: "Et ego (sum affirmans) (est) in Arcadia."

At the heart of *The Arcadian Shepherds*, which is also the central moment of the represented scene, we encounter a sentence *without a verb*, a sentence that nonetheless allows the subject to name itself: "Ego."

The *theory* (of judgment, of the representation of the subject of enunciation, of discourse, but also of history and the story) collapses at this point. This theoretical unraveling is also theory reverting to desire, the desire for theory reverting to the blinding brilliance and lack of unity that is peculiar to the *jouissance* and delectation of Arcadia. Utopia, then, would be a kind of nonmeaning.

Let me try to pull together the various threads of my "argument." I have claimed that "Et in Arcadia ego" is a truncated version of what might be translated as "Even in Arcadia, me (I am here-now)." Yet who might plausibly be identified as the speaker of this phrase? One possible answer is the Tomb, the sememe of Death. However, to opt for this answer would be to move too quickly. For what can Death actually say? I am Death or rather, an Allegory of Death. We bring death to life in order to make it speak. But if this is the case, then we are no longer dealing with death. Let us instead, then, consider death as such. Yet without the aid of allegory death cannot speak: it is silent, mute, and quite precisely the present instant of discourse, of all human discourse. As Benveniste has made clear, discourse has only one tense, the present, and this present is never *signified* in discourse; that is, no signifier marks the presence of *ego* in the present tense. The past and future tenses, on the other hand, are marked discursively by signifiers, for they are identified as points of view preceding and following the present. In Poussin's painting, for example, the shepherds on the right and left have a temporal significance of this kind. Enunciation, then, is paradoxical in the following sense: discourse is always constituted by signifiers signifying what it is not (the past, the future); at the same time, these signifiers can only convey a particular signification based on what discourse never signifies (the present). Ego, the present presence of the ego? A crucial difference separates the mute self-referentiality of the I (the ego that does not speak) from the expressive meaning of the nonpresent, which includes the past, memory, and all future projects. Put differently, there is a rift at the heart of the sentence, in the middle of the tomb's wall, at the center of the painting. *It is written [C'est écrit]*: "Et in Arcadia, ego." Thus speaks death.

Let us now consider the second interpretation of "Et in Arcadia, ego:" "Even in Arcadia, me (I died)." This statement may be rephrased as follows: "Here/now me, I affirm that I died." Construed in this manner, the utterance raises the question of the speaking I's identity. It may well be that it is the Deceased who speaks out from within his tomb. Once again, however, we would be moving too quickly if we were simply to embrace our initial conception. After all, how can the Deceased speak? Given that he is dead, how can he say in the here and now, "I died"? Nor is the situation rendered any less puzzling by substituting "I have lived" for "I died." For we know all too well that the cogito of death, like my death, is unsayable. I can only pronounce myself dead through an act of retrospective anticipation, through a ruse of writing. Writing allows me to claim that I will be dead by the time you *will read* the utterance "I died." Here and now, then, "I died" essentially means "I will have died." What we have here is the paradox of autobiography, a paradox linked to the fact that I cannot enunciate the concluding or final sentence. This impossibility is a consequence of my being, at the end of my life history, my own narrator. Someone else, then, must read what I have written while I become, for myself, an "it," a nonperson, something without a name in any language, the cadaver in the tomb.

## The Nominal Sentence according to Benveniste

It would be useful at this point to recall the existence of what Benveniste calls "nominal sentences" (*phrases-noms*):

> Briefly characterized, the nominal sentence consists of a predicate nominative, without a verb or copula, and it is considered the normal expression in Indo-European where a possible verbal form would have been the third person of the present indicative "to be." . . . Nor could one describe its various manifestations in identical terms. It includes varieties that must be distinguished. Nevertheless the fact remains that the most varied linguistic structures allow or require, under certain conditions, that the verbal predicate not be expressed or that the predicate nominative be sufficient. To what necessity is the nominal sentence bound for it

to be produced in similar ways by so many different languages, and how does it happen—the question will seem strange but the strangeness is in the facts—that the verb of existence, out of all other verbs, has this privilege of being present in an utterance in which it does not appear?[10]

Benveniste responds to the questions he raises with a complete and coherent theory of Indo-European nominal sentences that seems crucial to my argument concerning the formula "Et in Arcadia ego," an argument that to some extent is inspired by Panofsky's work. We saw that Panofsky, at a strategic point in his study, includes this formula in the same category as that of nominal sentences (example: *summum jus summa iniuria*).

> We shall say that the nominal sentence in Indo-European constitutes a finite assertive utterance whose structure is similar to that of any other utterance having the same syntactic definition. The term with the verbal function is likewise composed of two elements: the one, invariable and implicit, which gives the utterance the force of an assertion; the other, variable and explicit, which this time is a form of the morphological class of nouns. . . .
>
> Now it is possible to describe more precisely the functional structure of the verbal form in the assertive utterance. It comprises two elements, one explicit and variable, the other implicit and invariable. . . . Once one has decided to consider them as the same type, and hence as equally justified, one sees more clearly *how they differ, depending on whether the verbal function resides in a form of the verbal class or in a form of the nominal class.* The difference comes from the properties that belong to each of these classes. *In the nominal sentence, the assertive element,* being nominal, *is not* capable of the determinations that the verbal form conveys: modalities of tense, person, etc. The nominal assertion is inherently timeless, impersonal, nonmodal—in short, expressive of semantic content alone. A second consequence is that the nominal assertion cannot share, either, the essential quality of a verbal assertion, which is to relate the time of an event to the time of discourse about the event. The nominal sentence in Indo-European asserts a certain "quality" (in the most general sense) as belonging to the subject of the utterance, but outside any temporal or other determination and outside all relation to the speaker.[11]

As Benveniste effectively demonstrates, a study of the use of nominal sentences in the work of Pindar, Homer, Herodotus, or in certain Latin texts reveals that nominal sentences always serve to affirm permanent truths. They inevitably presuppose an atemporal and absolute relation, and are always used in direct discourse as an argument by authority. "In contrast, only the verbal sentence (with εστι) is suited to the narration of a fact, the description of a manner of being or of a situation."[12] A nominal sentence is thus significantly different, in two respects, from a sentence with the verb "to be."

> The nominal sentence and the sentence with εστι do not make assertions in the same way and do not belong on the same plane. The first is from discourse, the second, from narration. The one establishes an absolute; the other describes a situation. These two features are connected and they both depend on the fact that, in the utterance, the assertive function rests on a nominal form or on a verbal form. The structural connection of these conditions stands out clearly. In being suited to absolute assertions, the nominal sentence has the value of argument, of proof, of reference. It is introduced into discourse in order to influence and convince, not to inform. It is a truth offered as such, outside time, persons, and circumstances. That is why the nominal sentence is so well suited to those statements in which, actually, it tends to be confined, maxims or proverbs, after having once had more flexibility.[13]

Is "Et in Arcadia ego" a nominal sentence then? Such an interpretation is problematic for reasons having to do with the presence of "ego" in the formula, that is, of the proper name of the speaker "I." The present here and now that "ego" implies is the present of enunciation as well as the obligatory referent of any utterance in the past tense. For example, when I say "I (who speaks to you), I lived in Arcadia," the past tense that is enunciated in the sentence is part of the past by virtue of its relation to the present moment in which I enunciate it.

## A Fragmentary Sentence

Is "Et in Arcadia ego" a fragmentary or incomplete sentence, a sentence that has been partially effaced? Might not this sentence be considered doubly incomplete on account of the absence of both a verb and the proper name of the "ego"? Let us, for example, compare the formula to Daphnis's epitaph in Virgil's "Eclogue V," which, much like Sannazaro's *Arcadia*, is one of the iconographic referents for Poussin's painting:

> Daphnis ego in silvis hinc usque ad sidera notus
> formosi pecoris custos, formosior ipse.[14]

"Daphnis ego in silvis . . . notus (sum)": "ego" is doubly determined both by a proper name, Daphnis, and by a verb *in the past tense.*

> I woodland Daphnis, blazoned among stars,
> Guarded a lovely flock, still lovelier I.[15]

The identifying presence of a proper name is a constant trait of funerary poetry. This remark, however, does not resolve the more general questions raised by utterances that are written in the past tense and that comprise an enunciative I and a proper name. I am thinking, for example, of autobiographical stories or memoires in which the I that writes about itself is at once an I and a he, I as he, I-as-another. What is striking is that in these writings the identity of I and he is nonetheless pronounced across this rift of difference. The autobiographical I is thus permanently in a divided state as a result of writing. At the same time it is writing that constantly discloses *and* neutralizes this very division. What we are dealing with here is the paradox resulting from the separation of the "writing I" and the "written I," a paradox that epitaphs push to the extreme.

My hypothesis, in this case, is that the inscription is best left indeterminate, for its semantic undecidability may well be the meaning of Poussin's painting, which is a beautiful meditation on the writing of history. The effacement of the name associated with "ego" in the epitaph makes that epitaph a "floating signifier" waiting to be anchored in our reading. The effacement of a conjugated verbal form has the effect of positioning the sentence between the present and the past, between identity and alterity, at their limit, which is the limit of representation itself. In other words, a certain representation of death refers to the process of representation as death. Yet, at the same time, death is tamed and neutralized by writing, and by the work of art more generally, as the living read and contemplate the painting. The dual effacement of a name and a verb in the inscription effectively points to the operation that is realized by the process of representation/narration: the effacement of the enunciative structure itself. The effacement of this structure is what allows the past, with its element of loss and death, to be revived before the living, in and through representation, in the here and now. The very function, then, of the historiographical exercise is to stage the past as an object of serene contemplation permitting an exorcism of angst.

## A Funerary Interlude

A dialogue is established in most poetic epitaphs, a feature that can be traced to the influence of Roman funerary poetry. The passerby is essentially enjoined to tarry, and the epitaph thus becomes a vehicle for an injunction to read the inscription and thereby to articulate a prayer for the deceased-who-speaks, a prayer that is said also to be beneficial to the person who reads it. The addressee is the anonymous "you" evoked by a speaker who calls himself "I." Not only does the deceased speak out as an I, but he constitutes himself, through writing, as the author of the poem that he invites the passerby to read in the here and now. This absent presence in the tomb of the deceased speaker is underscored by a number of referential and self-referential terms: *these* lines of verse, *this* tomb, *here* lies. . . . It is the poetry inscribed on the tomb that constitutes that tomb as imaginary, as a monument of language.

All the paradoxes of inscribed utterances, of autobiography and history, are present in condensed form in the epitaph, in the funerary poem that is also the tomb of enunciation. "Passerby, tarry a while and read the poem here and now." Although this present-tense proposition involves a passive construction, it does refer to a speaking "I." However, the I, speaking now and in the present, appears in the past evoked by the funerary poem as a "he," as the author of the verses that he now presents to be read. These verses about the self, we know, are part of the past, having been written before the author's death. Yet the "I" who now speaks in order to say that he wrote these verses in the past is in fact writing them now, for the words he utters are precisely those inscribed on the tomb. Thus, the impossible cogito of death reveals the blind spot of a cogito of life.

The structure of the funerary poem does indeed establish itself as a dialogue with a "you," a passerby. Yet this dialogue of writing and reading is merely the frame—provided by the dual injunction to tarry and to leave—of a story, or history of the self in which the "I" narrates itself as "he," even sometimes naming itself. "John went as he came . . ."

The Epitaph for Pierre Patrix (1583–1671)
Passerby, tarry a while. Beneath the words that you here may decipher,
Lie buried the bones of their author.
With one foot already in this grave,

He himself composed these lines to cover his ashes,
A sad and funereal duty,
Which, as you see, he expected no one else to perform.
The forgetfulness that surviving friends
Commonly demonstrate toward deceased friends obliged him to do it,
For he knew that once his soul had departed,
This too would be how his own friends would act.
Yet, you should not believe, Passerby, that he invites you to tarry
In order to teach you his name, or describe his virtuous life,
What he was in the world or what he was not,
The loss that his century suffered upon his death,
Or, in short, how in abandoning this earth,
His glorious soul went to Heaven,
A new star enhancing the fires of the firmament:
Ridiculous discourse, monumental jargon,
That he refuses to have inscribed on his tomb
So that future generations may read it;
He well knows that this would be a mistake, and that, in all sincerity,
He, damned sinner, has merited no honors.
On the contrary, continuously hardened in his crimes.
Of a hundred loves the eternal victim,
Infamous plaything of a thousand vanities,
These, while living, were all his qualities.
Oh, what happiness to have been born
Capable of correcting the vices he was able to identify!
Passerby, go your way, and assure yourself today
That in praying for him you pray for yourself.

While positing himself as a "he," the author, Patrix, indicates that the author takes the place of the "other" as the only real source of memory. Thus the autobiographical "I" can only narrate and constitute itself by tearing apart the *ego*, dividing it between "I" and "he." We here encounter yet another paradox that identifies what is at stake in Poussin's *Arcadian Shepherds* and its inscription. More specifically, the poet announces to the reader/passerby the neutralization of the auto-biographical story in the very same moment that he articulates it. In short, the poet reveals his own denegation.

1. The neutralization of the narrative enunciation proceeds by stages, the first of which is the effacement of the *proper name* and of its *narrative expansion: his life,* what he was and was not while part of the

world. The I who speaks and writes in the here and now has a dual nature: he is the author of the verses composed long ago in retrospective anticipation of the present moment in which they are enunciated and read; he is also the author of his own anonymity, for he only authors the poem in order to say that he will not speak his name, just as he evokes his past life only in order to indicate that he will tell nothing about it.

2.  The act of negation in and beyond the present subverts the temporal categories of both past and future in what is a decisive moment of truth; it is in the moment of negation that death is demystified and demythified as a result of myth itself. The mythical element resides in the promise that the deceased will be forever present in the form of an eternal constellation of stars. Thus, in much the same way, Daphnis, in Virgil's "Eclogue V," is transported to the stars by poetry, just as one of the poem's protagonists experiences a vision of, and describes, the transcendent utopia of a golden age.

3. But this discourse, writes the deceased in the inscription inscribed on his tomb, is a kind of "monumental jargon." What we have here is yet another instance of denegation, for the demythified death-apotheosis becomes a sincere confession, a narrative of personal failings. Although this story involves knowledge of the self, it does not amount to a practice of self-reform. The deceased's prayer with its optative of unreality is converted by the final formula, and through the prayer itself, into a kind of identification between the passerby, the "you," and the "he," since praying for *him* is praying for *yourself*. Yet, by the same token, the subject of enunciation withdraws definitively.

"I assure you that praying for yourself is equivalent to praying for him (who is me)."

# A Letter, a Shadow, and an Interpretive Key

Let us occupy once more that site between rigorous proofs and playful musings, between perception and phantasm, analysis and projection, reading and contemplation. What I am proposing is that we return to that undecided and central zone of the painting and its tomb, a site of delectation.

It is a matter of reflecting once more on the central spacing of the two groups of figures and, more precisely, on the index fingers of the two shepherds who necessarily point to this spacing. We may begin by noting that the finger of the shepherd on the left rests on the letter R in "Arcadia," on the circular part of the letter. Now, this R is not only the middle letter in the inscription, but the central point in which the vanishing point of the painting's horizon is displaced onto the wall of the tomb. It enigmatically provides the first letter in the proper name of the individual who invented the formula "Et in Arcadia ego": Cardinal Rospigliosi, the future Clement IX. The letter R is a signifier inscribed on the tomb where the point of view and vanishing point coincide, a site occupied by both the painter and the viewer of the painting. The letter R functions here as a sort of *hypogrammatical signature* indicating the name of the individual who coined the formula and commissioned the painting. A Name is thus evoked in the painting, and this Name occupies and takes the place of the painter/viewer. Rospigliosi is known to have commissioned two other paintings from Poussin—*The Dance to the Music of Time* and *Time Saving Truth from Envy and Discord*—and the meaning of their dual allegory may well figure in the symbolism that "Et in Arcadia ego" both reveals and hides, a symbolism that is identified by the letter R.

The following passage from Félibien is worth reflecting on at this point in the discussion:

> Do you want to know how he dealt with ideas of a moral and allegorical nature? I shall mention only three examples. The first is a picture of life, represented by four dancing women, who have some relation to the four seasons, or to the four ages of mankind. Time, in the figure of an old man, sits playing the lyre, while the women—Poverty, Work, Wealth, and Pleasure—dance in a ring to its sound. The women seem to be holding out alternating hands to each other, thereby pointing to the ongoing

changes that mark life and the fortunes of men. . . . Near the figure of
Time, and at his feet, there are two young Children. The one holds an
hourglass, and while studying it carefully, seems to count life's passing
moments. The other is playing with a reed, using it to blow bubbles of air
and water that immediately burst, which signifies the vanity and brevity
of life.

In the same painting there is a statue of Janus. The Sun, seated in his
chariot, is visible in the sky, in the middle of the Zodiac. Dawn marches
before the Sun's chariot, spreading flowers on the ground: the Hours that
follow seem to dance while flying.

The second example is that of Truth thrown to the ground. Suspended
in air by means of the wings on his back, Time, in the figure of a venerable
old man, extends a hand, lifting up Truth by the arm; with the other hand,
Time chases away Envy, who bites his arm while fleeing, shaking the serpents surrounding her head. Meanwhile Slander, who never leaves Envy
and is seated behind Truth, seems to be enflamed with anger and to be
about to throw the two lighted torches she holds.

The third painting represents a reflection on death in the midst of life's
riches. Poussin paints a shepherd who, with one knee on the ground,
points to the following words engraved on a tomb, Et in Arcadia ego.[1]

Having discussed the significance of the posture of the shepherd on
the left, we may now usefully consider that of his companion. His index
finger is placed on a vertical fissure in the tomb's wall, directly above
the rift that divides the scene's foreground and thereby sets apart the
woman to the shepherd's left. Now, this fissure *cuts* vertically through
the horizontal inscription, which is the painting's legible syntagm.
More precisely, whereas the crack runs between two of the words in the
first line—"In" and "Arcadia"—it divides "E/go." This configuration
points to the central play in the entire painting, to what is at stake: the
play at stake in the divergence between the two pointing gestures, between the letter of the name of the Father (of the inscription and of the
painting) and the division in the self who represents Death in Arcadia
by means of writing and painting. It points to the division of the
painter's absent name. Yet the painter did produce the painting, perhaps suggesting in this way that he, too, is in Arcadia, although he is
absent from the site of happiness that is none other than the painting
itself.

In the fissure that marks both the word "E/go" and the tomb on
which it is inscribed, I thus perceive and read a *letter,* and with it, a

*name,* the name of the Author who somehow surfaces to fill the breach from which meaning, the present, and the subject all escape, a breach where meaning and the present continuously reconstitute themselves.

But it is at this point that another eye intervenes. This eye is situated in the wings, is a source of light, and produces the narrative anamorphosis that occurs in the depths of the mirror/window. This eye is the second eye of representation. It projects the shadow of the reading and interpreting shepherd onto the wall of the tomb in an open-air version of Plato's myth of the cave. This shadow, which is also the shepherd's double, is the originary form of the fiction of painting. It appears, within the painting, on what may also be called a painting, the tomb's smooth and opaque wall. The tomb is like a painting, for it functions as an apparatus that reflects, albeit only shadows and simulacra. This tomb is where the reality of happiness, that is, Arcadia, is lost and found, but only in the form of a representation. More precisely, the shadow cast by the arm and hand also designates the letter R that stands for the name of the Author (of the inscription and of the painting). The shadow effaces itself in this letter and in the immediacy that is the mark of pure contact. At the same time, the shadow neutralizes the letter as a result of a blindness that occurs in the absence of distance. But what this shadow outlines on the tomb's wall is not properly speaking an arm or a hand, but a *scythe.* The scythe is an attribute of the god Saturn, who presides over the Arcadia of the golden age, but also of Cronos, who castrated his father Uranus, and of Chronos, who brings death to everyone and everything. This scythe, which recurs as an allegorical sign in one of the other two paintings painted for Rospigliosi, functions here as the *painter's iconic hypogram,* as the trace of his gaze.

Can my reading be justified in the manner of a rigorous demonstration or is it instead a kind of phantasmatic projection? Can it be attributed to Poussin's conscious intentions, to the artist who modestly claimed to have "overlooked nothing"? Or is it simply the result of the enigmatic operations that always exceed the work of art, the "Golden Bough" in the painting itself, which casts open the doors of horn and ivory through which real shadows and imagined memories enter into the painting. My discourse has no other justification than delectation, the *jouissance* derived from a painting by Poussin, the painter whom Bernini once described as a great *creator* of fables and stories.

The inscription in Poussin's painting—"Et in Arcadia ego"—makes clear that the story told in a historical painting is a myth that can always be retold. And as this story unfolds, we move from the writing of history, which is a representation of death, to painting, a deadly presentation of utopia.

*Plates*

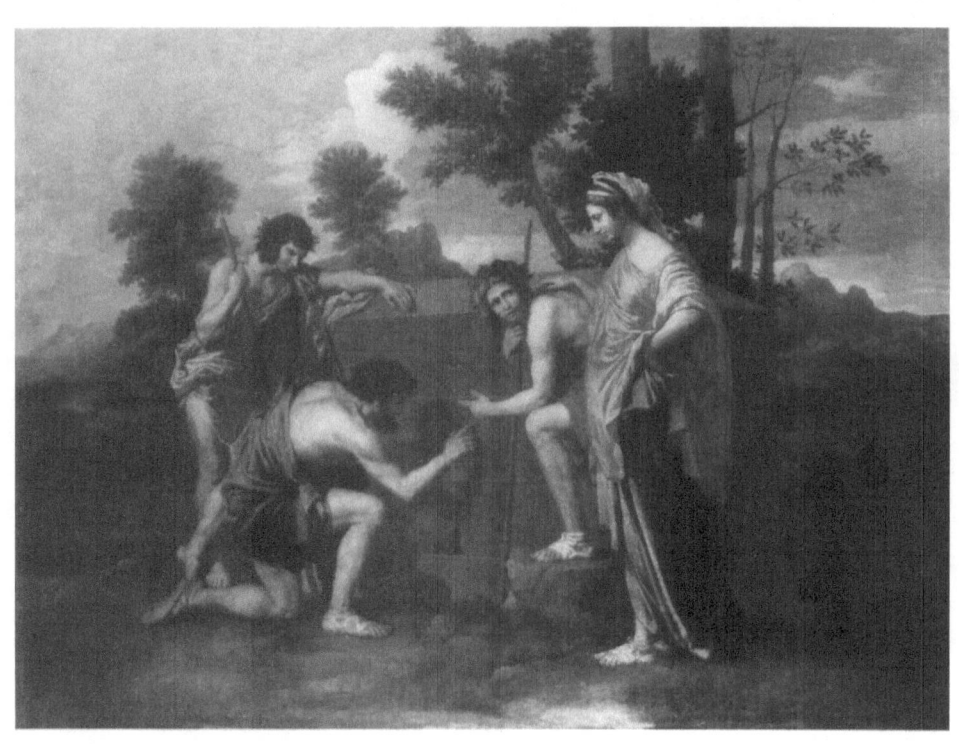

1. Poussin, *The Arcadian Shepherds*. Louvre, Paris. Giraudon/Art Resource

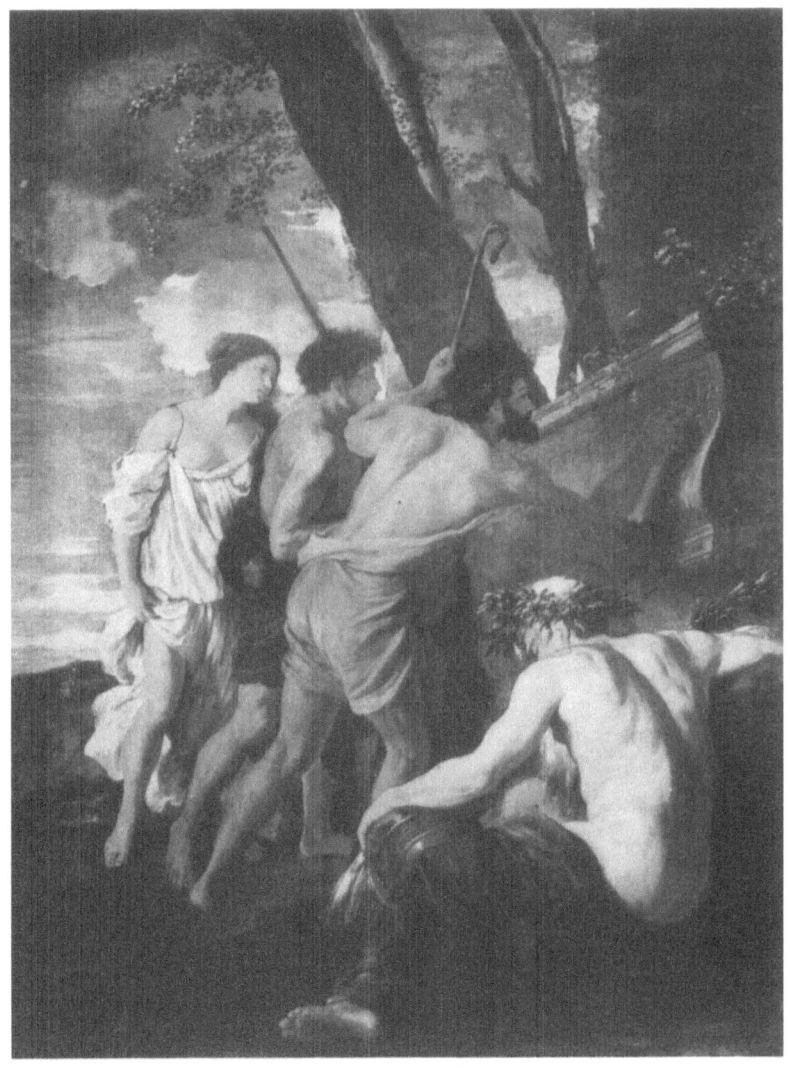

2. Poussin, *The Arcadian Shepherds*. Duke of Devonshire, Chatsworth
Settlement Trustees. Art Resource. Photo © Erich Lessing

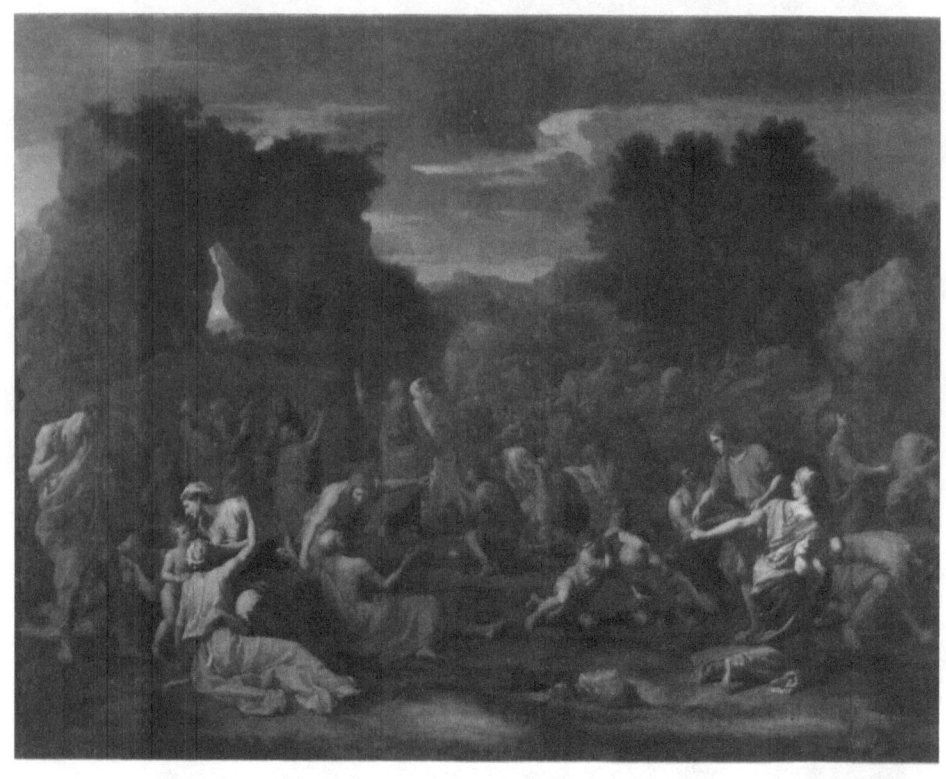

3. Poussin, *The Israelites Gathering Manna in the Desert*. Louvre, Paris.
Giraudon/Art Resource

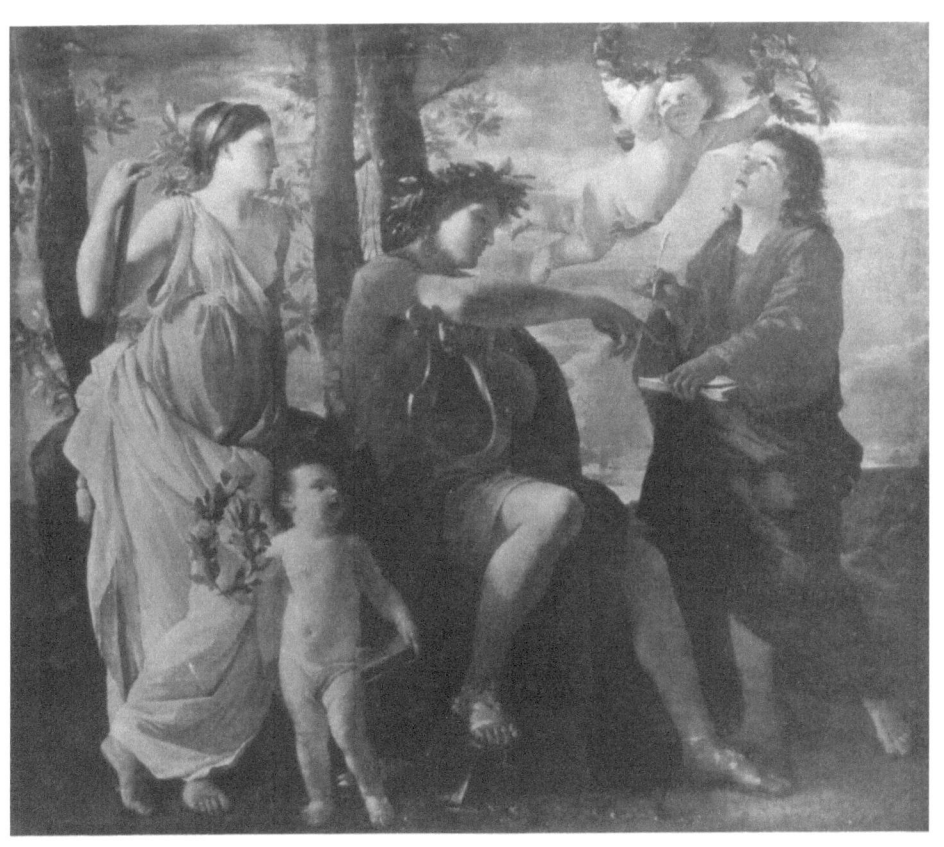

4. Poussin, *The Inspiration of the Poet*. Louvre, Paris. Giraudon/Art Resource

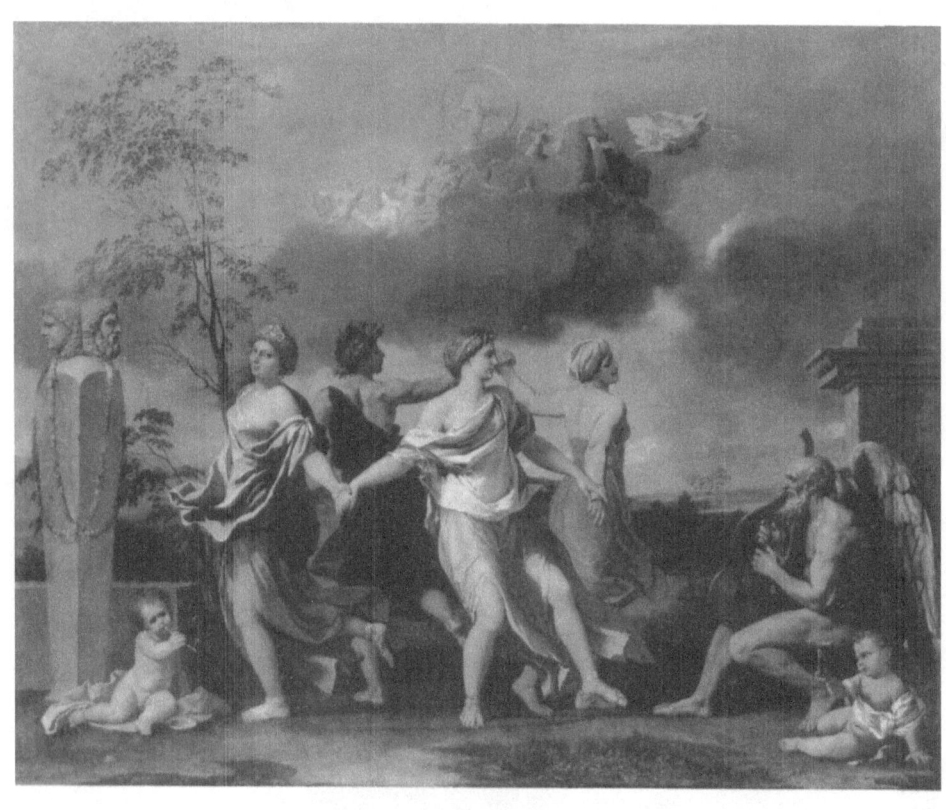

5. Poussin, *The Dance to the Music of Time*. Wallace Collection, London

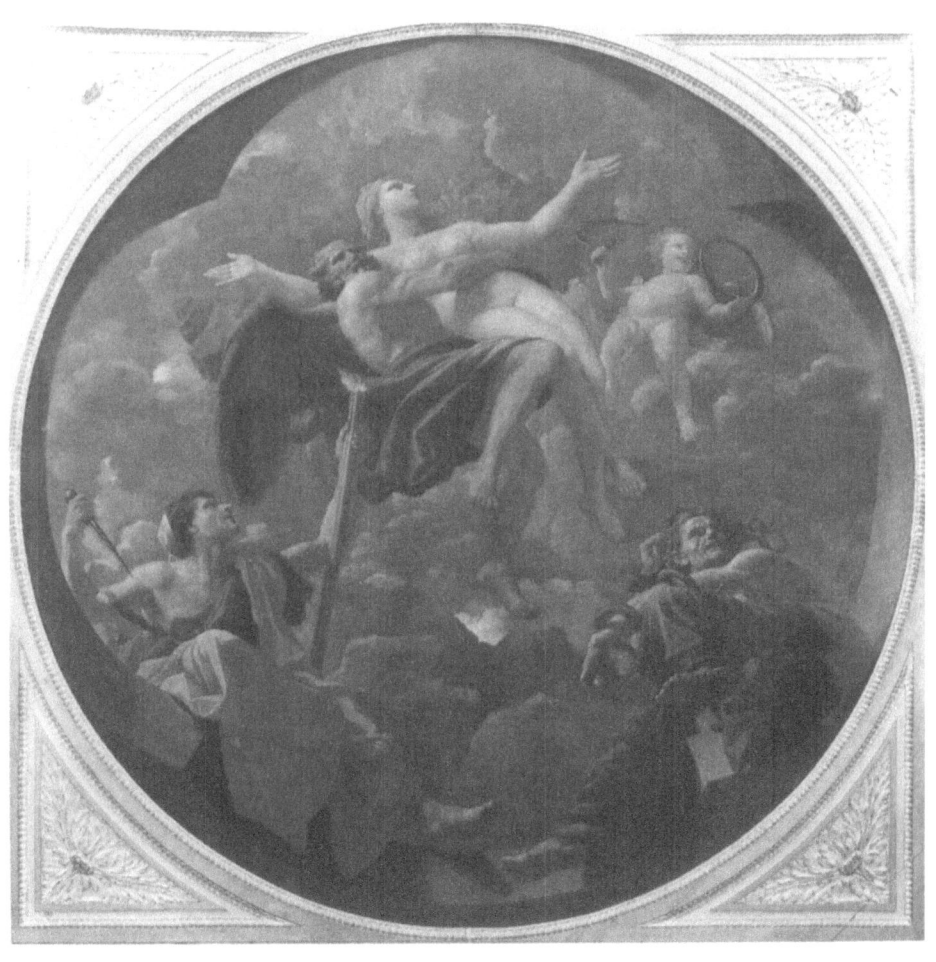

6. Poussin, *Time Saving Truth from Envy and Discord.* Louvre, Paris.
Giraudon/Art Resource

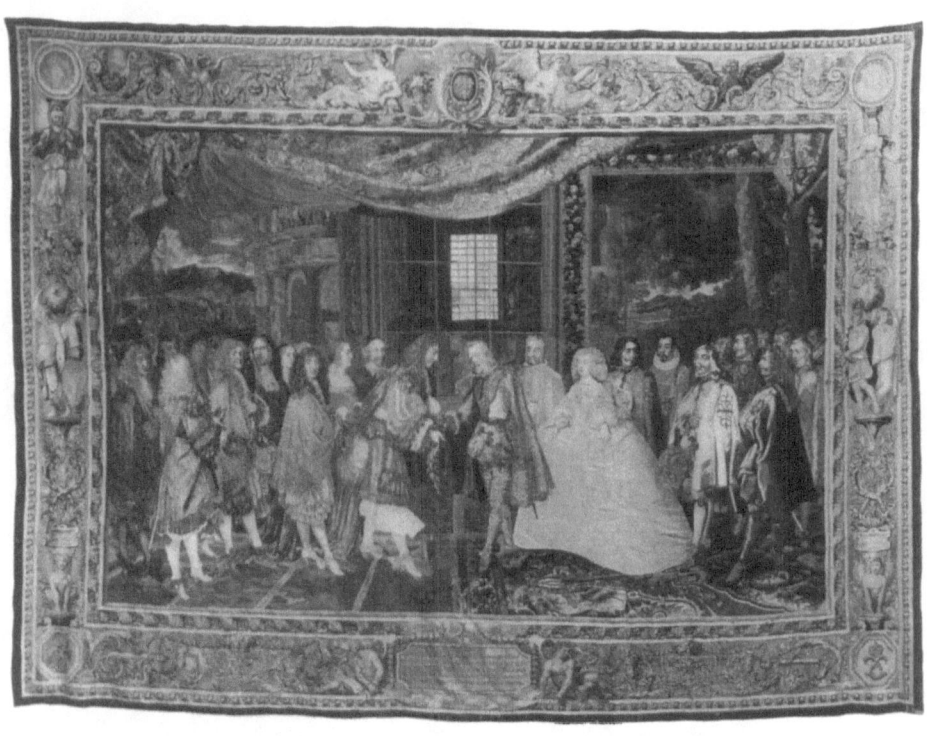

7. Le Brun, *Meeting between Louis XIV and Philip IV of Spain*. Mobilier National, Paris. Giraudon/Art Resource

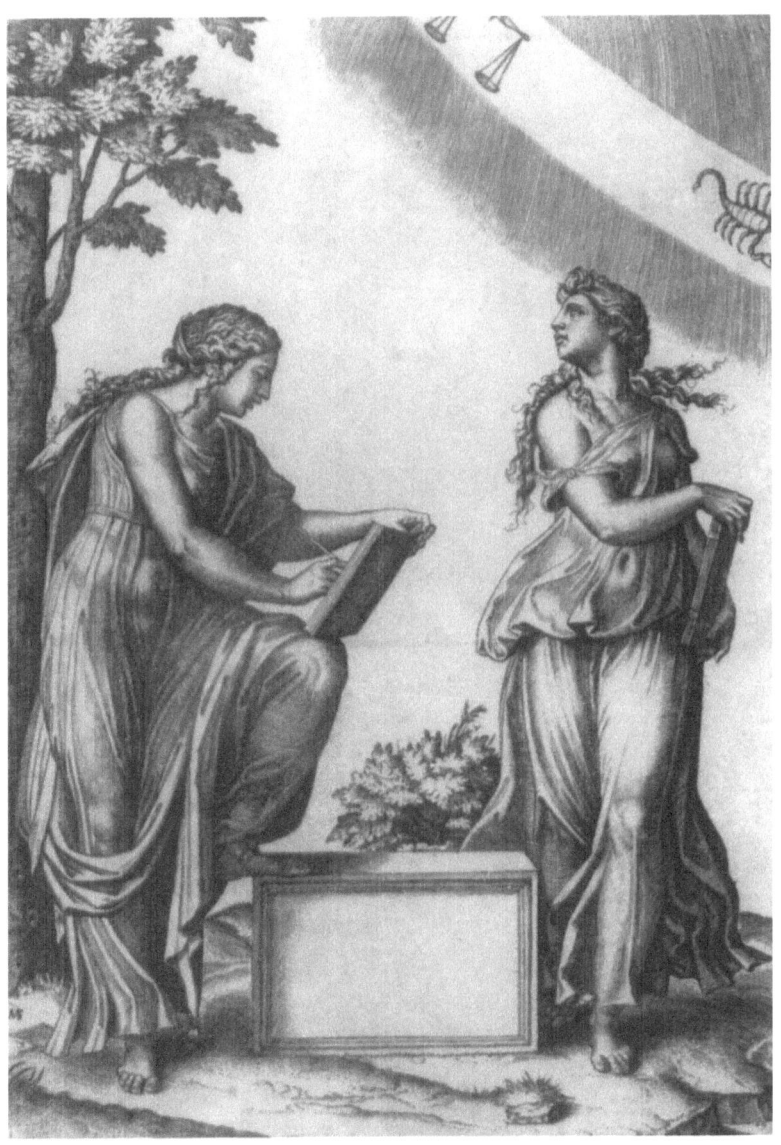

8. Raimondi, engraving after Raphael, *Two Women with the Zodiac*. Gift of
W. G. Russell Allen, © 1993 National Gallery of Art, Washington, D.C.

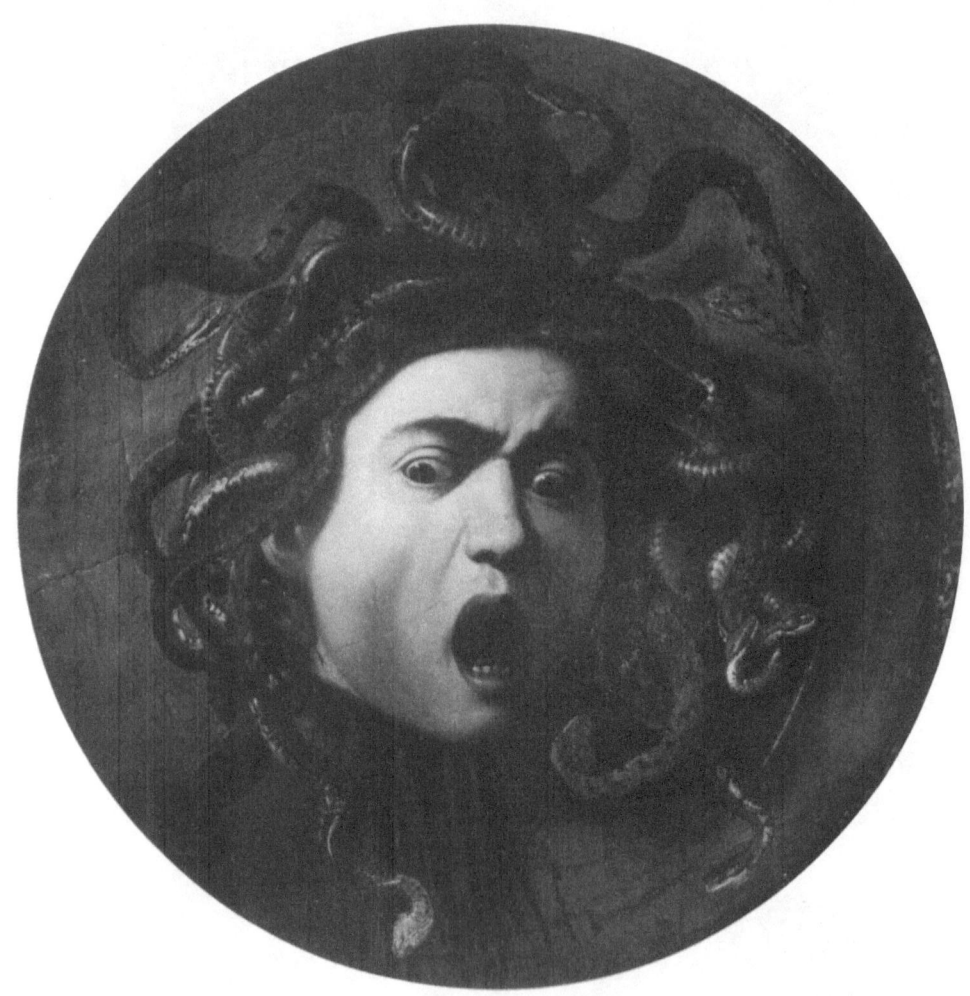

9. Caravaggio, *Head of Medusa*. Uffizi, Florence. Alinari/Art Resource

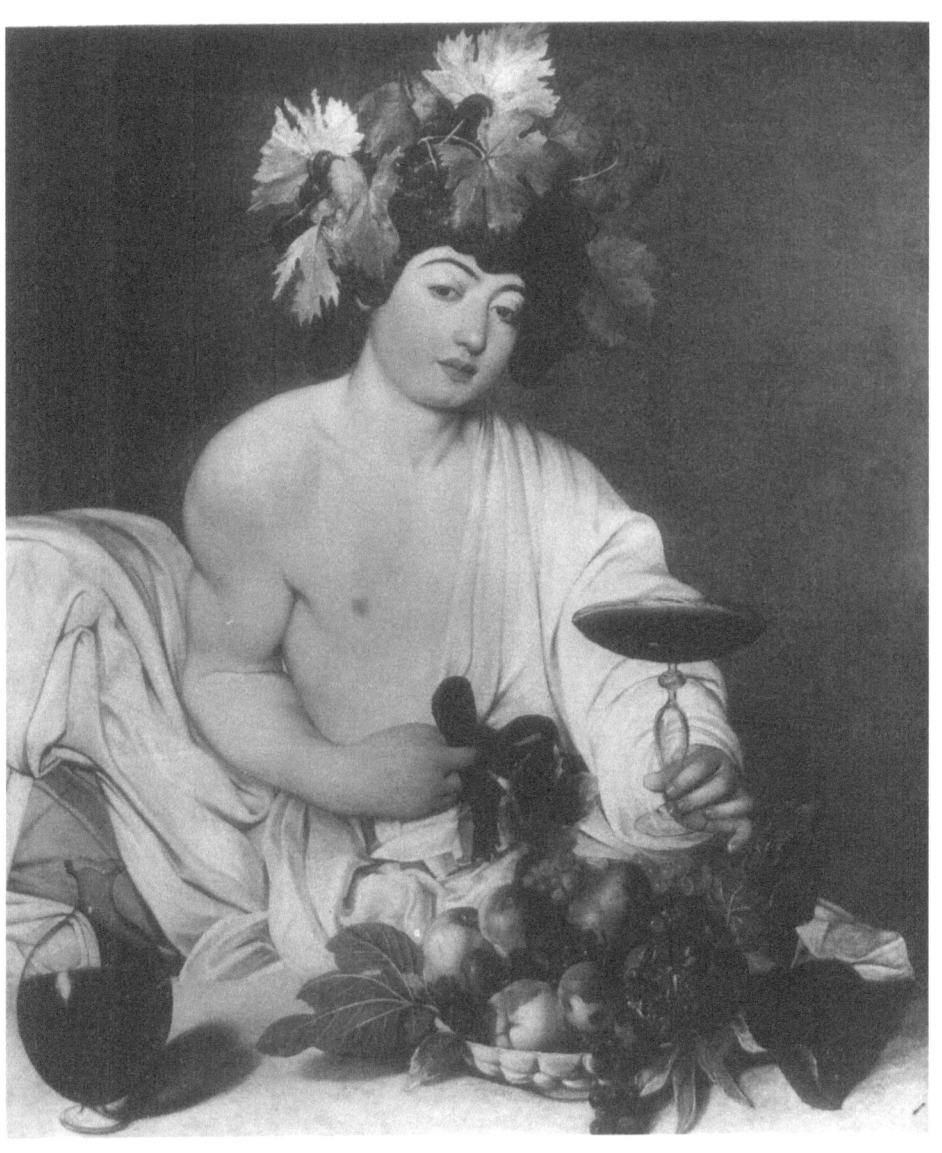

10. Caravaggio, *Bacchus*. Uffizi, Florence. Alinari/Art Resource

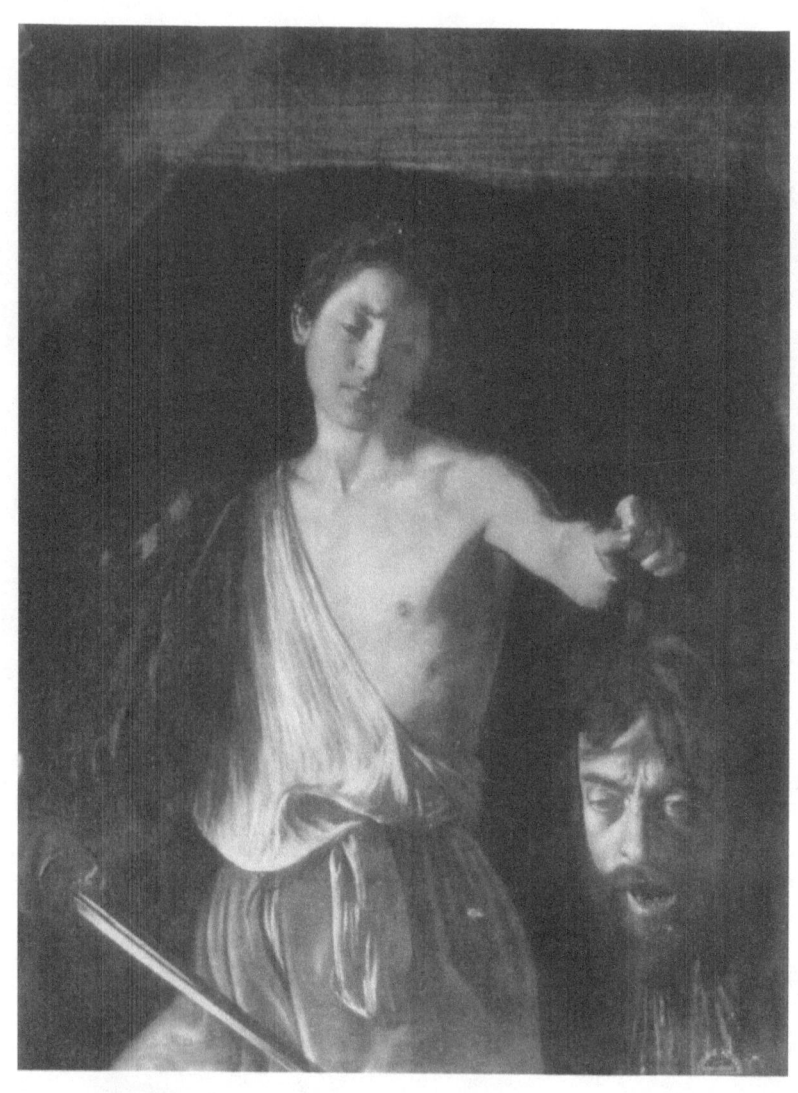

11. Caravaggio, *David with the Head of Goliath*. Galleria Borghese, Rome. Alinari/Art Resource

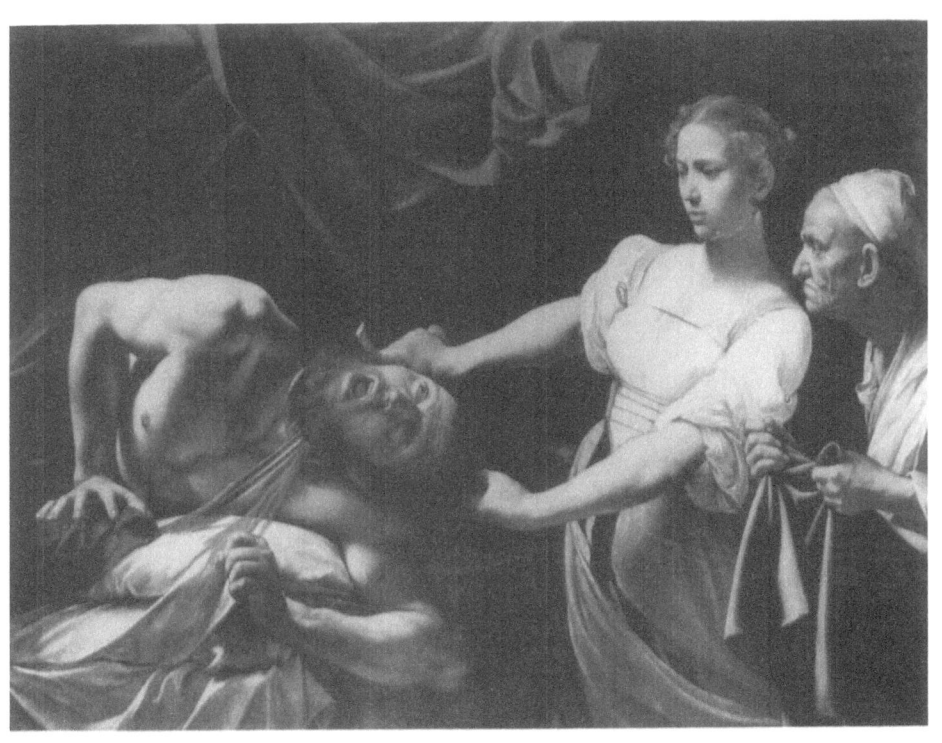

12. Caravaggio, *Judith Beheading Holofernes*. Galleria Nazionale d'Arte Antica, Rome. Art Resource. Photo © Nimatallah

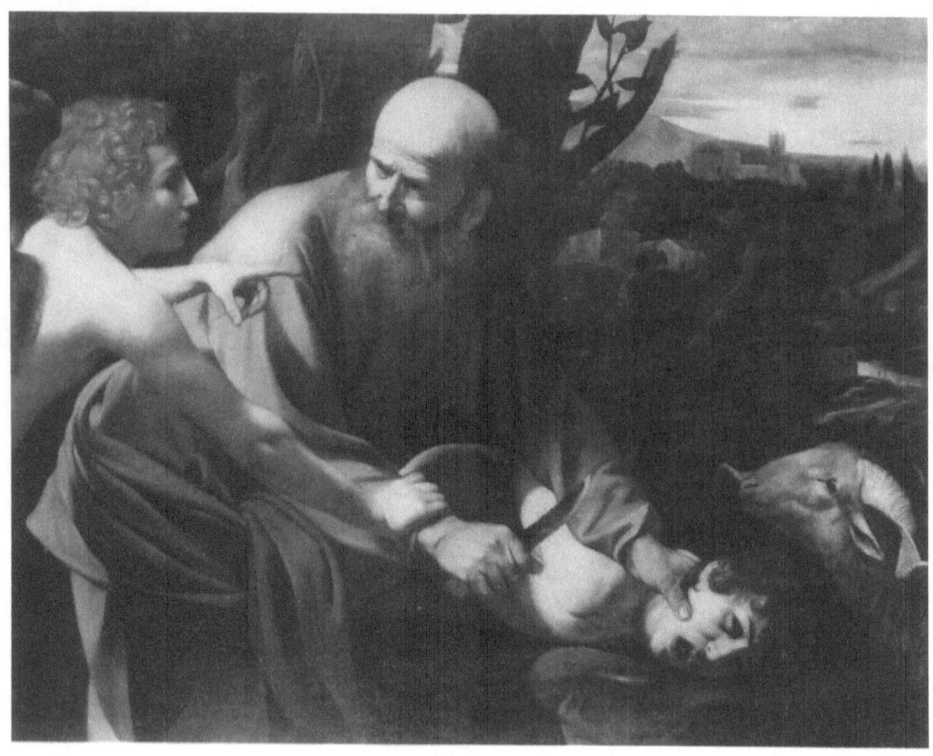

13. *(above)* Caravaggio, *The Sacrifice of Isaac*. Uffizi, Florence.
Alinari/Art Resource

14. *(right)* Caravaggio, *The Resurrection of Lazarus*. Museo Nazionale,
Messina. Scala/Art Resource

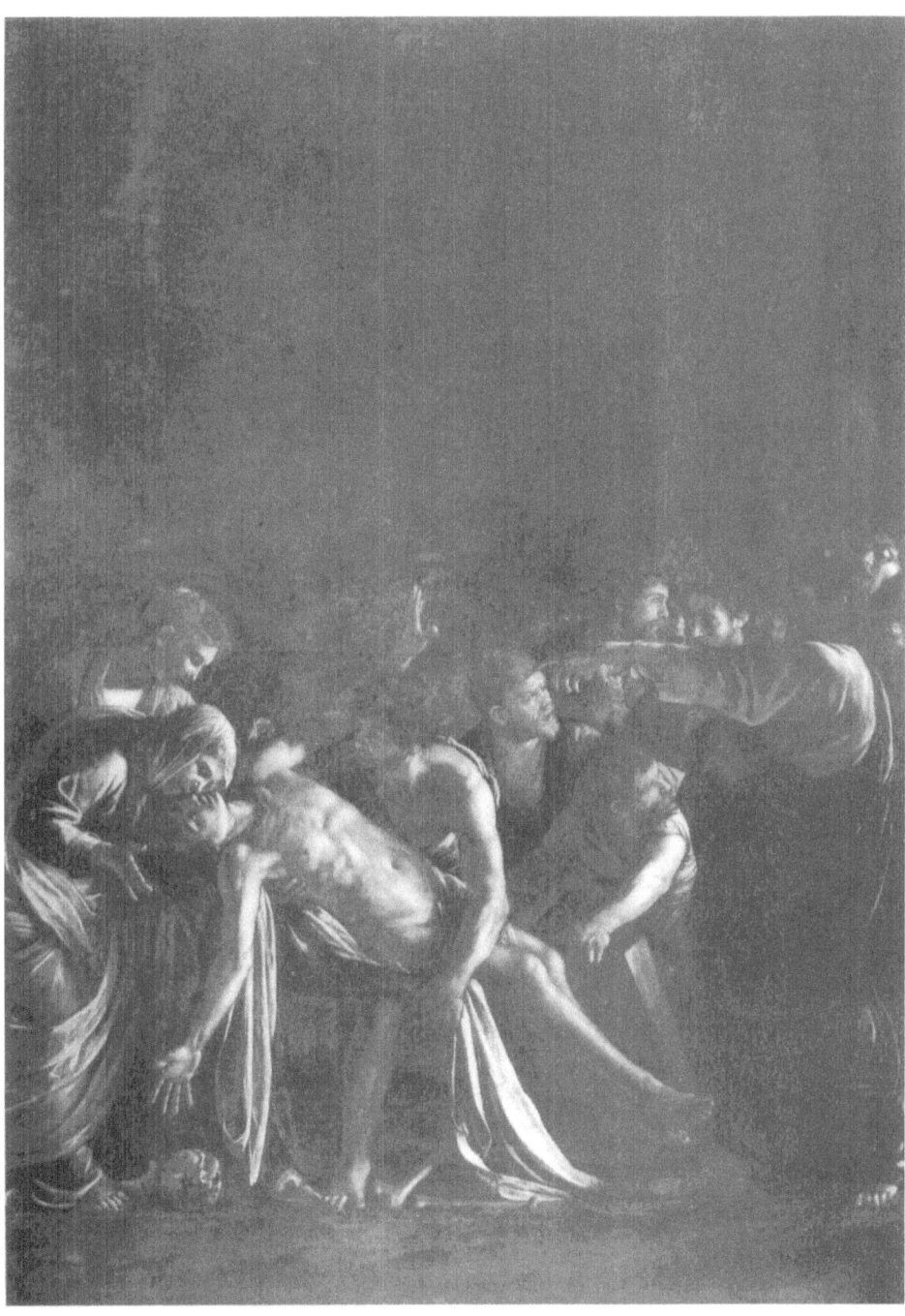

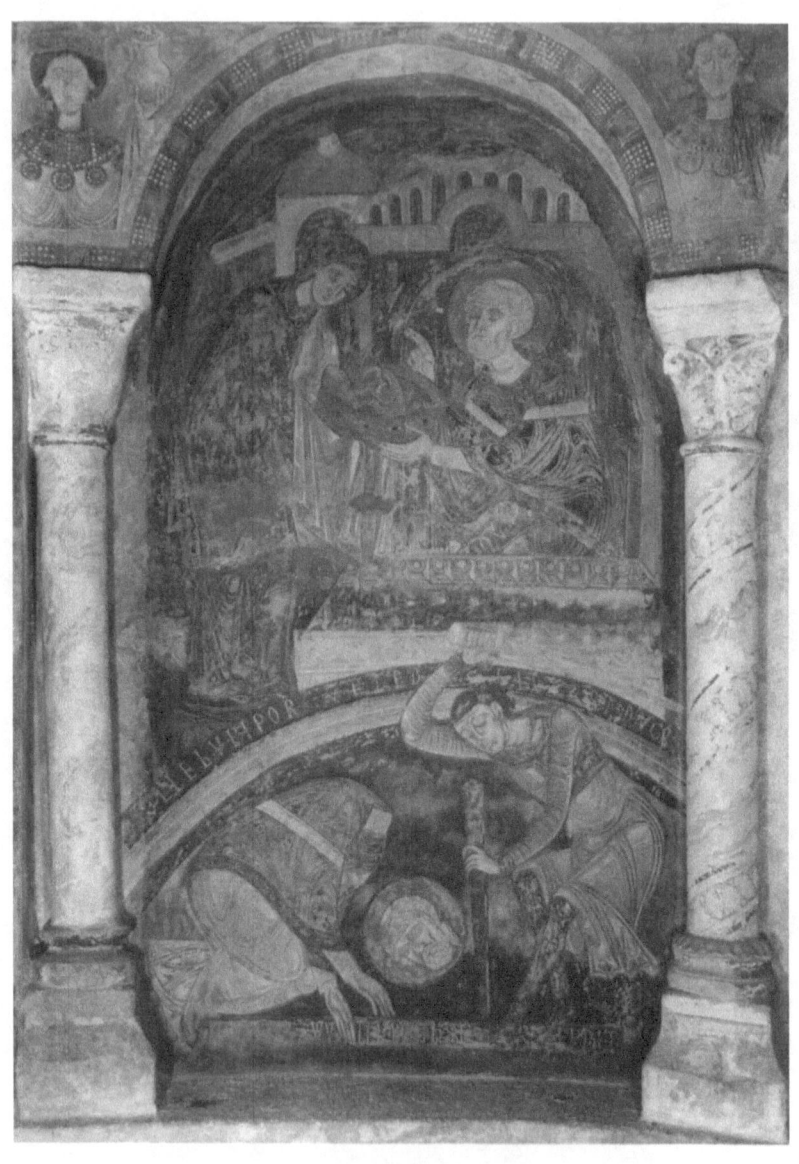

15. Fresco in Berzé-la-ville depicting an episode from the life of Saint Blaise. Giraudon/Art Resource

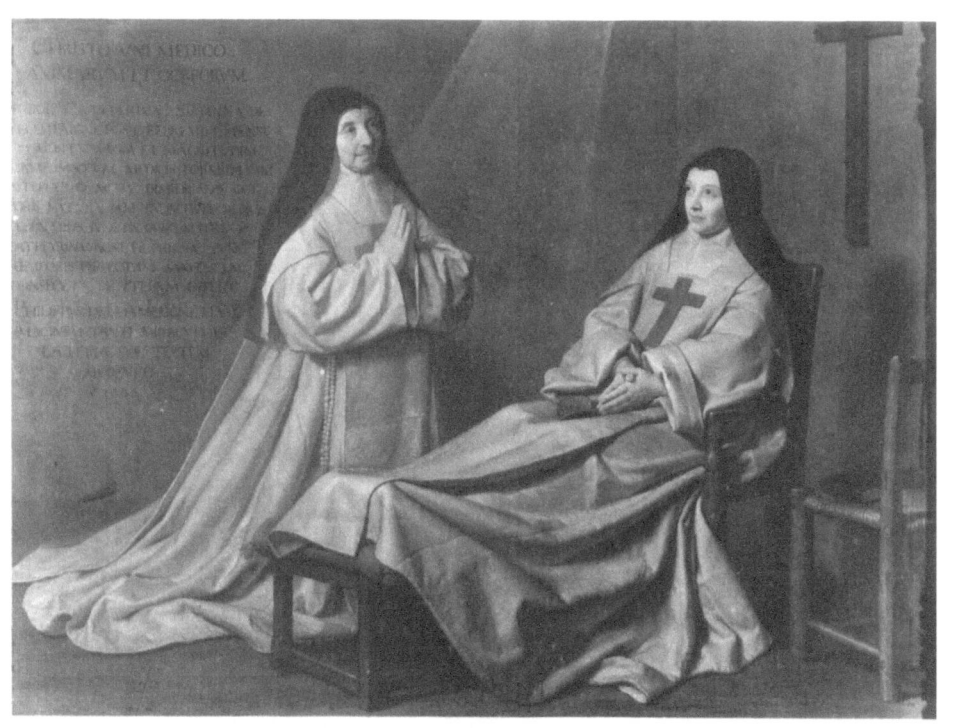

16. Champaigne, *Ex Voto of 1662*. Louvre, Paris. Giraudon/Art Resource

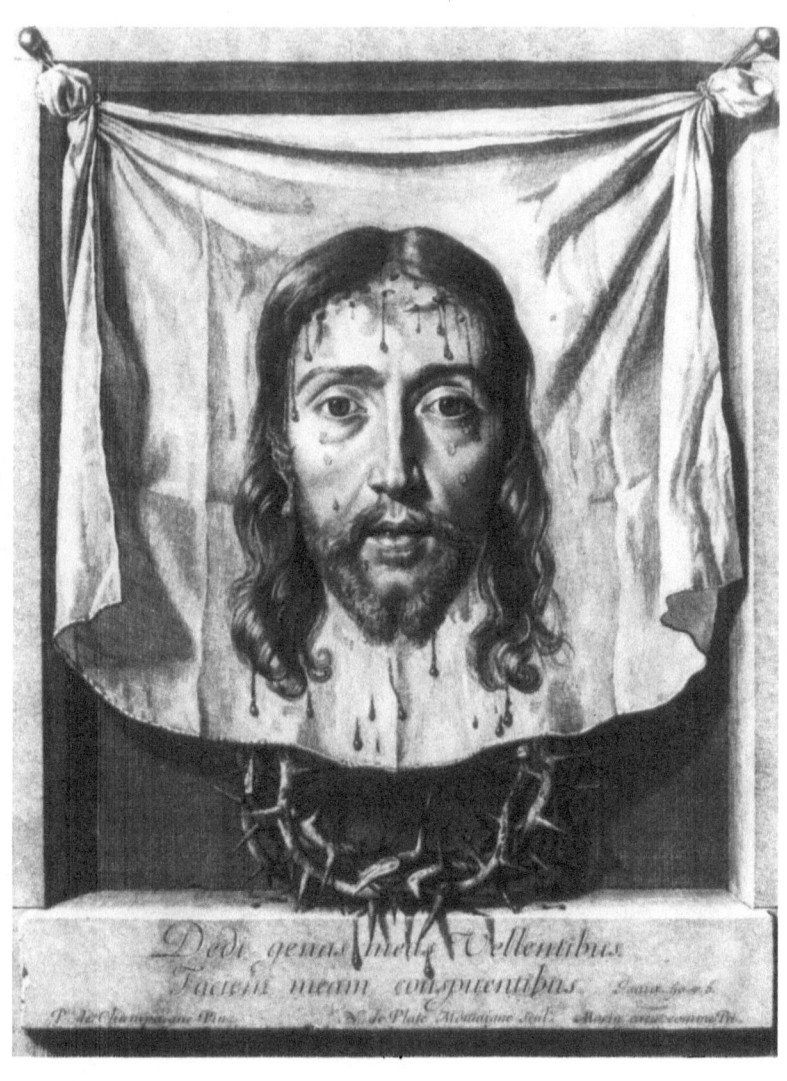

17. Champaigne, *Veil of Saint Veronica*. Bibliothèque Nationale, Paris. Giraudon/Art Resource

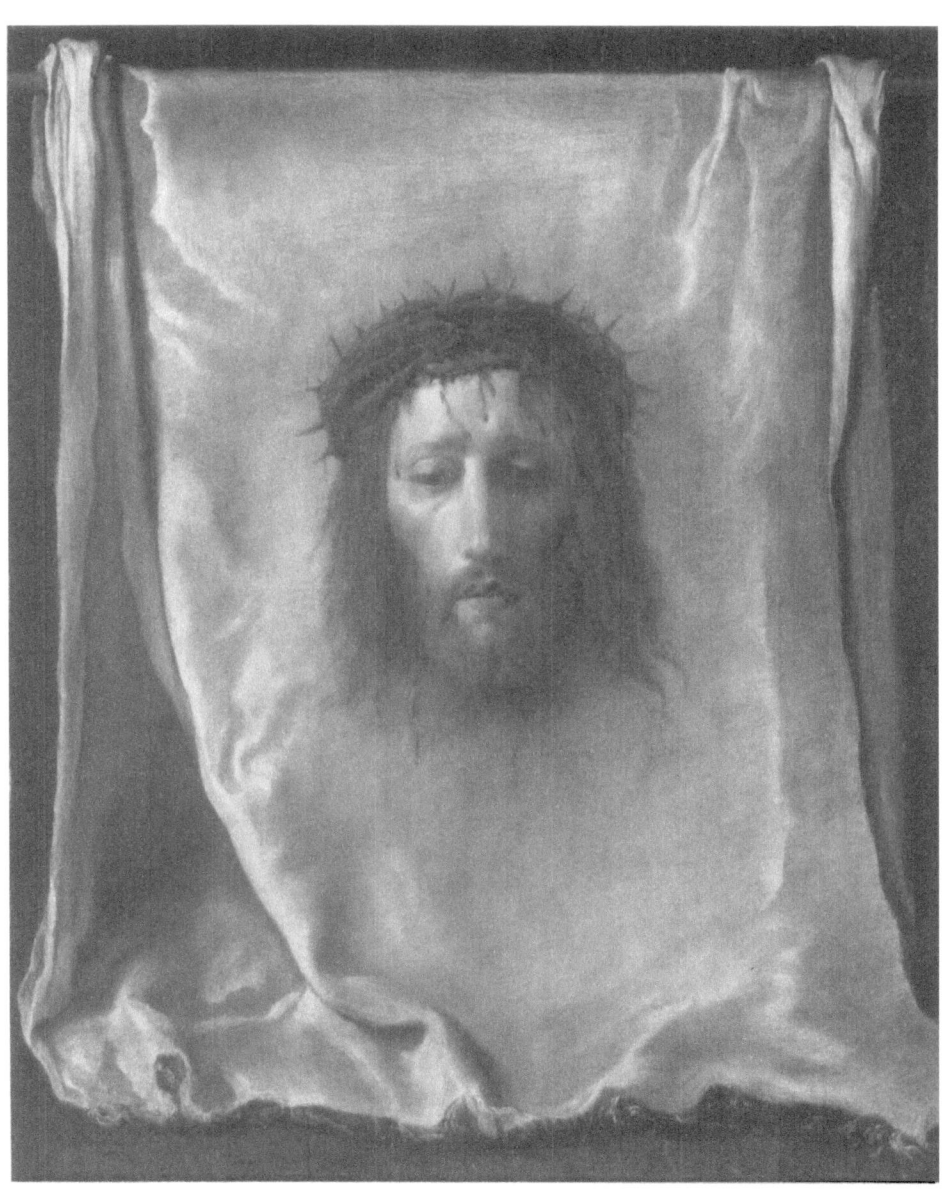

18. Fetti, *Veil of Veronica*. Samuel Kress Collection, © 1993 National Gallery of Art, Washington, D.C.

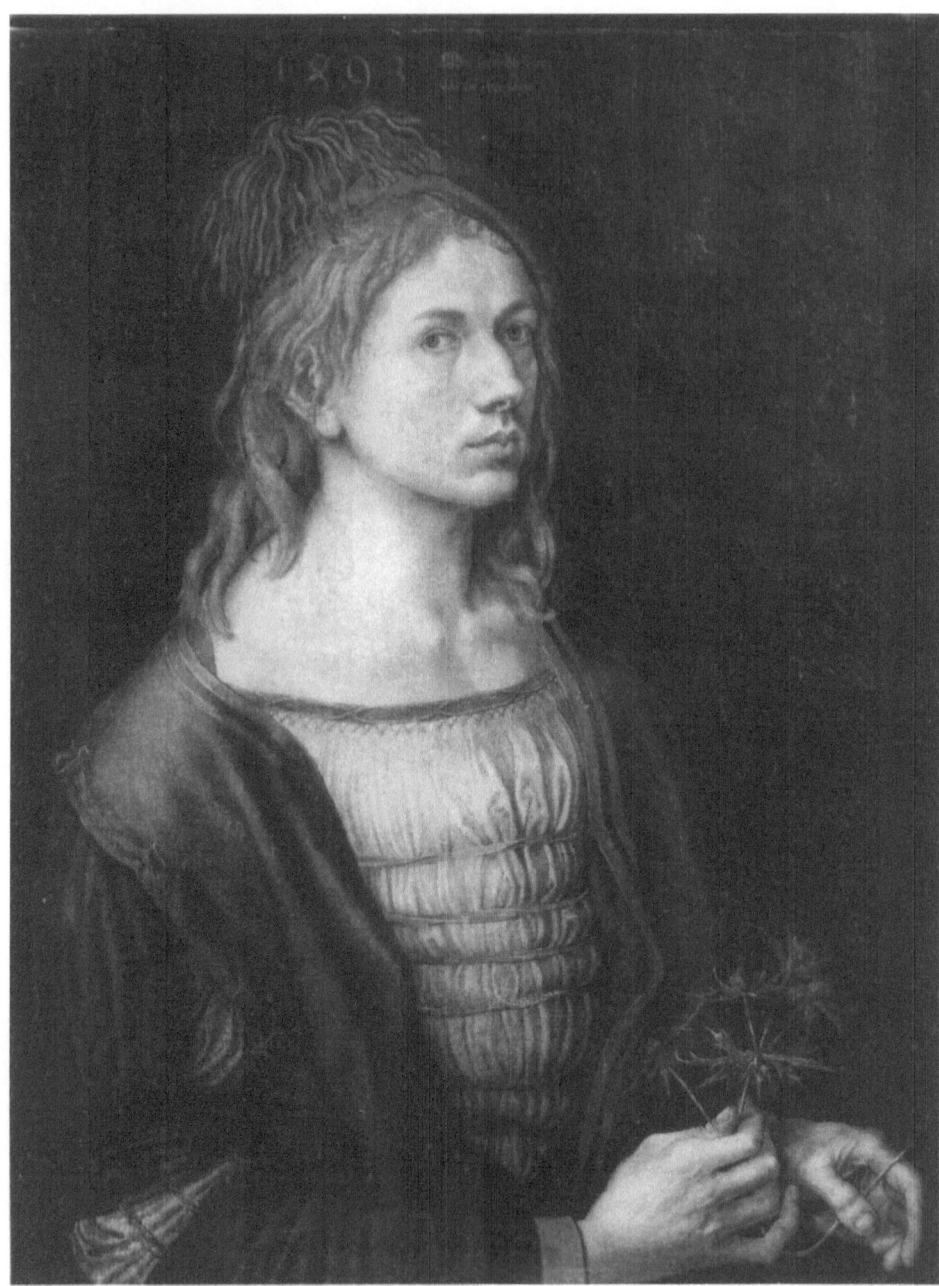

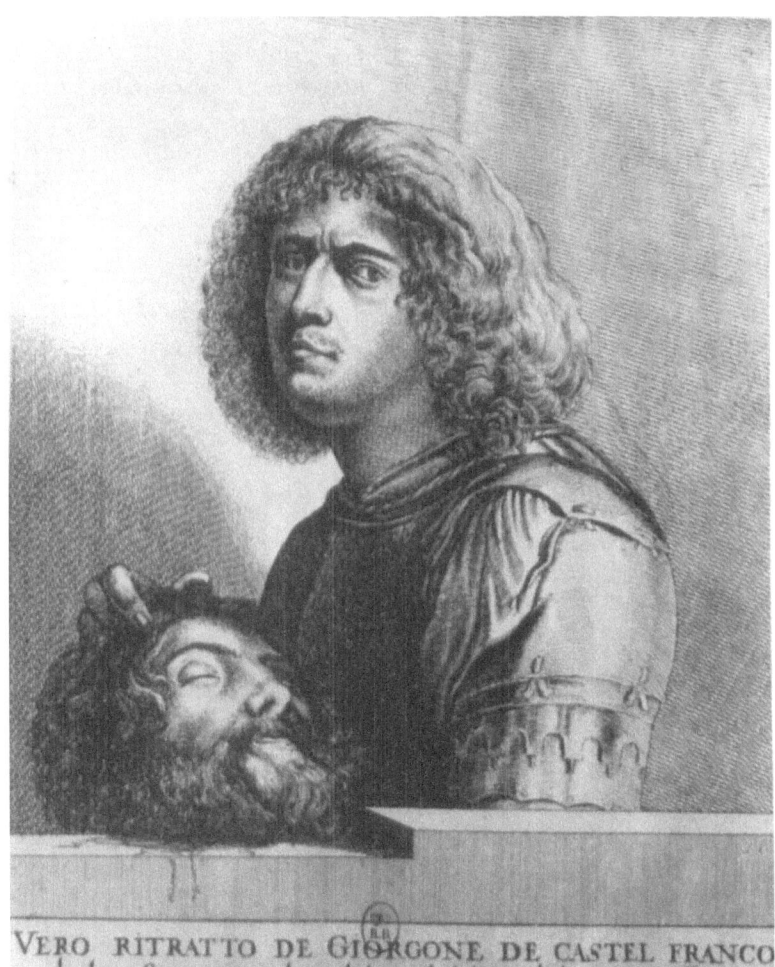

VERO RITRATTO DE GIORGONE DE CASTEL FRANCO
da luy fatto come lo celebra il libro dei VASARI.

19. *(left)* Dürer, *Self-Portrait*. Louvre, Paris. Giraudon/Art Resource

20. *(above)* Hollar, engraving after Giorgione's *Self-Portrait as David*. Bibliothèque Nationale, Paris. Giraudon/Art Resource

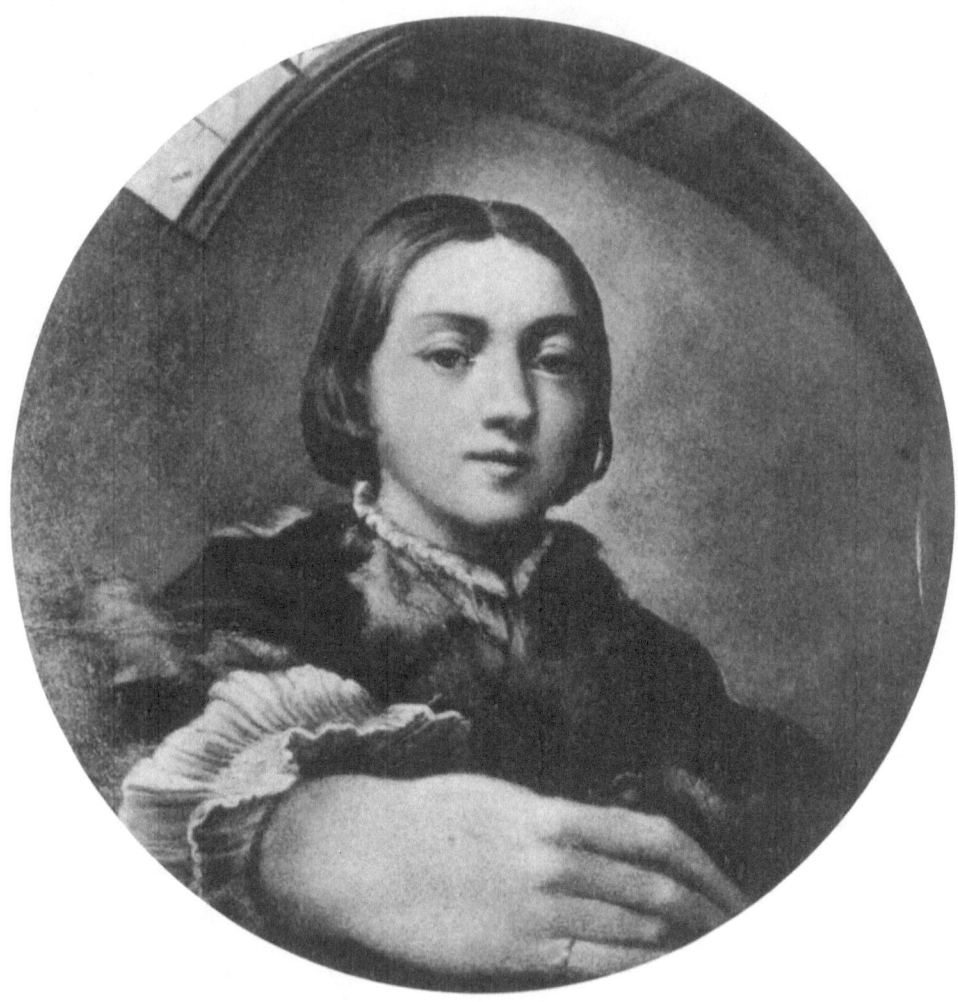

21. *(above)* Parmigianino, *Self-Portrait in a Convex Mirror.* Kunsthistorisches
Museum, Vienna. Bildarchiv Foto Marburg/Art Resource

22. *(right)* Master of the E-Series Tarocchi, engraving of *Philosophy* (attributed
to Mantegna). Rosenwald Collection, © 1993 National Gallery of Art,
Washington, D.C.

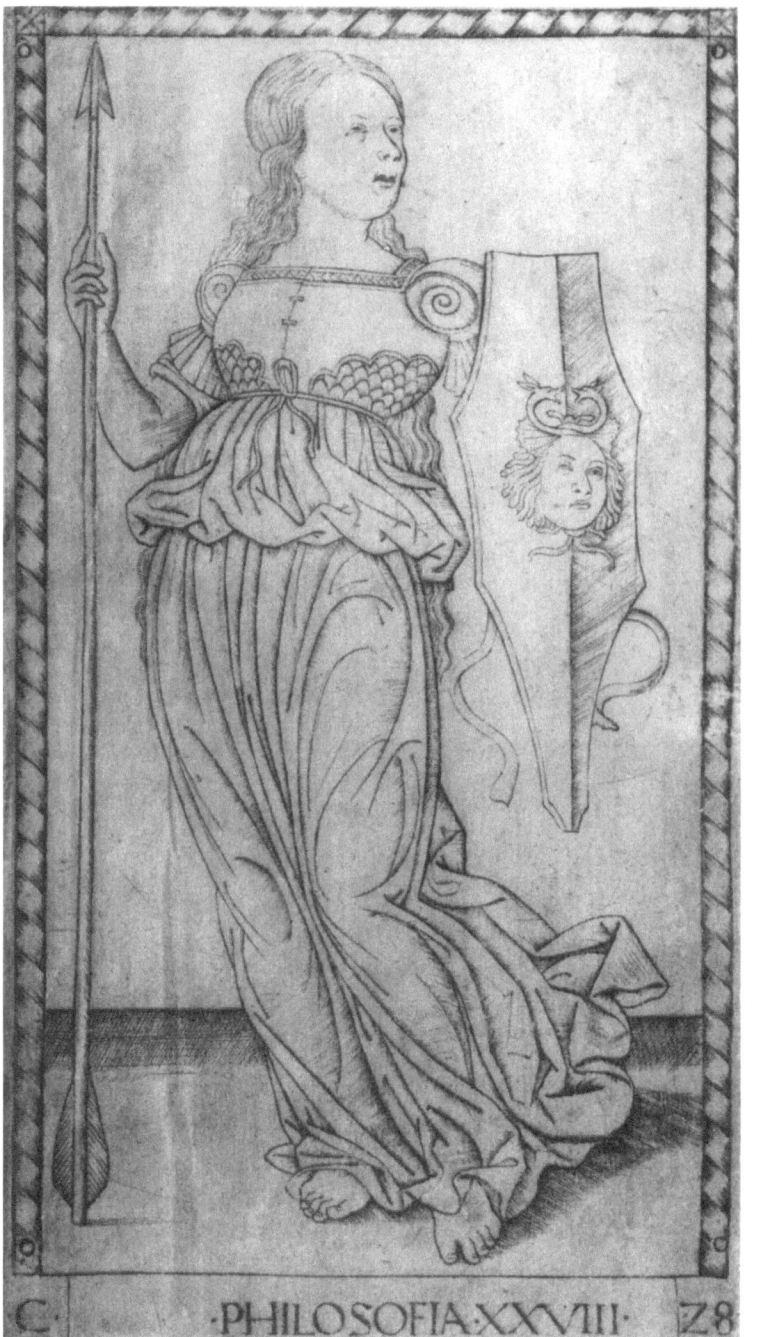

·PHILOSOFIA·XXVIII·

# Part II: Et in Arcana hoc

But, in fact, the eye sees itself in the above phenomenon merely as it does so in ordinary optical reflexion.

If the visual organ proper really were fire, which is the doctrine of Empedocles, a doctrine taught also in the *Timaeus*, and if vision were the result of light issuing from the eye as from a lantern, why should the eye not have had the power of seeing even in the dark?

—Aristotle, *De Sensu* 437b. 9–14

# Theoretical and Methodological Introduction

We may usefully begin by considering the following passages from Michael Fried's *Three American Painters: Kenneth Noland, Jules Olitski, Frank Stella:* "But if the inadequacy of almost all contemporary art criticism is not surprising, it is undeniably ironic, because the visual arts—painting especially—have never been more explicitly self-critical than during the past twenty years."[1] If this is so, it is because this "modernist" painting, to use Greenberg's phrase, "may be characterized in terms of the gradual withdrawal of painting from the task of representing reality—or of reality from the power of painting to represent it—in favor of an increasing preoccupation with problems intrinsic to painting itself."[2] According to Fried, it is not surprising that the language, procedures, and methods of a certain kind of art history should fail to deal adequately with modernist paintings. He has in mind the kind of art criticism that essentially aims at an understanding of the topics and themes of a painting, of its propositional content, the goal being to grasp the ever more complex codes that allow these themes to be identified and recognized by viewers. The main thrust of Fried's argument is that all paintings, particularly representational ones, are implicitly if not explicitly self-critical. That is, in a pictorial manner, they raise the fundamental problems inherent in painting or in painterly representation itself. To say that representational paintings use pictorial means to raise the fundamental problems of painting is to claim that they represent or make evident representation itself, the very process by which they are produced. Poussin's *Israelites Gathering Manna in the Desert* is a striking example of this kind of painting, as is made clear by the painter's own statements in his letter to Chantelou. *The Arcadian Shepherds* in the Louvre is an even clearer example of the genre, if only by virtue of a comparison with the Chatsworth version of the same title. A representational painting is self-critical to the extent that it is self-referential or self-generating. That is, a painting is self-critical if the fundamental characteristic of the representational system in question is self-referentiality, self-designation, or self-regulation. This situation is definitively described by Spinoza's phrase: *Veritas*

97

*index sui.* That is, Truth designates and represents itself as truth, and requires no external criteria.

By the same token, the role of critical discourse can be derived directly from this feature of self-referential representations. Critical discourse is nothing more than a making evident, in discourse and language, of this law of self-referentiality characteristic of the representational system. In short, critical discourse is merely the linguistic reproduction of this law. In this sense, it is not in fact a discourse *about* a given painting, but rather a discourse belonging *to* the painting itself. These remarks may be summarized in the following "graph":

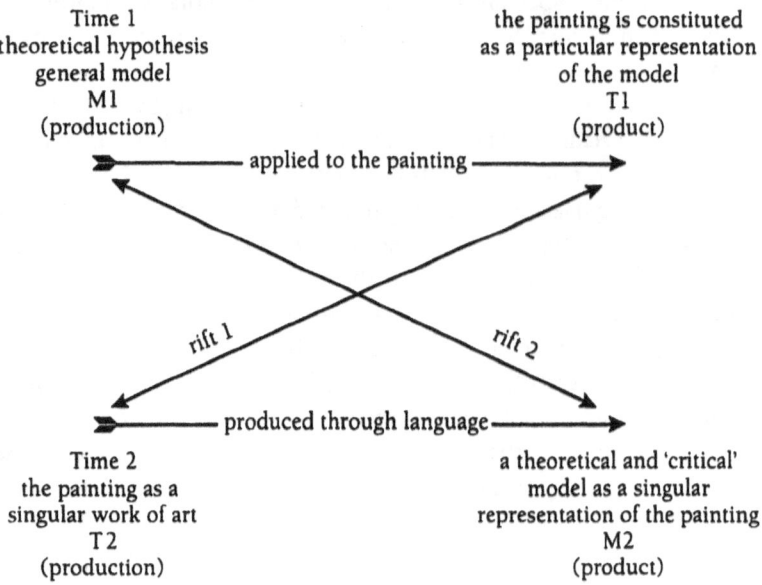

Time 1
theoretical hypothesis
general model
M1
(production)

the painting is constituted
as a particular representation
of the model
T1
(product)

applied to the painting

rift 1    rift 2

produced through language

Time 2
the painting as a
singular work of art
T2
(production)

a theoretical and 'critical'
model as a singular
representation of the painting
M2
(product)

M1 is not M2; T1 is not T2. Critical discourse in this case is quite simply the trajectory involved in this chiasmic structure. Indeed, the discourse in question brings to light the rift between M1 and M2 (rift 1) and between T1 and T2 (rift 2). It is especially important to underscore that the "critical" theoretical model that is produced as a particular representation of the painting (M2) differs from the more general theoretical model defining, for example, the laws and rules of the representational system.

The trajectory defined by M1–T1 and M2–T2 is not a circle, not even a hermeneutic one. Rift 1 (M1/M2) is the self-critical site of the critical model itself; rift 2 (T1/T2) may well manifest one and the same painting—Poussin's *Arcadian Shepherds* or his *Israelites Gathering Manna*, for example—according to radically different structures. This is the case if for no other reason than that T1 is a *product*, that is, a representation of a general model, while T2 *produces* a theoretical model, a discursive substitute for the painting. What we have here is a graph of the rifts separating the discourse *on* painting (M1/T1) from the discourse belonging *to* the work of art itself (T2/M2).

## Poussin Revisited

"Poussin could not bear Caravaggio and said that he had come into the world in order to destroy painting."[3]

This citation reports an *utterance* by the great master that merits reflection and even inspires a commentary by his *pupil*, who reveals himself somewhat disobedient as he plays with the meanings of that utterance. I hear you clearly, Master: you detest him, you hate him. Having succeeded in Paris, it was not easy for you similarly to succeed in Rome, for the entire field of your career had already been staked out. Paintings that were executed in a baroque style, that were inspired by Caravaggio, or that were painted by the Bolognese were favored by the market. "Poussin," says Félibien, "could not bear Caravaggio." The statement allows for none of the exceptions that might confirm the rule. You see red, Master, when you see a painting by him or by one of his many "pupils," who have cast themselves and their products onto the market that he created. His paintings make you *suffer:* in your hatred, in your impatience, there is a certain *pain*.

Yet there is something strange about the way in which Félibien reports the words of the great Master. Indeed, earlier I noted a certain hesitation, a kind of oscillation in Félibien's text. On the one hand, Caravaggio's paintings are said to be a source of pleasure, of "fullness and marvelous force," there being "nothing more beautiful." On the other hand, his paintings are described as disagreeable (there is no "agreeable light").[4] More specifically, we are to understand that Caravaggio's work does not lead to the "end" of painting, to its proper finality, which is delectation, contemplation informed by theory and knowledge. On this view, paintings are what Kant would call "hypotyposes." They are symbols of morality, figures of an unknown and unspeakable unity between perception and understanding, figures of a harmony within the agent, a harmony that reconciles the viewer to herself. Although this harmony cannot be proved, it can be shown and made present, "*subjectio ad aspectum,*" in paintings that are both beautiful and learned. The Master's suffering is articulated in turn by the fact that he cannot bear Caravaggio, whose paintings maintain and reveal the scission, the caesura between the parts that his own paintings reconcile. Indeed, Caravaggio's work not only maintains this scission but explores and exploits it. This is ultimately Wittkower's point when he speaks of the paradox of Caravaggio, describing the Italian as a painter of antitheses.

Caravaggio allows himself to be drawn to the truth of nature as it appears to him. What results is imitation, an illusion capturing the mere appearance of truth. According to Félibien, who speaks for Poussin, the latter's suffering is caused by noticing that, in the work of Caravaggio, representation or mimesis is turned inside out like a glove. A given representation, more specifically, does not refer to a corresponding idea, for we are told that Caravaggio never articulated an idea of his own, that he lacked the ideas needed to choose between options, and that he had no beautiful ideas. Instead, representation in Caravaggio's work refers to the appearance or mere aspect of things, and as a result, to antithesis and caesura.

The paradox of Caravaggio's work, to put it somewhat differently from Félibien while drawing on the intuitions of Félibien, Bellori, and countless art historians, consists in copying the truth of what appears in so slavish a manner that the *pictural representation becomes a mere effect.* That is, truth is an effect of the painting and not its origin. In his paintings Caravaggio irritatingly and sadomasochistically raises the question of truth in painting. Because a Caravaggio painting slavishly subordinates itself to the thing itself as it appears before one's eyes, it cannot be a representation of this thing. Instead it is the presentation of this thing's double. What we have here is a simulacrum, a trompe l'oeil, an excess of mimesis. It is true that imitation is defined by the classical age as the art of tricking the eyes. Yet this process should be pleasant and should involve the kind of choice and discernment that bespeaks the influence of the law of beautiful ideas. The trompe l'oeil is thus a supplementary mimesis, its excess. In fact, imitation maintains the distance between the copy and the model, thereby allowing the mind and theory to examine the law by which mimesis is controlled and mastered. By eliminating the distance between the model and its copy, a trompe l'oeil traps the perceiving eye at the level of appearance-as-essence. At the same time, it exposes the body-eye to the *fascination* of its double, its simulacrum. Inasmuch as the trompe l'oeil generates stupefaction, it can have neither a contemplative nor a theoretical effect. Instead its effect is surreal, an impure mixture of fear and shock.

Two texts, among others, are relevant here. First, Pietro Bellori:

> Demetrius, the ancient sculptor, is said to have been so eager to render the likeness of things that he cared more for imitating them than for their beauty. We have seen that the same is true of Michelangelo Merisi: he recognized no other master than the model and did not select the best forms of nature but emulated art—astonishingly enough—without art. . . . The painters then in Rome were greatly impressed by his novelty and the younger ones especially gathered around him and praised him as the only true imitator of nature. Looking upon his works as miracles, they outdid each other in following his method, undressing their models and placing their lights high; without paying attention to study and teachings, each found easily in the piazza or in the street his teacher or his model for copying nature.[5]

And second, Francesco Scannelli:

> A unique prodigy of naturalism, [Caravaggio was] led by a natural instinct to imitate, to ascend from the imitation of reality to the copying of flowers and fruits, from imperfect bodies to the most sublime, from imaginary figures to portraits, until he finally painted figures in their entirety, and, on occasion, historical compositions. This he did with such truth, such power, . . . that frequently, although nature is not equalled and defeated by his art, his *paintings nonetheless fool the viewer by tricking his eyes, thereby fascinating and delighting all humanity.*[6]

Scannelli points out that Caravaggio's genius led people to believe that he surpassed all rivals. However, according to Scannelli, Caravaggio's particular genius could not entirely compensate for his failure to acquire the basic skills that make the truly great Masters worthy of praise and admiration.

It is first of all a question of a Medusa's head.

## Recapitulation

The notions implied by, or explained in, the theories of painting and art cited above—representation, the imitation of natural beauty, judgment, choice, discernment, models, and pleasure—form a theoretical and critical network, the principle of which is that the representation of nature always must be subordinated to the law of representation. And this law authorizes the mastery of reality, its appropriation or its appropriateness. This law has a unique status, for in relation to the representational process it is at once transcendent or external and internal or immanent. It is transcendent inasmuch as it remains absent from the representational process and immanent in the sense that this process must conform to the law if it is to unfold at all.

From this point of view, Caravaggio's paintings are scandalous. What we have here is the paradox of a type of representation that at once reveals and cancels its own law while the painting becomes a simulacrum and thus ceases to be a re-presentation. By the same token, this painting becomes improper or impure by virtue of an excessive degree of propriety. A characteristic feature of Caravaggio's paintings, then, is that they reveal and represent the excessive nature of representation, which grounds and authorizes them.

I am raising a very general question here: what is the relation between truth and painting, between a work of art and the internal structure that aims at this central referent and serves as its representation? For this is essentially what the theoretical texts that we have read or reread on this particular occasion are all about. I am thinking, for example, of certain passages in Félibien's text, passages that seem somewhat contradictory although they are only a few pages apart. At one point Caravaggio is said to find his spontaneity in the relation between painting and truth, for he allows himself to be carried away by the truth of nature as it appears to him. Yet it is in this same relation that Caravaggio is said to discover the law of his own servitude, for "he had no ideas of his own"; "he made himself a slave to nature and not an imitator of beautiful things."[7] The relation to truth is so dominant that Caravaggio's flights of inspiration are conceived as the active receptivity —an expression that may not be as contradictory as it seems at first— of nature as he saw it. There is a certain insistence, here and there in the texts of the art historians, on what one might call the *surface* of things, an insistence that is used to characterize Caravaggio's art and to explain his extraordinary success. The surface is neither the outside nor the inside of things, but the plane where the outside and inside coincide in a blurred and undecidable boundary. It is here that the outside and inside are at their most intense and attain their greatest power, a power so overwhelming it cannot be resisted.

"What vanity is involved in a painting that inspires admiration by resembling things that would hardly be admired in the originals." It is the enticing or "vain" nature of certain paintings that creates the power to attract the viewer's gaze and to turn it away from the thing itself. What a marvelous thing is the painting that locates, within the incoherence of a symbolic effect, not a logical contradiction in its system but the all-powerful nothingness or vanity of its force. And if we are to believe Van Mander or other art historians, Caravaggio seems to echo Pascal in this regard and to respond in advance to Poussin by turning against him his phrase about the destruction of painting: those who try to escape the seductions of the surface, the mere aspect of things, or Nature as it appears to the perceiving eye, create only puerile and unimportant art; they are doomed to produce only insignificant work, no matter what the subject of the painting may be. The surface, with its mere aspects and appearances, is the most serious thing in the world. It is perhaps the site of tragedy—in its very undecidability—and the site of the tragedy of painting. According to Pascal, and no doubt Poussin, its vanity is its tragedy, the place where painting destroys itself. Pertinent here as well is Bellori's remark about Caravaggio, a painter whom he was little inclined to favor: the surface is where Caravaggio "emulated art—astonishingly enough—without art." The surface, then, emerges as the site where the art of painting achieves its greatest intensity as well as the power to attract and fascinate the viewer's gaze, thereby causing the viewer to turn away from the thing itself in stupefaction.

Of relevance in this context is a somewhat ridiculous, but perhaps no less *radical*, aspect of Pymandre's response to Félibien's rhetorical and pedagogical question, asking him to articulate his impressions of a painting by Caravaggio and another by Titian: "Caravaggio is not agreeable. There is nothing that a painter must seek more than to make his works agreeable. But this is what Caravaggio never did."[8] Félibien seems to suggest that the painting's "attractiveness" has no other function than to diminish what I have called the tragic dimension of the surface, to attenuate the tragedy of a representation that destroys itself, perhaps by means of a travesty of the *subject*.

It is for this reason that I shall attribute particular importance here, albeit in a parodic spirit, to what could also be seen as a farce: a painting in the Uffizi representing the head of Medusa. All the issues raised thus far come together in this painting, where the theoretical-critical network of representation erupts.

I am interested in painting as representation, but also in the irresistible pull, and stupefying effects, of what I see in the mirror it creates. Although what I see is intolerable, everything else seems trifling and childish in comparison.

## Theoretical Interlude: Remarks on Margot Cutter's "Caravaggio in the Seventeenth Century"

In her article Cutter introduces an important distinction between the theorists of art and those who quite simply love Caravaggio's work. Although Cutter's use of this distinction within her argument more generally is somewhat debatable, she is right to consider it important.[9]

The painting in question here is Caravaggio's *Death of the Virgin*. On the advice of Rubens, Giovanni Magno, the duke of Mantua's agent, buys this painting, which had been rejected by a chapter of the de la Scala Church. Rubens is enthusiastic about the painting, and his enthusiasm increases when he sees it for the second time. Magno, however, admits to being one of those people who prefers paintings that are pleasant to look at. He further remarks that he was more impressed by the testimony of the experts than by the painting itself; he indicates that he was incapable of understanding those "occult artifices which place the picture in such high esteem."[10]

Margot Cutter quite rightly points out that the decision to justify or explain one's stance on a given painting through *writing* is to identify, at least in part, with an academic point of view. To write is to approach the painting from a *theoretical* point of view, which is tantamount to adopting the discourse of the Masters. This discourse about painting is an "academic" one, a discourse that divorces the theory of painting from its practice. I am using the term "practice" to refer not only to the "making" of paintings, but also to the "seeing" of paintings. What I have in mind here is the opposition established above between the discourse *about* painting and the discourse *of* the painting itself. "Theoretically," the question raised by this distinction is important: how does one write a discourse that is not a discourse about the painting but a transposition (translation, transversion) into language of the discourse that the painting itself engages in, assuming, of course, that the painting could *engage* in a discourse? Discourse about painting is always academic, which essentially means that it is metadiscursive. That is, it is based on a system of norms, transcendent references, previously established principles of aesthetic judgment, and codes, all of which have an a priori status in relation to the painting under consideration. In that sense, terms such as "theory" or "theoretical" are synonymous with "academicism." Now, we know that Caravaggio's paintings played a very important role at the outset of the seventeenth century, to the point where it is legitimate to speak of something like a Caravaggian "revolution." The importance of his work can be explained primarily in terms of its *effect* (see Rubens). I want to suggest that a painting by Caravaggio provokes what I shall call an "effect of seeing." As a result, a painting by Caravaggio cannot be considered as the application of a system, or as the result (or message) of an a priori code that finds theoretical expression in the discourse on painting. The situation is quite the opposite, for in producing an *effect* of "seeing," the painting in question constitutes itself as a force, thereby distributing a series of visual effects. If a painting is construed as a function of an a priori code, it is nothing more than the representation, in an "iconic language," of a preexisting theory. If, on the other hand, a painting is viewed as having a certain efficacy, then the discourse *about* it will be the *product* of this very painting. In other words, the crucial task here is to articulate the effect of painting construed as a force in the field of *sight*. In the first case, the discourse on painting is quite simply the *power* of an institution; that is, the metalanguage is the expression of an a priori code and theory of painting; an expression of institutional power. In the second case, the painting is a *potency*, and the discourse on painting is the *effect* or *impression* left by this potency at the level of representation. How, then, are we to produce a discourse about painting that captures the impression left by a painting without being "impressionistic"?

Bellori makes a number of remarks about Caravaggio, one of which is that this painter restored the power of color by reviving the mimetic dimensions of art. What is the secret or occult artifice (see Magno) behind the power of color in Caravaggio's work? Malvasia tells us that Alessandro Tiarini liked the work of Caravaggio "for the purity, truth and force of his color, marvelling indeed at the stimulating effect it had upon him even though it was completely lacking in decorum, majesty, and erudition."[11] The painting's force, or potency, which produces a discursive effect, is quite simply the force and potency of color. We are led, then, to contemplate the nature of a semiology of color: can there be a "theory" of color, in the strict sense of the term, if color is a force? What, more specifically, would a dynamic theory of color look like? How would such a theory be linked to a semiotics of painting?

What is also strange, to say the least, is that the issue of the force of color and its effects seems to have been linked to a recurrent seventeenth-century critique of Caravaggio's work. The claim was that Caravaggio's historical paintings were completely devoid of *action*. Thus, for example, Bellori says of *The Conversion of Saint Paul* that the "story is entirely without action."[12] Referring to *The Martyrdom of Saint Matthew*, he states that "the composition and the movements . . . are not adequate for the story, even though Caravaggio repeated it twice."[13] The "Academician" is surprised to discover just how powerful Caravaggio's painting is in spite of the absence of action. An opposition (which should be explored further) begins here between what Bellori calls action—that is, painting as a *narrative representation* of agents engaged in action—and the *force of painting* as a set of colors unleashing visual effects. The ultimate effect of this force in a painting presented as a narrative representation (as is the case of both *The Conversion of Saint Paul* and *The Martyrdom of Saint Matthew*) will be an annihilation of action. In a painting that presents itself as a narrative representation, the force of color has the effect of stupefying the action, of foreclosing the possibility of a story about human actions. It does so by unleashing in the viewer a desire to see (scopophilia). In light of my earlier analyses of the representational moment in historical paintings, as these are construed by Le Brun (or Poussin), the task at hand is to try to understand the transformation painting, and the criticism of painting, have undergone as a result of Caravaggio's efforts. More specifically, it is a matter of articulating the opposition between the moment of representation and what I, lacking a better term, shall call the moment of sight.

I want to return here to the basic model I developed of historical painting from the "classical" period. This model, we recall, was kinetic and mapped out a certain transformation undergone by a formal network comprising the painting's point of view and vanishing point. That

is, the model indicated the manner in which this network was lat-
eralized and displaced into a linear network running parallel to a plane
of narrative utterances articulated symmetrically as "circumstances"
around a center. Together these utterances constituted the moment of
representation. My aim at this stage is to show how the moment of
sight erupts within representation, how the drive for color has the effect of stupefying or annihilating the narrative representation. I am
interested in certain features of Caravaggio('s) criticism, both the "criticism" resulting from his practice of painting and the academicians'
critical discourse about the painter. These discourses share a tendency
to disengage the powerful visual effects produced by color from the
other fundamental parts of the painting and from the system of painting itself. I am thinking, for example, of terms such as "idea," "grace,"
"decorum," "architecture," and "perspective," terms that name the
very properties of a drawing or sketch. There is a tendency to overturn
the order of the relevant parts and to give free rein to the powerful visual effects produced by color, the Medusa-effects of representation.

It is helpful at this point to draw once more on Baglione's *Le Vite
de' Pittori, Scuttori, et Architetti* (1642). I am particularly interested in
the following passage, in which Baglione cites a statement by Poussin,
a statement that Félibien also attributes to Poussin in his "Entretien"
dedicated to the French painter:

> However, some people consider him to have been the very ruination of
> painting, because many young artists, following his example, simply copy
> heads from life without studying the fundamentals of drawing and the
> profundity of art and are satisfied with color values alone. Thus they are
> incapable of putting two figures together or of composing a story because
> they do not understand the high value of the noble art of painting.[14]

In his attempt to explain why certain individuals insist that Caravaggio
destroyed the art of painting, Baglione presupposes that the art of
painting is basically a constraining cultural institution or power. He
further assumes that Caravaggio's imitators, by following his example,
called into question the codes, norms, and rules that are the very *basis*
of the art of painting and of the disciplinary knowledge constituted by
the didactic and pedagogical system of the arts. This destruction stems
from a fissure that is minuscule, but that expands to the point of becoming *catastrophic:* the attempt to paint a face after a living model.

The theoretical and practical implications of this gesture are far-reaching. They can be summarized as follows:

1. The design (of both painting and painter) is placed in a secondary and nondominant position. Design is no longer either the organizing principle or the basis of the art of painting. It does not exist as an "idea" (*disegno interno*), a *judgment* that is wholly in the mind of a painter, nor is it the basic organizational structure of the painting, its *prospect*.

2. As far as the issue of pedagogical practice is concerned, it is a matter of rejecting the tradition of copying or imitating ancient models, essentially sculpture, that enshrines the primacy of drawing in two ways: paradigmatically, since a work of art, a statue, or a bust is already the model for another work of art or painting; and practically, since the imitation of sculpture entails a privileging of drawing.

3. Caravaggio's gesture reveals a preference not for the depth of art but for its appearance or surface. We recall that as far as the "classical" logicians and philosophers were concerned, the sketch constituted the painting's invisible-visible dimension. The sketch, they believed, was hidden deep within the painting, giving the latter its "soul." Color, on the other hand, was viewed as the painting's visible-invisible dimension, its surface quality.

4. The result is an interdiction on historical painting, for history does not exist in the *hic et nunc*, does not immediately manifest itself in the present before one's very eyes. Whether a given history is derived from mythology, historiography, or fiction, it is always first and foremost a written text that is read and contemplated by the painter, who imagines the figures, their relations, and those expressive signs that are embodied emotions. The painter composes this text as he imagines an idea for a sketch, an idea that he then transforms into a preliminary sketch and finally into a sketch on the canvas itself. This final sketch, we know, will ultimately be covered over by the colors the painter manipulates at will. Incidentally, Caravaggio never made any preliminary sketches.

These points evoke the institutional power of painting, the network of constraints that connects a series of concepts, such as sketch, depth, invisibility, nobility, idea, subject matter, and history.

It is helpful now, by way of contrast, to consider a different series of questions. How, in the case of Caravaggio, is the effect of color produced? What is the relation between the effect of color and the use of light, or, more precisely, between the function of light and the effect of color? Between light, color, and the depiction of history by means of painting? How does the intensification of light—of the contrast between darkness and light—raise the question of the effect of representation as stupefaction? Bellori, for example, clearly picks up on Caravaggio's characteristic tendency to cast intense light on the main parts of the body while leaving the rest in darkness. What is more, Bellori is not the only one to grasp that in so doing Caravaggio produces the painting's force, which takes the form of an intensely surprising, realistic-plastic effect.

Could it be that the stupefying effect and power of the narrative representation is produced by an intensification of the contrast between darkness and light, a contrast that somehow increases the force and violence of the color drive?

*We must be dealing here with the workings of Medusa.*

## A Methodological Objection

I would like at this point to respond to a possible objection to my analysis. One might argue that my commentaries on citations from Félibien, Van Mander, and Scannelli involve a radical displacement of these authors' texts as well as a series of misinterpretations resulting from a penchant to overinterpret. My reading of two sentences may seem particularly illegitimate, which is potentially problematic since they play a central role in my analysis. I am thinking of "Poussin could not bear Caravaggio" and "he had come into the world in order to destroy painting." It could be argued that my interpretation of the first of these sentences is obviously excessive, the point being that Félibien simply intended to say that Poussin did not like—absolutely did not like—Caravaggio's work. In the second case the claim would be that I misread the sentence, a point that I would have to recognize if I were to reread the passages from Baglione that figure in Bellori's text.

I would like to respond to this objection by considering the following question: What does it mean to *displace* or *misappropriate* a text?

We may begin to propose an answer to this question by reflecting on the methodological implications of the phenomenon. To displace or misappropriate Félibien's commentary—and perhaps even Poussin's sentence—is not to misinterpret it, but to manipulate it in such a way that it cannot properly perform the function for which it was originally intended. The task of the discursive units in question is to establish the art of painting as a mimetic process capable of "mastering" reality or nature and of subjecting it to the law of a transcendent truth. This function, we note, is none other than that of representation as it is defined in the critical vocabulary of Bellori, Félibien, and *perhaps even* Poussin. To displace a definition, or a commentary on a phrase by Poussin, is in a sense simultaneously to affirm this definition in its entirety (as well as its paraphrase). The process of displacement makes the definition more "appropriate" [*"propre"*] than it was when the theorists of art first articulated it. Yet, as a result, the definition is practically destroyed. By positing it as wholly "appropriate" [*"propre"*], we in fact "compromise" it.

Now, what is at issue here is the destruction of painting. Although we may assume, along with Bellori and Félibien, that Caravaggio's paintings destroy painting, it is important to grasp that in a sense Caravaggio's mission of destruction destroys the very process of representation that is the basis of painting. As a result the art of painting collapses, for the self-reflexive moment within Caravaggio's paintings reveals painting to be a representation without a basis, without foundations. The method of textual analysis being discussed here is strategic, for although it relies on the "art" of systematization, it does not reveal the law of its own construction, the principle governing its system. On the one hand, this strategic art would seem to identify a set of procedures for the displacement and misappropriation of texts. On the other hand, this art appears to maintain the very plurality of the procedures (proper to different fields or regions) that make displacement and misappropriation possible in the first place. It is indeed, then, a matter of appropriating notions from other fields and of making them serve quite different ends. By altering the position of certain concepts, we create something like a parody of any process of systematic construction or integration. In this particular case, the historical and semantic analysis of a theoretical text by an art historian is taken so seriously as to become parodic. That is, some of the text's explicit or underlying notions are discussed in an attempt constantly to destabilize their possible meanings and thereby to bring to light certain semiotic or meta-semiotic, psychoanalytic or metapsychoanalytic dimensions. The idea is not to create a new *theory* in the sense of a new way of systematically comprehending paintings or works of art. The aim, rather, is to enable several different theoretical fields to intersect in a productive manner that makes possible an ongoing circulation of meaning. The displaced and misappropriated notions thus acquire a plurality of references. I should add, and this is perhaps the main point, that the kind of parodic displacement I have in mind here neither denigrates nor caricatures the original text. Rather, the parodic process of displacement repeats the very operation in which painting destroys itself: the parody mimicks itself, as it designates its own operation of collapse and thereby avoids any claim to embody the truth.

*It will thus be a matter of the painted head of Medusa the Gorgon, "sopra una rotella rapportata."*

## Catalogue

*Baglione*, 136: "Among the works for the Cardinal del Monte, Caravaggio painted on a round shield (sopra una rotella rapportata), a frightful head of a Medusa with snakes for hair, which the Cardinal sent as a gift to Ferdinand, Grand Duke of Tuscany."

*Bellori*, 205: The head of the Medusa, given by Cardinal del Monte to the Grand Duke of Tuscany, was especially praised by Cavaliere Marino, first in glory among men of letters, whose portrait Caravaggio had painted.

*Marino, Galeria*, 1620, p. 28: "*La Testa di Medusa* in una rotella di Michelangelo da Caravaggio nella Galeria del Gran Duca di Toscana." . . .

*Head of Medusa*. Florence, Uffizi, tondo on wood, diam. 55.5 cm., Cat. 1926, p. 94, Mostra No. 5.
   The head of the *Medusa* is painted upon an old tournament shield of the sixteenth century with a border of gold ornaments on a dark background; pieces of leather and velvet are still visible.
   The wedding of Cosimo, to which Cardinal del Monte was invited, took place in 1608, and the *Medusa* was undoubtedly given in celebration of this event. . . . The painting is connected with the juvenile period, but certainly comes at the end of it.[15]

Why start here? One might ask whether the choice is arbitrary, but I insist that it is not. I insist that it is logically necessary given the issues that confront us here, beginning with the question of truth in painting, the problem of the relation between painting and the truth that the critical texts call "nature," or "natural," a relation that is termed "representation." Félibien essentially said as much: "One must imitate nature, but only up to a certain point," for one must *know* how to be selective and how to regulate the process of imitation by means of knowledge or the idea of beauty. The goal, then, is to imitate nature, but according to a certain idea or *design*.

The key issue, then, may be stated as follows. It is necessary to start with a singular painting, one that may be singular only to the extent that it is organized around the point of truth in the place of the center. What is at stake, then, in the truth of a painting when the work itself destroys painting, because, as we are told, it is not merely true, but *too* true?

Why the *Head of Medusa*? Because it is a painting of *decapitation*, not first and foremost the iconic depiction or story of a decapitation, but decapitation itself, since the painting is in itself a decapitated head. There are many decapitations in the work of Caravaggio, but I know of only this one painting that is itself a severed head.

Imagine, then, that nature, truth, idea, and design regulate pictorial mimesis, providing the law of beautiful representation, or, in short, the "head" of the artistic process in the eyes of Félibien, Bellori, and all academic critics. Imagine as well that Caravaggio came into the world in order to destroy painting. If this was his destiny, then I, too, am fated, at the head of my discussion, to encounter the one painting that is a Medusa head—or, more precisely, a severed head of Medusa.

## History

It seems that the first of Caravaggio's paintings, after his years of apprenticeship in Lombardy and Milan, depicted half-figures and were sold in the streets of Rome.[16] The *Head of Medusa* was painted for Caravaggio's first patron in Rome, the Cardinal del Monte. He bought the *rotella* and gave it to Cosimo, the future Grand Duke of Tuscany as a wedding present in 1608. This was in no way surprising or exceptional, as such "parade shields" were fashionable and "often painted or repainted by fairly reputable artists."[17] Now, on many of these round or oblong shields prevalent in the sixteenth and seventeenth centuries, a Medusa head was represented, sometimes in relief, often painted. In all the examples known to us today, the head played the classic, pro-phylactic role of the apotropaion. In other words, its symbolic function was to petrify the enemy of the Prince, which helps explain the allegor-ical and philosophical meaning that Cesare Ripa, for example, attri-butes to it in his *Iconologia* (1603).[18] The enemies of man are construed as internal enemies, the evil and disruptive passions. Ripa "therefore defines the head of the Medusa as a symbol of the victory of reason over the senses, the natural foes of 'virtue,' which like [the political and] physical enemies [in the myth of the 'origin,'] are petrified when faced with the Medusa."[19] The head of Medusa, then, is the defensive and offensive weapon wielded by wisdom in its war against the passions.

> Cavaliere Marino, in his small book *Galeria Distinta*, dedicated a short poem to Caravaggio's "Head of the Medusa in the Palace Gallery of the Grand Duke of Tuscany," in which the shield is praised solely as an apo-tropaion having the power to change the Duke's enemies into "cold marble." [But he concluded that] the true protector of the Duke, is his own valor (la vera Medusa è il valor vostro).[20]

## Iconography

There were three Gorgons: Sthenno, Euryale, and Medusa, all three daughters of the sea gods, Phorcys and Ceto. Only the last, Medusa, was mortal, the other two being immortal. We commonly call Medusa "the Gorgon" because we think of her as the Gorgon par excellence. These three monsters lived in the Far East, not far from the kingdom of the dead, the land of the Hesperides. Their heads were covered with serpents. They had large tusks like boars, bronze hands, and golden wings that allowed them to fly through the air. Their eyes shone with looks so penetrating that whoever faced them was turned into stone. Mortals and immortals alike were terrified of them. As Hesiod says, Medusa "was mortal, but the other two immortal and ageless; and with her the god of the Sable Locks [Poseidon] lay in a soft meadow among the spring flowers."[21] Once Medusa's head had been cut off by Perseus, Athena placed it on her shield. Henceforth her enemies would be petri-fied at the very sight of the goddess.

The legend of Medusa undergoes various changes as we trace it from its beginnings to the Hellenic period. The Gorgon starts out as a mon-ster but is later presented as the victim of a metamorphosis:

Her beauty was far-famed, the jealous hope
Of many a suitor, and of all her charms
Her hair was loveliest; so I was told
By one who claimed to have seen her. She, it's said,
Was violated in Minerva's shrine
By Ocean's lord. Jove's daughter turned away
And covered with her shield her virgin's eyes,
And then for fitting punishment transformed
The Gorgon's lovely hair to loathsome snakes.
Minerva still, to strike her foes with dread,
Upon her breastplate wears the snakes she made.[22]

We have, then, two Medusas in one: a horrible monster as well as a striking beauty: the fascination of contraries mixed together.

Vasari tells us that the young Leonardo painted a Medusa head with serpents in the place of hair, one of his most extravagant and bizarre inventions. But Leonardo also took a circular piece of wood and painted on it something so horrible that one could barely look at it: there were lizards, serpents, and frogs, all of them so dreadful that they recalled the head of Medusa. Leonardo kept this object in his private collection, and it is rumored that his father sold this "animalaccio" to the Duke of Milan.

One more comment should be made here. Contemporary art historians debate the resemblance between the Uffizi's *Head of Medusa, Bacchus,* and other portraits of young boys (*Boy Bitten by a Lizard, The Lute Player,* and *The Musicians*). Are these the painter's self-portraits, studies of his own features and emotional expressions created by looking at himself in a mirror? Could they be studies in physiognomy? But if so, what emotion was the *Head of Medusa* meant to depict? Could they also be so many disguises, a kind of travesty of the subject's identity?

# An Analytic Strategy and a Mythical Ruse

How should we go about looking at the Uffizi's *Head of Medusa?* How, like a new Perseus clad in Hermes's sandals, can we attack this painting?

My strategic, analytic calculation was initially to apply to Caravaggio's painting the operative model that I used in studying both Poussin and Le Brun. It was a matter of first constructing a model of the dynamic network of the representational process itself in order subsequently to analyze the transformations brought about in and by the particular object or scene represented in the individual work. Yet applying this method to the *Head of Medusa* does not work, a fact that gives us a first indication about how we must proceed if we are to articulate this painting's discourse. When we attempt to apply the method in question, we soon realize that the discourse cannot remain stably situated on either the level of representation or on that of what is represented: a discursive slippage takes place between the two levels. Something similar was at work in *The Arcadian Shepherds*, which represents the very process of representation itself. In the *Head of Medusa*, however, the turbulence that affects the discourse of representation is much more immediate. In *The Arcadian Shepherds*, the folding back of representation upon itself is "mediated" in a symbolic manner by the tomb, the epitaph, the name "Arcadia," the word "Ego" and the dialogue of gestures and gazes. No such symbolic mediation is at work in the *Head of Medusa*, for Caravaggio's painting not only makes representation visible in what is represented but also uses mimesis to *destroy* the mimetic process.

How exactly did Perseus kill Medusa? How did he "encounter" the Gorgon in the military sense of the term? There would seem to be an insurmountable and irresolvable aporia at work here insofar as the enemy in question wields the absolute weapon, the look that kills at any distance, a deadly invisible ray. Perseus can only hope to triumph over such an enemy by using a *ruse,* the trick of the mirror and its reflecting power. And this ruse is preceded by another trick that is of great symbolic interest in the present context. Both ruses concern the three poles of the perspecitval apparatus, the Poussinian "prospect," that "function of reason [that] depends on three things, that is, on the eye, on the visual ray, and on the distance between the eye and the object."[1] We must reread Poussin's phrase in light of Ovid's narration of Perseus's adventure:

> And Perseus told him of the place that lies,
> A stronghold safe below the mountain mass
> Of icy Atlas; how at its approach
> Twin sisters, Phorcys' daughters, lived who shared
> A single eye, and how that eye by stealth
> And cunning, as it passed from twin to twin,
> His sly hand caught, . . .[2]

The first trick involves using a hidden act of substitution to obtain the Gorgons' single eye. In this manner Perseus enters an unknown space and occupies what is essentially the "point of view." In a sense, then, he adopts the position of the viewer, taking the place of the painter. This is similar to my looking at the Church of St. John depicted in the painting while covering one eye with my hand, just as if I were Filippo himself with his easel set up on a tripod immediately inside the central portico of Saint Mary of the Flowers. The first of reason's three terms—prospect (or the eye)—is indeed the first element in a rational model. However, it is also the first move—an act of substitution—within an apparatus of entrapment, a machination or trick, the beginnings of a snare: . . . "and then through solitudes,/Remote and trackless, over rough hillsides/Of ruined woods [here the aporia resumes: Perseus may have dealt with the first aporia now that he has the eye, but he still must cover the distance between the eye and the object, which means he must trace the trajectory of the visual ray] he reached the Gorgon's land."[3] What does Perseus find in this aporetic space? Dispersed here and there in the domain of the Gorgons he finds a variety of stony figures—those of men and savage beasts, which have been grasped and transfixed by the Gaze, "all changed/To stone by glancing at Medusa's face."[4] How can Perseus conquer this gaze now that he has the eye? How can he, in turn, begin to produce figures? The answer is: by means of a second ruse involving a mirror, the ruse of representation. "But he, he said, looked at her ghastly head/Reflected in the bright bronze of the shield/In his left hand."[5]

The aporia that Perseus must resolve resides in the impossibility of contacting and killing an enemy who keeps her distance by immobilizing the opponent wherever he is, using her petrifying gaze to hold him at the point of view. Thus Medusa remains at the vanishing point, at the very limit of the depth of field, poised at the aporetic position of infinity. And, at the moment of his *death,* she occupies the enemy's point of view, reconnoiters him. The ruse Perseus employs in order to encounter and kill Medusa, while also keeping his distance, is a kind of retaliation in which the Gorgon's own power is turned against her. Perseus substitutes Medusa's gaze for his own, replacing his weakness with her strength, positioning Medusa's deadly gaze in the round bronze eye of his shield.

The representation of Medusa's gaze in the reflecting and reflexive mirror is a ruse and a machination. An element of reason—prospect—reversed or overturned, results in the reflection and retaliation of reason. The gaze is trapped by the eye in the confrontation between weakness and strength, life and death. The painting is, first of all, Medusa petrifying herself with her own gaze in the present and immediate moment of polemical violence, before assuming a place of power on the breast of Jupiter's daughter as an attribute of the latter's divine institution.

## Humorous Features

Let us return to Ovid's narrative as we read Caravaggio's painting over the shoulder of the poet of metamorphosis: "and while deep sleep held fast/Medusa and her snakes, he severed it/Clean from her neck."[6] It would seem that the beautiful and elaborate ruse described above falls short, since Medusa is asleep when Perseus decapitates her. The ruse is useless, then, unless we take pleasure in its sheer beauty, or in its elegance, as mathematicians would say. If Medusa and her serpents are asleep, none of them can look at the adversary, and thus there is no need to employ the shield's bronze mirror. The lesson is simple: the strong, the powerful, and the absolutely powerful cannot ever afford to sleep. Power depends on distance and abolute vigilance, and no one with power can afford to rest or sleep on the job. This point is amply illustrated by the many examples of wakeful attention and failures to remain vigilant described in Marcel Détienne and Jean-Pierre Vernant's *Cunning Intelligence in Greek Culture and Society.*[7]

In my reading of the legend, I carry Perseus's trick to its extreme: I imagine a Medusa who petrifies herself by looking at her image in the shield's mirroring eye. In keeping with this myth, the French verb *méduser* means to petrify, to turn someone into a frozen, marble statue. But if we read the legend this way, one question remains unanswered. If Medusa was transformed into marble the very moment she saw herself in the bronze mirror, then how could Perseus possibly have decapitated her with his golden sword? Would he not have broken his sword against the hard stone? Perhaps he cut her head off the very instant her self-transformation took place, or, rather, the very instant it was about to occur or was *in the process of occurring*. Perhaps the decapitation happens when the tender flesh of the beautiful Medusa, who had been ravished by Neptune, is no longer quite so tender but is not yet as hard as marble. Neither flesh nor stone; still flesh, already stone; Medusa hovers in the instant of the now, that is, the neuter, the complex moment of the transformational process.

How can we look at the *Head of Medusa?* We must be tricky, attentive, and vigilant. At every moment we must avoid the trap of this painting, which represents the trap laid by Perseus. We must in turn set our own traps, since strength can be weakness, and weakness strength. Such was Medusa's gaze and Perseus's eye or glance.

My first move, then, is to "begin" with the gaze and with the orientation of the represented head. This seems an appropriate starting point since we are dealing with Medusa and the "subject" of the painting is the gaze—mine, hers, the painting's, Perseus's, and the painter's. Medusa's head is turned to the left at a forty-five-degree angle. Properly speaking, Medusa does not look at *me;* she looks down and to the left. I try to position myself within her gaze, but this proves impossible: what we have here is yet another aporia. As far as Medusa is concerned, I am transparent. Indeed, she looks at me as though I were nothing, as though I did not exist. Why does her head tilt forward and to the left? Why is there this imperceptible movement, a movement that is oblique in relation to the plane of the painting? This is essentially the same movement, but in reverse, generated by the tomb in Arcadia, which opened up a space in which the scene and its figures could take on meaning. The answer, in part, is this: the painting is not a plane but a gently curved convex surface, which makes the left part of the face stand forward and the right part withdraw. Thus we can say that in the very "subject" of the painting, which is the *gaze*, we find an effect created by the representation's material support: *the represented object is affected and troubled at its surface by the support.*

By the same stroke, we see that what at first glance could appear to be one of the dimensions of the representational apparatus—namely, the "I-thou" correlative subjectivity—is displaced from its function of reciprocity by the partial effect of an element that is foreign to that apparatus. As a result, the *Head of Medusa* is a full-face portrait, but not entirely.

In a full-face portrait, the represented model looks at me; the model looks me in the eye, focusing on my gaze at the very point of view. In a kind of silent dialogue, she returns my gaze. She is "I," and I am the "thou" who corresponds to her, but also, the "thou" that *I* look at. She is "I" because she is internal to the representational utterance and external to the "thou" that I am (for her). But she is "thou" for me, as viewer, since "I" am always transcendent in relation to "thou." When I go outside of myself in order to enter into a living relation with someone else, Benveniste writes, I necessarily posit a "thou" who is, besides myself, the only imaginable person. A full-face portrait doubles and *animates* this correlative subjectivity, because it is a (frontal) *representation*. Although it is discreetly hidden, we can discern a conflict of forces here, an opposition having no equivalent, for the polarity does not signify either equality or symmetry. "Ego" always has a position of transcendence with regard to "thou," although neither term can be conceived in the absence of the other. The terms are complementary, even reversible, although their relation is one of interiority and exteriority. "Ego" has a position of dominance. Represented full face on the canvas, "ego" seizes my viewing and receptive eye by means of her gaze. But as viewer I do the same to her. I seize your gaze with my viewing and emitting eye. There is a struggle in this linguistic structure, but it is not Hegel's mortal combat in language because the opposition between us is a matter of the complementary and reversible relations of conversation. What is strange about the iconic dialogue—and here we find the very enigma of visibility more generally—is that the mortal combat coincides with its pacification, as conflict is replaced by an alternation of dialogic positions. It is not a matter of there first being an

"I" who speaks to a "thou," for "thou" becomes the "I" who speaks to an "I" who has become a "thou." Indeed, an immediate oscillation occurs, an instantaneous shifting of the terms "I"/"thou." Essentially, we here have the story of Perseus and Medusa. Yet, in the iconic dialogue, the mortal combat has no final winner or loser. Both parties are at once master and slave in a warlike entrapment of warfare.

The *Head of Medusa* is a full-face portrait, but not entirely. I *almost* look at Medusa as though I were looking at an "it." And in the viewer/reader's second step, which is the second moment of "theory," she looks at me, *but not really.* Medusa and I are doubly located somewhere between "I" and "thou," between "I/thou" and "it." In other words, what I reflexively look at is a rift or a gap—a nothing-in-between—within what is represented. What Medusa reflexively gazes at is a gap in the representation itself. Here we find a positioning of a double gap, one within the space of what is represented, the other within the space of what can be represented. Rather than witnessing the resolution of the conflict in an appeasement of the reversible positions of enunciation and representation, we encounter *two violent forces that miss each other* in a *parodic* mortal combat. It is critical not to miss this point, for otherwise I would lose my head, would fall headfirst into nothingness, lack, castration, the primal scene. *For the painting is all this as well.* It turns out that I ran the risk of being decapitated by this painting of a severed head. For every trick there is a countertrick. The painting wanted to make me say "nothing" when in fact what one should say is "almost." It wanted me to say "lack" when in fact "rhythm" is the right word, to say "always already" when I should say "every time until now."

Everything I have described takes place, at least partially, because the canvas is slightly curved. But of course it's curved. After all, it's a shield. What remains unclear, however, is the identity of the shield's owner. Is the shield Perseus's instrument of war or is it simply an ornamental object presented as a gift to the Grand Duke of Tuscany? In response to this question I find myself once more saying "either-or," "both-and."

What I see is the shield, the bronze mirror wielded by the clever mythical hero. But what I see on the "wood" is also the reflected image of the head of Medusa, floating in a deep space, standing forth in the virtual and illusory space of the mirror. Look, for example, at the shadows cast by the head and serpents on the right.

The head, however, has already been severed and the blood on the Gorgon's neck has already coagulated. The sword has already struck. It follows that the head I see here is not the image of the head reflected in the bronze mirror, so the shield must be the shield of the Grand Duke of Tuscany. Or, more precisely, the ornamental shield is a representation of Perseus's shield after the struggle, when it was decorated with the fearful head. And that is why the head stands forth, in relief, from the surface of the *rotella*.

However, because it stands out, the head is at once decorative and apotropaic. What is more, the head's relief serves to invert the convexity of the representation's material support into an illusory concavity. This inversion produces a certain depth, which is, once again, where the reflected image of Medusa's head floats. And this brings me to the hero's bronze mirror. The spurts of blood are not curved by the convexity of the painting's surface, which they would have been had the head "really" been lying on the *rotella*.

Yes, of course, one may respond, but the fact remains that the head has already been severed and is thus merely represented on the surface, in relief. And it is not only the head that is distorted by this surface (the left cheek in particular), but also, and perhaps most of all, the spots of light on the serpentine hair all around Medusa's head.

In other words, the head of Medusa is simultaneously inside the represented space and outside the space of representation. It is inside and outside, but also neither inside nor outside. The shield is both the shield of Perseus *and* the shield of the Grand Duke. It is the specular tool of the violent heroic ruse *and* a spectacular ornament symbolizing the Duke's virtue and power. The head is a reflected image, and thus the product of a representation, but it is also a simulacrum and a double; as such, it is representation itself. The head is a reflection made at the very moment before death. It is a double of the dead Gorgon, her petrified figure, forever frozen immediately after her death. This head exists in the here and now, yet it is also part of the past, frozen in representation. It plays the topological game of standing at that boundary which is the very surface of representation. As an effect of the support and of the surface, it disturbs all of the spaces enclosed by the painting within its representational system. The space of representation is the curve of the support; the represented space is the undecidable hesitation between convexity and concavity. And the space of representability—the viewer's space—is the double positioning and rift between correlative subjectivities and personalities.

## A Comparative Digression on Three Examples of Presentation and Neutralization

### First Example

A painting by Philippe de Champaigne, the *Ex-Voto of 1662*, provides an excellent example of the neutralization and presentation of a representation's material support and surface. On the right of the canvas, the painter depicts the miracle experienced by his daughter, a nun at Port-Royal. She is shown stretched out on a chaise longue, her hands folded, a small reliquary open on her lap. Beside and behind her stands another nun, Mother Agnes, who is also praying. Next to her, but in front and on the right, there is a chair with a closed book lying on it. The walls of the cell are blank with the exception of a cross, cut off by the picture's frame. The scene is lit from the left, but another ray of light, which illuminates nothing, falls from above, between the two nuns. What we have here is a narrative representation of the miracle's transcendent moment; or, rather, a representation of the moment before and after a miracle that is present only in the figure of an almost absent, vertical shaft of light.

The entire right side of the canvas is taken up by a long inscription. The narrative of the miracle is inserted between a formulaic reiteration of the nun's vow, her mystical and permanent marriage to Jesus, who is described in the inscription as "the sole doctor of bodies and souls" ("Christo uni medico animarum et corporum"), and the formula of the Ex Voto properly speaking—that is, the painter's own signature, "Philippe de Champaigne," which identifies him both as the author of this image and as a witness of the miraculous healing.

In a sense, this painting, with its "icon" and inscription, is Champaigne's *Et in Arcadia ego*, the key difference being that the double formula of the nun's vow and painter's Ex Voto, as well as the narrative framed by them, are not written on any object represented by the painting, such as a tomb or a painting within a painting. Nor is the inscription situated outside the painting, as is often the case in an Ex Voto, where the space of the votive formula tends to be separated from the "icon" itself by some kind of boundary. Thus the formula is neither inside the represented space nor inside the space of representability. Instead, it is positioned within the space of representation, that is, *on* the transparent surface of the mirror/window that is representation itself. By the same stroke, the inscription allows us to see the surface that is theoretically, ideologically, and technically invisible in its transparency. But since I am a viewer as well as a reader, I see the narrative scene and contemplate the story of the miraculous scene through the fourth wall of the cell, which has become transparent. The grace or illusion of painting allows me to *neutralize* the opaque surface-support on which the signs are written. As it becomes transparent in its turn, a deep space opens up beneath the signs. The signs become figures, for as I realize the transparency of the surface-support of representation, I begin to see what was once invisible. While remaining inscribed in the represented space of the scene, the figures of the two nuns become signs. It may be an oscillation of just this sort that Poussin symbolizes in *The Arcadian Shepherds.* Champaigne, on the other hand, *presents* the oscillation, making it visible in his *Ex Voto of 1662.*

Both Caravaggio and Champaigne construct their paintings at the very limit of the representational system, causing this system to vacillate. In the case of Champaigne, the painting is in itself a sacrament or sacramental sign. The representational system is doubly destabilized insofar as both the writing and the icon are affected. The vacillation points to the boundary and exterior of both forms of "semiosis." Each kind of semiosis is produced in such a way as to point outside itself, thereby calling attention to the other as its producer. Caravaggio's painting, of course, does not make use of writing in order to produce its own vacillation. Rather, it transgresses its own boundaries within itself, that is, within the diverse spaces that it brings together and encloses.

*Second and Third Examples*

I have in mind Fetti's *Veil of Veronica* (1613–21) and Champaigne's *Veil of Saint Veronica* (Musée des Beaux-Arts, Caen). In both works a Sacred Face is presented frontally against the "illusionist" background provided by the representation of Veronica's veil. This veil, this material [toile], is itself represented on a piece of canvas [toile], the representation's surface and material support. What differentiates the two paintings are the folds in the veil's material (setting aside the depictions of the fixtures from which the veil is hung—in Fetti's work, a horizontal, wooden rod, and in Champaigne's, clamps on each end; yet one may well ask whether these elements are part of the painting's "frame" or of what it represents). In both works it is striking that the folds in the cloth in no way affect the Sacred Face depicted on it. And, unless I am wrong, the face is supposed to have *printed its features on* Veronica's veil, or, more precisely, on the texture of its cloth, on its surface and support. This, at least, is so in the case of the first and original Edessa icon, which is the matrix of all Byzantine icons of Jesus. The negative effect I have in mind here is especially striking in Champaigne's painting. And the effect of this effect is that the face of the tormented figure somehow floats above the surface depicted as supporting it, the veil, and above the canvas, the surface-support. As a result, the Sacred Face is situated in and on the space of representation, in and on the represented space, but *also* in and on the space of representability, the space of the viewer. The Sacred Face comes toward the viewer, occupying a strange limiting position on the border between the spaces that this limit separates. As a result, the figure is no longer a representation in mimesis, becoming instead a presentation, a hypotyposis in Kant's sense. In a parody of the well-known Lacanian formula, we may say that "what was excluded from the real returns in the symbolic." Recalling the inscriptions of the *Ex Voto of 1662*, we may add that in the *Veil of Veronica* it is as if the icon has become a sign of writing, a pictogram, or, more precisely, a hieroglyph and a *sacrament*, neutralizing the material support of both writing and image while remaining an icon.

What is more, in the case of Champaigne's painting, the face looks me directly in the eyes, which has the effect of interrupting the diabolical game of the full-face portrait. In this instance, I can hardly occupy, in turn and simultaneously, the position of "ego" and that of "thou." The indefinite oscillation of mortal combat comes to a halt. The Sacred Face is somehow a portrait that stands as an exception to the conditions of representation governing portraits. For it is a transcendent Ego or Master that stands outside the representational system, dominating me as "thou." But this is surely the strangest of Masters, for the Dead Man seizes the Living, the tormented slave takes hold of the viewer's eye and subjugates it to himself as Master: a *sacred* sign of domination.

If Champaigne's *Ex Voto* is his *Et in Arcadia ego*, Caravaggio's *Head of Medusa* is his parodic *Veil of Veronica*. The face of the saint has become the head of Medusa, the crown of thorns worn by the King of the Jews and of the chosen people has become a head of serpents, and the drops of red blood on his forehead or on the veil (Fetti) have become the spurts of blood produced by the decapitation. Yet these are features that are, as it were, external to the parody. What is essential is the gaze, which is neither veiled, as in Fetti, nor direct and penetrating, as in Champaigne: Medusa *almost* looks at me, but as an effect of a convex support. Yet this support is concave and, as a result, a certain kind of depth opens up, so that the ornamental shield of the Grand Duke becomes the mirror of Perseus.

# The Portrait in the Convex Mirror

I want to return to the young girl who was decapitated for having been raped by Neptune in Minerva's temple. I want to return to Medusa and to the *portrait in the convex mirror.*

The painting's support is convex, but in the representation it looks concave. Medusa's head rests on the shield as its apotropaic decoration. But in the representation the head is reflected in the shield the way an image is captured in a mirror. The monster's evil career ends when her eye is reflected in her own gaze.

Let me begin with the aporia generated by convex and concave surfaces. Why, one might ask, isn't the mirror convex? Had that been the case, it would open onto an illusory space beyond its surface, a virtual concave space. Convex mirrors are numerous in the history of painting. I am thinking, for example, of Memling's *Diptych with Virgin and Child and the Donor Martin van Nieuwenhove* (1487), which André Gide evoked in his diary with reference to the *mise en abysme:*

> Behind the Madonna, the little convex mirror, which reflects her back, also captures the image—given the supposed angles of the panels—of Martin Van Newenhoven, this time in profile, adoring the Infant Jesus. Although he is excluded from the reflected scene, His supernatural presence does appear in the rays of light from His aura, which pass through the mirror, sanctifying and uniting in a single communion the two characters who are re-presented.[1]

Another example is Jan van Eyck's *Arnolfini Marriage* (1434) where

> what is invisible is made visible by the same device. But here the artifice is even more subtle, since the little convex mirror hung on the back wall allows us to see, behind and between the couple, people standing in the doorway of the room, whom only the couple can actually see. These are the wedding guests, among whom (if we are to believe the famous inscription above the trick mirror—'Johannes de eyck fuit hic') was the painter himself.[2]

Of interest in this context is also the convex mirror in the painting in the Louvre by Quentin Massys, entitled *The Money Changer and his Wife.* Mirrors depicted in a scene sometimes allow us to see what we would not see otherwise. Sometimes they show things differently from how they otherwise would have been seen, serving as devices to reveal what perspective necessarily hides from the eye. Certain painters, then, use mirrors to mobilize depicted reflections capable of introducing secondary points of view into the scene. These reflections play a crucial role, for they essentially allow the viewer's eye, which is situated at the point of view, to see the back side of things.

But why opt for a *convex* mirror? And what happens when the convex mirror is quite simply the painting itself, as is the case in the self-portraits involving a mirror?

Without trying to account for the frequency with which convex mirrors appear in the history of Northern European art, I would like to point out that this specular arrangement has a specific technical and theoretical importance. Namely, the distortions it causes alter the central axiom of linear perspective, the basic principle of the representational and enunciative apparatus. The formal apparatus of representation is in fact based on an axiom that I propose to call the "Medused Cyclops." Ovid narrates this axiom when he describes how Perseus overcomes the aporias on his way to conquer Medusa. Like the Cyclops and the two formidable Gorgons, the viewer has only one fixed eye. What is more, the plane that defines the plastic surface, the transparent screen of the painting on which the "icon" is traced, is considered, following this axiom, to be an adequate reproduction of the visual image.

## Humor

The perspectival apparatus creates distortions in the visual impression of space, for it neutralizes the spherical character of the visual field as well as the curved structure of the retinal image. The convex mirror, which has the same dimensions as the painting itself, neutralizes these very neutralizations, these effacements and distortions, by means of the distortions it introduces into the perspectival apparatus.

This is the source of the humor of Caravaggio's *Head of Medusa* and of the mirror/shield and/or ornament of Perseus and/or Cosimo de Medici. The humor in question can best be evoked by citing the words of Jean-François Lyotard:

[Humor] resides in the conviction that the laws governing sight and movement are not natural, but instead are strange, arbitrary, and random.

These constraints are "precise, yet inexact" (as Duchamp points out to Steefel), and have no identifiable reference. It is a matter, then, of a self-referential law, of a contract with oneself. Furthermore, the fact that the law in question is not itself legitimate, regulated by something beyond law, all-powerful, all-good, all-order, means that there can be no guarantee that one is abiding by it. God has to be good for him not to mock you, once his orders have been carried out, by saying: "Mistake, that wasn't what I meant; that wasn't what you were supposed to do." If God is not wholly good, but somewhat tricky, . . . then there is bound to be a certain play, in the mechanical sense of the term, between the establishing of contracts (projects) and their accomplishment (execution of works). As a result one will never know whether the work is good, or perhaps bad, because the artist exactly carried out the plan, or whether the work is good, or on the contrary bad, because something happened that was not anticipated by the contract.[3]

## Serious Variations

Let us consider: (1) the *serio ludere* with which Renaissance philosophers and painters were so familiar;[4] and, (2) some key passages from Erwin Panofsky's *Perspective as Symbolic Form.*[5]

A painting constructed according to the laws of legitimate perspective makes us *see* what we never see, which, we may say in passing, is a perfect definition of a model. Such a painting realizes and shows, in its representation of space, something of which immediate experience has no knowledge, namely, homogeneity and infinity. As it designates and makes them visible, allowing them to be experienced, it "transforms psychophysiological space into [geometrical and] mathematical space."[6] Following Panofsky, let us identify the nature of these transformations:

1. "We see not with a single fixed eye but with two constantly moving eyes, resulting in a spheroidal field of vision" rather than a four-sided box. We experience an all-englobing sphere divided into qualitatively different areas, not a single empty space defined as an abstract and continuous quantity. The space of our experience is marked by a "front and back," a "right and left," a figure and a ground.[7] So the first transformation is one of *abstraction and formalization.*

## 2. The second transformation is a matter of *discounting*

the enormous difference between the psychologically conditioned "visual image" through which the visible world is brought to our consciousness, and the mechanically conditioned "retinal image" which paints itself upon our physical eye. For a peculiar stabilizing tendency within our consciousness—promoted by the cooperation of vision with the tactile sense—ascribes to perceived objects a definite and proper size and form, and thus tends not to take notice, at least no full notice, of the distortions which these sizes and forms suffer on the retina.[8]

The stability of these shapes and sizes is the product of a psychic "interpretation" of the many variations in the retinal image.

3. The third transformation is a matter of misrepresenting and forgetting.

> [The] retinal image . . . is a projection not on a flat but on a concave surface. Thus already on this lowest, still prepsychological level of facts there is a fundamental discrepancy between "reality" and its construction.[9]

The result is a series of what Panofsky calls "marginal distortions." Panofsky has shown that these spherical transformations were well known to the theorists and artists of antiquity. As a result, their architectural and pictural works were better adapted to the *real structure of subjective visual impressions* than those guided by Renaissance theory. Panofsky points out, more specifically, that the theorists of the sixteenth century ignored Euclid's eighth theorem (which states that sizes vary not in function of distances but in function of the angles from which they are seen), a theorem that puts the laws of vision into a mathematical formula. In so doing, these theorists acted as though they were perfectly aware of the contradiction between a *natural and common* perspective and an *artificial and learned* perspective that aims only at the *practical construction of the painting's flat surface*.[10] It is easy to see why, for how could the surface of a sphere be unfolded onto a plane without putting in question the very idea of a painting? How could this be done without disrupting the representation of reality?

In light of these remarks, we can say that the *Head of Medusa* is a topological play upon the perspectival apparatus and its constraints, a learned game played at the expense of the instituted, institutional eye, a game played by this very apparatus as it represents itself according to

its own presumed identity. The goal of this game is to clear a path leading beyond the perceiving body to the unapproachable *impression* that
things in themselves make upon the flesh.

4. I shall juxtapose two polemical citations from the seventeenth
century in order to demonstrate that what is at stake in this discussion
of the convex mirror is the apparatus of representation and enunciation and the question of light and color in the perspectival "design."
One comes from C. A. Dufresnoy's *Art of Painting;* the other is from a
work by Abraham Bosse, a dogmatic theorist of Poussin's prospect;

> As in a Convex Mirror the collected Rays strike *stronger and brighter in the*
> *middle than upon the natural Object,* and the Vivacity of the Colours is in-
> creased in the Parts full in your Sight; while the goings off are more and
> more broken and faint as they approach to the Extremities, in the same
> manner Bodies are to be rais'd and rounded.[11]

Bosse responds as follows:

> They do not understand how to make objects recede and turn into the
> distance by using an arrangement of parallel planes. For these gentlemen
> are, as you know, accustomed to making an entire painting have the same
> *spherical, mirroring effect,* which amounts to representing objects *the way*
> *the eye sees them,* which is an absolutely false and ridiculous thing to pro-
> pose.[12]

## Self-portraits

The mirror with the same dimensions as the painting is, first and in its
essence, the portrait seen in the mirror, and, more specifically, a self-
portrait. Painting one's image in the mirror is the only method that allows a painter to *see* and to *make* himself at the same time, to look at his
image and to inscribe it on the rectangular or circular piece of canvas.
At that point, the painting is the mirror and the mirror is the painting.
Here we have a case of perfect reversibility, an ongoing movement back
and forth between the gaze and hand, following what is an almost immediate trajectory. And at the center of all this is the mirror that carries
the image it reflects, a mirror that is already a painting, a painting that
is still a mirror. But what happens when the painter looks at himself in
a convex mirror and paints himself on a canvas that reproduces the size
and shape of its surface? What happens is an acceleration and ampli-

fication of the distortions and turbulence of the curved surface, an intensification of the effects that this surface has on the reflection in the mirror and on the reflection of that reflection, which is the portrait.

It would be helpful at this point to reread John Pope-Hennessy's discussion of Dürer's self-portraits in *The Portrait in the Renaissance*.[13] Of special note are the distortions that a convex mirror produces of the face and hands, and more specifically, a shrinking of the left side of the face at the expense of the right side, the result being an impression that the head emerges on two different planes. The same is true of the left hand in relation to the right hand. (An example in which these effects are taken to the extreme is Parmigianino's *Self-Portrait in a Convex Mirror*, in the Kunsthistorisches Museum, Vienna).

To paraphrase Dufresnoy's remark cited above, we may say that it is true that objects take on a remarkable depth and roundness this way: the figure stands out more sharply than the original does and, as Bosse notes, is represented the way the eye sees it. But this claim would be ridiculous if made in relation to "reality," truth, and nature. This, at least, would seem to be Dürer's position, for he tries to eliminate and diminish the distortions of convexity, first by means of a series of artificial rectifications, and then, on his trip to Venice, by using the artifice of a flat mirror. I say *artifice* here because of the reasons Panofsky gives for denying that the perspectival apparatus renders a reproduction of the conditions of natural perception.

Another option, which was exploited by Parmigianino, is to have fun with the distortions, just as painters in the seventeenth century would tamper with linear perspective by making anamorphotic pictures.

But there is more. What happens when a painter attaches the head depicted and reflected in the mirror to a body? The mirror, we know, be it flat or convex, inverts the object through its image. Should an inverted head be attached to a "normal" body, or should the body be reversed as well? As Pope-Hennessy points out, Dürer initially seems to have opted for the first solution, which was the traditional one. As a result, the head seems to move from left to right *in the reflection*, but the exaggerated hand, which seems to be the left one, is in fact the right one. Only when Dürer started using a flat mirror did he opt for a complete reversal of both the body and the head. Here we have a new effect of the specular surface, for the mirror's reversal of the image gives rise to the problem of conjoining the head and the body, a problem having implications for the "truth" of representations produced in and by the speculum. In other words, the question of truth separates the head from the body: I paint an inverted head, but I correct the inversion of the body or else allow both head and body to remain inverted. As a result, the mirror and its surface effects come between the painter and his model (himself), dividing the subject of the act of painting into an "I" and a "thou." What is more, the mirror's effect *comes between the head and the body*, separating the site of the gaze and that of the gesture. By the same stroke, there is a separation of the representation to be painted (the idea, design, and subject) and the act of painting (the body and the hand that inscribe the mirror's reflection on the canvas). The mirror raises the technical and theoretical problems (problems that are indissolubly related) of a de-capitation and re-capitation of the painter, and the convexity of the mirror *intensifies* the issue.

The problem I encounter in Caravaggio's *Head of Medusa* is precisely that of the convex mirror and its effects, which are both within and beyond Nature and Truth. In this painting, I see the problem of a shield that is at once Perseus's mirror and the Duke of Tuscany's ornament. Here I see a self-representation, in a mirror and/or on the painting's surface, of the very subject of painting, namely, the petrifying *gaze* and the petrified *eye* (but also the reverse). I see a figuration of the subject's divided nature (and its play in representation: I look without really looking; I [almost] do not look). I see the mirror's decapitation of self-referential representation, or in other words, the separation of the painting's head from its body. I see a decapitation of the gaze that defines the "subject" to be painted and the "subject" of the painter's design. I also see the gesture of the hand and body that pose there, in the painting that is both mirror and support, in the painting and on its surface, as a represented object, the slashing of the subject: the painter's brushstroke, the stroke of Perseus's sword.

## Remark 1: The Disguised Subject

The fact that the painting of Medusa is not in any literal sense a self-portrait of the young Caravaggio does not in any way prevent it from figuring the act of painting and the scission that separates the painting's gaze from the gesture of painting. Whether one accepts the traditional hypothesis as reformulated by Walter Friedlaender or rejects it along

with Michael Kitson, the essential point is that the subject of the painting is disguised, a *travesty*. What is essential is the humorous light this
disguise sheds on the theoretical and practical "problems" of the self-
portrait, or in other words, on the *self-reflection* of the act of painting in
its relation to "truth" and "nature."

## Remark 2: The Decapitated and Decapitating Painter

Other paintings (by Caravaggio and others) illustrate the relation between disguise, even transvestism, and the motif of decapitation. By
employing the motif of decapitation, they point to the figurative or narrative disguising involved in the act of painting. Dürer's *Portrait of Joh-
annes Kleeberg*(Kunsthistorisches Museum, Vienna) is pertinent in this
regard:

> In the portrait Dürer's task was to systematize and to consolidate, and
> thanks to his unaided efforts, within a generation the intuitive painting of
> his predecessors was transformed into the rational likeness of Johannes
> Kleeberger,where the portrait type [descends] from the traditional German
> St. John's head shown on a charger, but the portrayal of the features is
> Ingres-like in its clarity.[14]

The model has been decapitated.

Another relevant example is Giorgione's *Self-Portrait* (Herzog
Anton Ulrich Museum, Brunswick):

> We first hear of it when Vasari, in Venice, visited the Patriarch of Aquileia
> and saw in his collection "a painting purporting to be a David with the
> head of Goliath," which was a self-portrait of Giorgione. Vasari was suffi-
> ciently convinced of the validity of the tradition to include a reproduction
> of the head in the second edition of his *Lives* as an authentic self-portrait,
> and the engraving by Hollar, through which the composition has come
> down to us, is perfectly consistent with that interpretation. If Hollar's en-
> graving is to be believed, the portrait was stamped with great intensity,
> and that is confirmed by a fragment at Brunswick which is all of the
> painting that survives.[15]

The painter, here, is "decapitating."

In *David with the Head of Goliath* (Borghese Gallery, Rome), Caravaggio, whose debt to Giorgione is well known, offers us a self-portrait—
*but in the decapitated head of Goliath.*

Friedlaender comments on this painting as follows:

The identification of himself with Goliath, the victim of a superior and in-
nocent power, may easily have been in Caravaggio's mind with all its
psychological implications. David is painted with uncommon tenderness;
his soft gentle face and sad expression are in sharp contrast to the
Medusa-like head of Goliath with its open mouth and blood trickling
down the throat.[16]

Another example is Christofano Allori's *Judith with the Head of Holofernes* (c. 1609). Rudolf and Margot Wittkower's remarks, in *Born under Saturn: The Character and Conduct of Artists*, are worth citing here:

Allori, a notorious rake, fell in love with an exotic beauty with whom he
squandered his considerable earnings. He portrayed her here as Judith
and himself in the head of Holofernes: a symbol of his sufferings 'by the
hand' of his beloved.[17]

Of interest here is also a text by Matteo Marangoni, "Note sul Caravaggio alla Mostra del Sei e Settecento," which Jean-Claude Lebensztejn
cites in "Au beauty parlour."

In the center of the mirror created by the wine in the flask, a recent clean-
ing has revealed, as if reflected, the minuscule head of a young man that
really does bring to mind the young Caravaggio's physiognomic traits:
large sockets, a broad-based nose, slightly snubbed, full lips and a half-
open mouth. Here we have yet another reason, if another is needed, for
including this work among the first to be painted by Caravaggio. My
friend Carlo Gamba helped me to see the similarity between this little
portrait and the figure that I, in my article in *Dedalo*, had taken for *The
Fruit Vendor* cited by Lanzi. . . , a figure that, according to Gamba, could
be that of a young man, and thus a kind of free self-portrait of Caravaggio
as a young man.

The likelihood of this assumption could be confirmed by Baglione's
testimony, for he claims that after Caravaggio left d'Arpin's "he tried to
support himself by producing some small paintings of himself in the mirror, of which the first was a Bacchus with clusters of grapes of different
kinds, made with great care, but in a somewhat dry manner." This *Bacchus*, as Longhi was the first to suggest, must be the one in the Uffizi,
which would thus suddenly become not only an original but also a *free*
self-portrait, given its close connection with the *Little Fruit Vendor* in the
Borghese Gallery. Incidentally, Fiocco made me realize that *Bacchus* is the
representation of a figure reflected in a mirror, for he holds the cup with
his left hand.

One must conclude, then, that the androgynous type, involving a combination of individual and ideal traits, that may be found in early works such as Petrograd's *Bacchus, The Fruit Vendor, The Lute Player,* and in the young man in the Louvre's *Gypsy* . . . , and even, I believe, in the Uffizi's *Medusa,* is a product of Caravaggio having used himself as his own model.[18]

Lebensztejn comments as follows on this passage from Marangoni: "The young Caravaggio (who 'thus' is androgynous) paints himself in the mirror and in the flask, inverting the reflection in order to insert it into the painting-mirror. Thus Bacchus joins Narcissus."[19]

To these remarks I would add that the artist painted his self-portrait in a flat mirror in a flask, a convex mirror, before he went on to bring together the painting-mirror and the flask in the *Head of Medusa.* I would also add that in the crystal vase of Bacchus he paints an image of his own head, but only the head, detached from the body. He paints, then, a "tiny little head of a young man," a doll's head, what the Greeks called a *korè,* the head of a young girl at the center of the eye—"the pupil." The young Caravaggio was truly androgynous, painting his own head, mocking the viewer's eye.

# The Medusa Head as Historical Painting

To stumble "headlong" into my topic, let me offer these scattered remarks as a re-capitulation of the preceding analyses.

Two different moments in the story of Perseus and Medusa are reflected in and on the mirror/shield, in a kind of condensation or overlapping of the story onto itself. This effect can be described by adopting an image Claude Lévi-Strauss uses in discussing music: the fabric of the narrative has been folded back over itself to produce what we, the viewers, perceive as a painting.

The first of the two moments is found at the level of what is essentially the story's represented "content": Medusa is stupefied and turned into a statue by her own reflection. The singular potency of her own gaze is applied intransitively to itself, reflecting itself and thereby producing its own petrifaction. The first moment represented in the painting, then, is the moment of this singular metamorphosis, the moment when the Gorgon's violence is immobilized in its very *expression, imprinting* itself on itself. In this regard, it is instructive to compare Caravaggio's work with other representations of the Gorgon (Friedlaender's study is a valuable source). Caravaggio captures the moment of petrifaction just an instant before it happens. The interval in question here is the most furtive, infinitesimal instant of time, but in its very evanescence it is also the most permanent moment of all. I would like to name it the *sculptural moment*. The metamorphosis is unusual because, properly speaking, it does not involve a change of form or external appearance. The Gorgon who has just petrified herself is exactly the same being that all of her victims have glimpsed at the moment of death. She bears the same terrifying gaze that these victims did not have time to perceive; she voices the same savage cry that they did not have time to hear. Instead of a metamorphosis, one might speak of an automorphosis in which Medusa immobilizes herself at the acme of her violence, which differs considerably from a metamorphic transformation of one form into another, a process during which a prior identity is lost. The automorphosis is also a *displacement* from one temporality to another, a passage from the moving, linear time of life and history to the time of representation with its immobility and permanence. The glancing blow struck by the gaze has become, in a fleeting moment, in an embryonic time, the wink of an eye blinded in its very gaze. The voice, the cry, has been lost in silence.

## A Humorous Objection

Why is it that the Gorgon does not look straight ahead, thereby staring into the eyes of the Duke's enemies, serving as an apotropaic ornament? Why doesn't she stare into the eyes of anyone who looks at the decorative shield, or into her own eyes, since she petrified herself by looking at her reflection in the shield? Were that the case, the viewer would be located in the external space of representability, would occupy the Gorgon's own position.

## The Answer

To respond to the objection, we may imagine the following arrangement. When Medusa saw herself in the shield, it was positioned lower and to the left in relation to the surface of the representational space. As a result, the viewer who occupies an external position is not in fact located in the position of the real Gorgon. Instead, the viewer is where Perseus was (a moment before), just after he cut off her head, when his sword was no longer reflected in the shield.

## A Counterobjection

Yes, but in keeping with this arrangement, the shield itself would have to be reflected as an ellipse inscribed in the circle of the shield/painting that is presented frontally to the viewer. This is not the case. What is more, according to the imagined arrangement, the convex mirror would no longer coincide with the convex support of the painting, for the painting would have to be an iconic story, or at least a fragment of one, a properly narrative representation.

An example is provided by Annibale Carracci's fresco, *Perseus and Medusa,* in the Farnese Palace in Rome. Athena (?) is shown holding up Perseus's shield like a mirror, while Perseus, positioned on one side, looks at the image—but not directly. Holding Medusa's head by the serpents, he aims his blow by keeping track of the head in the mirror. The viewer of this fresco sees the "round" shield as an ellipse inside the scene of the narrative. In other words, Carracci causes us to move from the representation-enunciation to what is represented and enunciated following the kinds of transformations I have formulated and formalized above. Caravaggio himself makes use of these transformations when depicting a number of mythical figures, for example, in his *Sacrifice of Isaac, Judith Beheading Holofernes, The Decapitation of Saint John the Baptist,* and *David with the Head of Goliath.* But he does not generate the transformations in painting Medusa, perhaps because of the extreme violence of her gaze.

These remarks do not settle the issue, however, for both the objections and responses to them stand. The debate must be continued.

The "represented utterance" of the painting comes first, then the representation itself, or, in other words, the total product that Caravaggio presents to the viewer. The latter includes everything that comes "after" the decapitation. We can call this the ornamental or decorative moment, when the mirror, Perseus's defensive weapon, becomes a shield bearing an image of a Medusa who is ready to go on repeating her deadly act. Medusa is capable, at this point, of renewing her violence because her gaze and cry were captured in that furtive instant located infinitesimally prior to the moment of self-stupefaction. The moment of decapitation left its traces, its writing, on the painting. These straight lines of streaked blood dried instantly on contact and serve to record the event as past. But the moment of decapitation is only a trace because Caravaggio's painting is not a representation of the moment when Perseus, with his back turned to the Gorgon, strikes his retroactive blow. Instead, the painting depicts Medusa's head as an ornament on the shield, an ornament, that is ready to go on working its powerful magic. Medusa's head is represented at the moment when it is made the object of a representation on the shield. From that moment on, the painting/mirror once again becomes the hero's shield. Yet the ornament remains dangerous and alive. What the Cardinal del Monte presents to the Grand Duke of Tuscany is indeed an ornamental shield, the persistent powers of which are allegorically praised by Cavaliere Marino. The shield still has the power to stupefy and petrify enemies and onlookers. The moment of self-representation and automorphosis is captured in the instant of representation, the moment when the object is exposed to sight. The Gorgon's face-off with her own reflection, seized and frozen at the moment of the original glancing blow, has become a face-off between the Gorgon and the viewer in a painting/shield that indefinitely repeats the unique, unlocalizable, signless moment of the initial scene.

Caravaggio's painting is a historical painting because it condenses two historical moments, causing each of them to envelop the other. The painting presents without presenting a model of the temporality of representation in its most powerful form. The rift or fold in historical time that I have just delineated is also indicated, pointed out, in and by the painting itself as a rift. The fact that the moment of the blow itself cannot be presented is designated by the folding together of the moments just before and after the blow. For what is absent from the painting is indeed Perseus's gesture of severing Medusa's head. The hero's stroke is absent, as is the stroke of the painter's brush in making his painting. In a sense, this painting recapitulates all of the historical and contemporary discussions of Caravaggio's work. It has often been said that in Caravaggio representation becomes nature's equal. This is indeed the artist's drama, for the very moment of art is to proceed, as Félibien puts it, from one inequality to another: an art that is perpetually inferior to nature is replaced by one that exceeds nature. Art is this very discontinuity or leap. With a single blow or bound, art crosses the gap between too little and too much. Such is the moment of the *Head of Medusa,* which in its very presence represents the moment of the leap and blow. Or rather, this painting mobilizes the story of the Gorgon to represent the rift in this leap. The moment after the blow envelops the moment before it, just as the painting designates itself as the blow's effect. At the level of contemplation and theory, this painting represents the moment in which art and Nature become equal, a moment when Nature is produced as an art, a moment that is unbearable and literally stupefying. I would add that it was precisely such a moment that Caravaggio sought to capture as nearly as possible.

## Digression: A Comparison of the Decisive "Moment" in a Romanesque Fresco and in Caravaggio's Two Paintings

The fresco I wish to discuss is in the chapel of the small priory of Berzé-la-ville and depicts the martyrdom of Saint Blaise. Having been decapitated, the saint's head rolls on the ground while his kneeling body collapses forward. Standing in front of the saint is the hangman who, leaning on the sheath of his sword, raises the sword above his head *in order to strike* the deadly blow with all his force. In the space of the narrative scene, the Romanesque painter cleaves apart the moments prior to and just after the decapitation; the unity of time's succession of instants has been broken in order to show "two aspects" at once. On the right is the inceptive moment in which the hangman raises his sword; on the left is the terminative moment when the saint's head rolls on the ground like a ball, surrounded by its circular halo. What is more, the whole scene is framed by two inscriptions reading from left to right, running in a direction contrary to that of the figures, who move from right to left. As a result, we are incited to read the narrative retrospectively, so that its surface-level, syntagmatic order runs as follows: he was put to death; the hangman raised his sword and the head rolled on the ground. When we read the text in this order, the first utterance describes the entire scene—Saint Blaise martyred through decapitation—and constitutes its end. In this totality, the causal concatenation is inscribed: the hangman's preparatory gesture—the raised sword—is the cause; the saint's head on the ground is the effect; and the fall of the headless body is a second effect. In other words, by *separating* the two limiting terms of the narrative, the Romanesque painter *shows what is not representable* in this moment, namely, its central instant, the instantaneous and decisive movement of the sword's blade slicing through the thickness of the neck, the acme of violence. But at the same time, by inverting the syntagmatic order of the represented narrative sequence through the presence of a legible text, the artist provides the viewer with a *typical figure* of representation, namely, the martyrdom of a saint, which is situated within the didactic and apologetic dimension of the narrative. Here is the painting's lesson, which coincides, we may note, with the end of the story it narrates. What comes *after the narrative* is the *figural ending* that gave the narrative its meaning *at the outset*. Between these two terms lies the unrepresentable moment when the head is severed by the sword.

Let us now consider Caravaggio's *Judith Beheading Holofernes*, a painting in which the inevitable servant appears to the right of Judith as she performs the act of decapitation. In this work Caravaggio shows us the "central" moment when the blow of the sword is being delivered, for the blade is pictured at the midpoint of its trajectory, halfway through the victim's neck. Judith's left hand holds Holofernes's head by its hair and three spurts of blood gush out onto the pillow and sheets. Here there is no before and after, only the unique, decisive, and deadly moment of an infinitesimal duration. But there is change, which is perhaps not as surprising as one might think. The moment of the action is immobilized by the very representation of its instantaneity. The sword blow freezes halfway to its completion. Judith will never stop cutting off Holofernes's head with her arrested sword. The story of her deed freezes there as well, having neither a past nor a future, as if it were truly atemporal. This permanence is not a matter of an obsessional or compulsive repetition, but rather the immobile "now" of a phantasm.

Finally, let us consider Caravaggio's *The Sacrifice of Isaac*. Here the story opens at the moment when Abraham stands leaning over Isaac, brutally pressing his head against the sacrificial stone, about to cut his throat with a knife. Entering from the left, the angel, God's messenger, stays the murderous arm of Abraham with his right hand. Abraham turns his head to follow the angel's left index finger, which *points out* to him what the Lord's angel sees: the ram on the right that will be *sacrificed* in place of the son. In this arrangement, where the retrospection moves from the center to the left, simultaneity functions as an inchoative and prospective immobilization. The gesture and gaze move from left to right where the future is being prepared. A story finds its starting point in the interval between the halting of the knife and the offering of the neck, the instant that serves as the matrix of a successive temporality. But something very strange happens in this space "between" two moments, this inter-diction of a sacrificial murder that *will not* take place. The viewer's eye is tricked into producing this moment. It is trapped by the *single eye* of Isaac lying on the stone, who, his mouth open as he cries in terror, looks at me with a gaze that is something like the look of Medusa. This gaze has no equal, unless it is the much more complex gaze of the head of Goliath/Caravaggio held by the young David, as depicted in the painting in the Borghese Gallery.

## Medusa Revisited

I spoke above of the absent gesture of Perseus the hero and of the absent gesture of the painter's act of painting. Yet suddenly the painter makes his entrance into the mirror/shield, not as a hand or a gesture but as a gaze and a head, as the "subject" of the painting and as its *means of execution*.

In order words, we still have some ground to cover. Or perhaps I should say that I have another move to make in the game of my encounter with Medusa.

The first part of my move involves studying the story told by Caravaggio in order to discover the gesture in which the head (the center, the chief, the top) is cut off. I should point out, however, that Caravaggio does not really narrate a story because the viewer cannot, on the basis of a representation of a single moment, silently tell himself the story. Yet, at the same time, the viewer is suddenly thrust into the middle of the *theory* of a story that has been painted. The onlooker is plunged into the center of a pictorial story in order to discover *the absence of this very center.* What the viewer has to discover, even if this has been contested and is at once hidden and revealed, is that the Medusa head is a portrait of the painter. This is a new and the most radical kind of self-reflexivity of painterly representation, since the painter, who is the subject of the representation, simultaneously occupies the position of the absent hero, Perseus the carrier of the shield, and that of the Grand Duke, the recipient of the shield. The painter has severed the head and carries it as an ornament on the shield he has painted, but he is also the one who is represented on the shield in the form of this very head. The blinding and blinded gaze and the silent scream belong to him. Thus the painter inscribes himself in the painting in a dual manner, for he figures there as the petrifying and petrified gaze of Medusa, but also as the caesura of what allows him to be a gaze, namely, the head, but a head cut off at the point of its greatest power and most extreme violence. The painter presents the very violence of the caesura itself. When we construct the series of gestures of decapitation that have constituted this painting, and when Caravaggio attempts to seize as nearly as possible the instantaneity of the cut in his painting, we can imagine that we are witnessing—in a single stroke—the very realization of the cut, a kind of maximal decapitation in which the painter himself has his head cut off. Isaac, Holofernes, Goliath, and John the Baptist are all merely representatives of this decapitated painter. By means of the same transformation, the shield, a defensive weapon, becomes the blade of the sword that does the cutting. Thus we are shown how all representation is a kind of power based on violence, for representation is founded and becomes an *institution* at the very place of the cut.

In the second part of my move, I note that the discourse that I have just written only gives voice to the pathos of the painting and could very well be a trap. The painter, after all, not only disguises himself as Medusa; he also cross-dresses as a Gorgon, a woman, or at least as the head of a woman. This is a woman of striking beauty, Ovid tells us, or at least she would be were it not for her hair of serpents, which she wears as a punishment for having been raped by Neptune. She is a headstrong woman, but also, like a freak in a carnival, a kind of detached, bodiless head. Here the most serious and essential question—and along with it, the metaphysics of representation—is disguised in a game of substitutions involving the headstrong woman, the woman without a head, and the head without the woman. And this game leads to the frivolous and superficial surprise of finding a woman who is only a head. This game is a humorous parody of the denegation of enunciation. And this motif leads me back to the story and to the enuciative modality that characterizes it, for within the story we discover that the subject who utters it is both effaced and disguised. The events *seem* to tell themselves (and we must underscore Benveniste's use of the term *seems* in this context). I have called this a denegation of the enunciation, by which I mean to identify a process of positing and suppressing, asserting and negating, in which the assertion is there only to lead to its negation and is posited only to be excluded. The concept of denegation is appropriate here because what is shown in the painting is the cutting off of the story's head, or rather, of its generative source, the subject of the enunciation himself. This subject's gaze and cry are cut off at the very moment when he looks and screams. What the painting shows us and allows us to see is representation as a cut, a cutting blade severing the story from the subject who tells it while also severing the scene from those who look at it and produce it as a scene. But how does this work? The operation is performed by showing the severed head on the plane of the painting-mirror-shield-sword. And this head, which is the painter's, is also the head of a transvestite.

Now that I have made this move, I am sure that you are waiting for me to speak of castration. You may in fact have been waiting for this from the outset. Given the nature of our modern "situation," a book is always more or less a kind of gratification, or at least it tries to provide some kind of gratification, and I can hardly disappoint my readers in this regard. After all, Freud himself wrote on Medusa.

Having played my game, I must follow the rules of the game that I have been playing backwards. In short, I must go along with the game. So I will cite and then comment on "Das Medusenhaupt" as a kind of interlude, an interlude being some kind of entertainment or amusement—such as a ballet, a dance, or chorus—included between the acts of a play.

# Psychoanalytic Interlude

Freud's essay "Medusa's Head" was written on May 14, 1922, but was published posthumously in 1940. I think it important to begin with an idea that has not been taken seriously enough in the literature on Freud. The psychoanalytic interpretation of the terrifying severed head of Medusa is *too easy* because it is readily suggested by the mythological theme itself. It seems as if the interpretation is already included in the theme of the story, so what need could there possibly be for any further interpretation?

We have not often attempted to interpret individual mythological themes, but an interpretation suggests itself easily in the case of the horrifying decapitated head of Medusa.

To decapitate = to castrate. The terror of Medusa is thus a terror of castration that is linked to the sight of something. Numerous analyses have made us familiar with the occasion for this: it occurs when a boy, who has hitherto been unwilling to believe the threat of castration, catches sight of the female genitals, probably those of an adult, surrounded by hair, and essentially those of his mother.

The hair upon Medusa's head is frequently represented in works of art in the form of snakes, and these once again are derived from the castration complex. It is a remarkable fact that, however frightening they may be in themselves, they nevertheless serve actually as a mitigation of horror, for they replace the penis, the absence of which is the cause of the horror. This is a confirmation of the technical rule according to which a multiplication of penis symbols signifies castration.

The sight of Medusa's head makes the spectator stiff with terror, turns him to stone. Observe that we have here once again the same origin from the castration complex and the same transformation of affect! For becoming stiff means an erection. Thus in the original situation it offers consolation to the spectator: he is still in possession of a penis, and the stiffening reassures him of the fact.

This symbol of horror is worn upon her dress by the virgin goddess Athene. And rightly so, for thus she becomes a woman who is unapproachable and repels all sexual desires—since she displays the terrifying genitals of the Mother. Since the Greeks were in the main strongly homosexual, it was inevitable that we should find among them a representation of woman as a being who frightens and repels because she is castrated.

If Medusa's head takes the place of a representation of the female genitals, or rather if it isolates their horrifying effects from their pleasure-giving ones, it may be recalled that displaying the genitals is familiar in other connections as an apotropaic act. What arouses horror in oneself will produce the same effect upon the enemy against whom one is seeking to defend oneself. We read in Rabelais of how the Devil took to flight when the woman showed him her vulva.

The erect male organ also has an apotropaic effect, but thanks to another mechanism. To display the penis (or any of its surrogates) is to say: 'I am not afraid of you. I defy you. I have a penis.' Here, then, is another way of intimidating the Evil Spirit.

In order seriously to substantiate this interpretation it would be necessary to investigate the origin of the isolated symbol of horror in Greek mythology as well as parallels to it in other mythologies.[1]

Fear of Medusa is thus a fear of castration linked to the action of looking for something and finding it missing. It is, in a sense, linked to the sight of a "lack." But how can one see a lack? We see only what is there. If I see what is not there, I must have been expecting to see something.

I shall try to delineate the scene in which the mother's sex is seen, and shall do so with a staging of the *Head of Medusa*.

1. The Head of Medusa is, *first of all*, a head, a raised head. Here I follow Freud. It is a penis, and when the Viennese master decodes the serpents as a multiplication of penises, it is this reference that he is noting. This is what I expected to see and indeed what I do see.

2. But the head of Medusa is *secondarily* a head that is a gaze, the sole function of which is to look. It is a head/glance of the eye, my own eye, and my own glance.

In other words, on the one hand we have the object we expected to see, which is there, but on the other hand we have the gaze of this very expectation, the eye. On the one hand, we have the object constituted by our expectations, by our foresight and knowledge; on the other, we have this foresight, knowledge, and gaze in the object itself.

In short, we have the "prospect" which according to Poussin depends on three things: the eye, the visual ray, and the distance between the eye and the object. Here is the distance in the story of Medusa.

3. The head of Medusa is, *finally*, a severed head, a decapitation. Freud identifies this as a castration, the lack or suppression of the expected object.

I have just told a story. Medusa stands erect and vigilant in the space guarded by her two sisters who share a single eye. Perseus is on his way toward her and encounters the aporia. He meets and sees Medusa, and, with a glancing blow, kills and decapitates her. Three moments are condensed into a single instance involving both a positing and a suppression.

How can negation be "figured"? A negative judgment, we know, is expressed by means of the word "not." But how can the function of "not" be represented by an image? The way to do this is to represent the object *first, then* its destruction. The head of Medusa and its gaze are the anticipated object, and the gaze doing the anticipating and performing the act of decapitation is the gaze that discovers the absence of the anticipated object.

What is a representation? Freud raises this question in his article "Negation."

> We must recollect that all presentations originate from perceptions and are repetitions of them. Thus originally the mere existence of a presentation was a guarantee of the reality of what was presented. The antithesis between subjective and objective does not exist from the first. It only comes into being from the fact that thinking possesses the capacity to bring before the mind once more something that has once been perceived, by reproducing it as a presentation without the external object having still to be there. The first and immediate aim, therefore, of reality-testing is, not to *find* an object in real perception which corresponds to the one presented, but to *refind* such an object, to convince oneself that it is still there.[2]

From this point of view, then, representation is generally accompanied by the conviction that the represented object is absent but not lacking. Representation targets and brings to mind what is not there, but this object was once there and can be rediscovered. An object is absent if it cannot be directly perceived yet is present in representation.

Given these assumptions, the severed head of Medusa would be a representation in a single figure, of a contradiction: (1) the perception of the penis by the gaze, and (2) the gaze's observation that the penis is lacking. We realize that this must be the case when Freud interprets the viewer's petrifaction as an assertion: "I am not afraid of you, I defy you, I have a penis, an erection."

Yet the central episode of the myth goes unanalyzed by Freud, and it is precisely this very moment that is represented (or perhaps figured) in the *Head of Medusa*. This is the moment in which Medusa petrifies herself and Perseus decapitates her. This central moment is *the moment of the ruse* by means of which the hero turns Medusa's own strength against herself, thereby overcoming his own weakness. This is, of course, the ruse of turning the shield's reflective power into a weapon.

Freud's story—perhaps one should add, Freud's myth—which subtends his remarks on the head of Medusa, elides the "central" moment of the ruse, focusing instead on the beginning and end of the event: (1) Medusa petrifies those who see her, and (2) the virgin Athena carries the head of Medusa, petrifying those who attack her. But to get from the one to the other we have to encounter the moment of the ruse. There is a sense in which the decapitation is secondary, for it would be impossible without the machination in which Perseus uses his shield, in a sort of *bricolage*, as an optical device, a mirror to capture Medusa in the trap of her own deadly gaze.

One can, of course, forget the essential element and fall into the trap of emphasizing the moment of decapitation and castration, thereby interpreting it as the moment in which the object is at once present and absent. I can let myself be trapped by the representation, the trap within the trap created by "Caravaggio," the very mainspring of representation in which the real itself is what is lacking. In the moment of representation, we are allowed not to see "the real," not to want to see it, for the "gap" where castration is made manifest is covered over by the erection of a substitute for the lacking penis; this substitute stands in the hole where sexual difference is revealed. But at the same time, representation marks this reality as a lack, underscoring it while trying to hide it. This is, in fact, a description of the simplest kind of trap, a hole in the earth covered over with branches, leaves, and some dirt. What looks like an unbroken surface is in fact just some leaves and grass hiding a discontinuity. The trick involved in a trap like this is that it is the animal's own weight that causes it to fall into the hidden hole. The victim, that is, contributes to the working of the trap. Indeed, the bigger and stronger the animal, the more quickly it falls, as its strength cleverly is *turned against* it.

In other words, the psychoanalytic interpretation of representation as a fetish overlooks the fact that the fetish (representation) is a trap and thereby makes it function as one. Better yet, representation is the trap of interpretation. Freud reveals the trap of his account of the myth by forgetting that Medusa's self-petrifaction is the result of Perseus's ruse. Freud thereby falls into a trap while trapping us.

Caravaggio's *Head of Medusa*, then, is a counter-ruse mobilized against the ruse of pictorial representation. In this context, it would be appropriate to cite Ellis Waterhouse's remarks on Caravaggio's *Conversion of Saint Paul* and *Crucifixion of Saint Peter* (both of which hang in the Cerasi Chapel, Santa Maria del Popolo, Rome):

> The arrangement of these two pictures, conceived as receiving their light from a painted glory in the ceiling of the chapel, is *deliberately* illusionistic. Caravaggio has done everything possible to bring home to the spectator the vivid immediacy of the scene, as if he were witnessing the incident himself, rather than as if he were looking at a picture of it. The intention is not different from that recommended by the Jesuit *Exercises*, and *the picture, viewed in this light, has the hallucinatory quality of a vision beheld by the spectator himself.*[3]

To conclude our interlude, we may define the trap and hole of the present. What Medusa's gaze provides us with is the representation of an embryonic time, an infinitesimal moment during which she has just looked at herself and is no longer doing so. This is the moment when her gaze has its effect on her. In a single enunciative and representational present, there are, in fact, two present moments, one that is an "up until now" in which the present moment brings an end to a story, and another present moment that is an "all of a sudden," a sudden moment that is only infinitesimally removed from the first present moment. In this *same* moment, "neither this nor that" and "both this and that" are conjoined. What is represented *here* is the gap upon which representation "is founded." This is the gap of the present, a point that is a hole, the hole of the eye through which the gaze of theory falls.

# Of Light, Shadows, and Narrative

Let us begin by recalling the words of Giulio Mancini:

> The salient feature of the school of Caravaggio is the use of a constant source of light that illuminates from above without reflections, just as this might occur in a room with only one window and with rooms painted black; the light is so bright and the shadows so dark as to create a certain sense of depth in the painting . . . In my mind these procedures are not appropriate to the composition of the story and the expression of emotion . . . for it is impossible to arrange within a single room illuminated by only one window a large group of figures who enact the story, who laugh, cry, and walk, and who at the same time stand still in order to be painted.[1]

Caravaggio, then, did not know how to tell a story. And the *Head of Medusa* proves as much. When it comes to the highest position in the hierarchy of genres of paintings—historical paintings—Caravaggio is a failure. And his failure is explained in terms of the kind of space that is peculiar to him, his special use of light and shadow, his particular mode of *painting*. What is at stake here is what is at stake in all *painting*, for the question raised by Caravaggio's work concerns the destruction of painting as well as the pleasure and *jouissance* that painting produces.

## Geometric and Aerial Perspective

We must take on the question of a destruction of painting, and, in order to do so, we must articulate it in terms of what I have called the perspectival apparatus, that is to say, the formal apparatus of enunciation and representation. We must begin once more with Poussin so as to be in a position to come back to Caravaggio. I begin, then, with the distinction between geometric and aerial perspective so as to return to the problem of light and darkness, *ciaro* and *oscuro*, fire and shadow.

This is what Le Brun says about Poussin's *Israelites Gathering Manna*:

> As for the light, he [Le Brun] observed, it is cast diffusely over all the objects. And in order to show that the action takes place early in the morning, some wisps of mist are still visible at the mountain's base and on

the ground's surface. This mist makes them a little dark and causes the objects in the distance to be less visible. This serves to make the figures in the foreground more apparent, and they are illuminated by certain beams of light that escape from openings that the Painter intentionally made in the clouds in order to justify the rays of light that he distributes in various places of his work.

One even notices that he tried to keep the air darker on the side where the manna falls; and on the side where the sky is darker the figures are more clearly illuminated than on the other side where the sky is lighter; this he did in order to introduce variation at the level of lighting and action, and to imbue his Painting with an agreeable diversity of light and darkness. . . .

Mr. Le Brun pointed out that the perspective of the painting's plane is perfectly observed, and that Mr. Poussin, having represented a site that is uneven and filled with mountains, made use of terraces, placing the figures on the most elevated ones; this gives greater flexibility and variety to the overall disposition of the individuals making up the Work. And this also helps to make visible a large multitude of people within a small space, and to situate advantageously the figures of Moses and Aaron, who are, as it were, the two Heroes in the story.[2]

Geometric perspective is a perspective composed of planes. These planes rationalize the drawing—the guarantee of technical correctness—and the design—the guarantee of the well-balanced distribution of the depicted figures. As a perspective of planes, the perspectival network makes possible a *complexification of pictorial narrativity* that in no way challenges the third dimension, namely, the depth of field that is, after all, the great theoretical and practical accomplishment of Renaissance art. Instead, complexification serves to link this depth of field to the story depicted in the work. It makes depth itself the organizational principle of the "subject" of the utterance. It would seem, then, that on the various planes, the different levels of depth in the painting, there is a lateralization like that which constitutes the "denegation" of the enunciation, making it *seem* as though the events simply tell themselves on their own. Poussin's *Israelites Gathering Manna* is exemplary in this regard, at least if we accept Le Brun's commentary on it. Perspective is indeed the organizational principle that produces the painting, but only because of the enunciative modality characteristic of narrative. More specifically, *the eye's direct relation to the point of view* is mediated by the utterances represented on the canvas and *displaced* onto them. The terraces in the desert and the different levels of depth in the image are occupied by figures in the story, each group incarnating one of the verisimilar possibilities of the passions that it is their function to represent. But the displacement is also a kind of *condensation* of the story's temporal succession and its various moments into a single moment of representation—as Le Brun would say. In other words, there is a single represented moment around which each successive moment in the story has left its visible and verisimilar trace, its inscription, in the form of the grouped figures in the desert. These inscriptions are a form of writing that allows the viewer to tell himself the story by means of anticipations and retrospections with regard to the central represented moment. Yet such temporal operations never compromise the unity of representation characteristic of that spatial object which is the painting.

Aerial perspective (which is also an airy or atmospheric perspective) is properly pictorial because it raises the question of color. The pictorial universe is a universe of color. So-called aerial perspective arises when the laws of geometric perspective are applied to the colored universe of a painting. As aerial perspective, perspective rationalizes color by diluting it, both in "quality and force," as a function of distance and the intervening atmosphere. How can the density of intangible air be measured? How can we measure the intensity of light and color?

In this regard Brunellesco's paradigmatic experiment is once again pertinent. As Hubert Damisch has rigorously shown, the spatial box constructed by the optical-geometric apparatus is not entirely perfect. The box remains open since it has no lid. What is more, the "specular structure on which the experiment was based is reduplicated."[3] In the painting of St. John's Cathedral, the sky is a burnished silver plate serving as a second mirror. What it mirrors is not the painted illusions but the variations in the actual sky and light, the clouds that pass, blown by the wind.[4] Damisch's analysis is especially valuable because he identifies a breaking point in the model. Representation gives way to presentation and to the thing in itself, or, rather, to something that is not a "thing" but the very condition of visibility of all things, namely, this place and supplement, this capturing of light in and by means of the perspectival apparatus that organizes the work of representation.

How can the law of perspective be *applied* to the color universe of painting? One solution, which is arrived at by extending the geometric theory of perspective, is to use the painting's perspectival network to construct successive levels of luminosity, shadows, and local variations in color. But how is such a construction to be achieved? Is it a mechanical or a physical operation? Is it of a theoretical or practical nature? The conflict between Gérard Desargues, Abraham Bosse, and Laurent de la Hire on one side, and Poussin and Roland Fréart de Chambray on the other (the Cassiano dal Pozzo-Matteo Zaccolini circle) is documented in Bernard Teyssèdre's book, *Roger de Piles et les débats sur le coloris au siècle de Louis XIV.* Teyssèdre points out that, for Bosse, Poussin's "perfection was *demonstrable,*" for "the Works of the said gentleman are made by *following a rule at all times and are governed by reason from beginning to end.*"[5]

For Fréart de Chambray,

> the talent for color is subordinated to "the science of shadow and light, which is . . . a branch of perspective, where the center of the illuminated body represents the eye; and the section that is constituted by its rays on the plane, or on any other surface, expresses precisely the real contours, and the form itself, of the illuminated body."[6]

In other words, Fréart de Chambray believes that the luminous source in a painting is a representative of the eye (the point of view and vanishing point) as a source of light. The eye that looks at a painting is a seeing sun, and the sun that lights up an object in a painting is a luminous eye. The sun or luminous source illuminates the objects that the painting represents—and that the eye sees—by serving as a delegate of the viewer's eye. The cross section of optical rays distributed on the painting's surface expresses the real contours and linear form of the drawn or represented bodies, just as the cross section of rays on the surface or plane expresses the real contours and form of the illuminated body.

Bosse gives us an even more accurate expression of the principle governing the construction of parallel perspectival sections on the plane of the painting. This principle is the *reason* or *ratio* of aerial perspective (in the dual sense of "rationality" and "proportional calculation"). In this sense, Bosse faithfully obeys the fundamental postulate of painterly representation, the effect of which is to deny that the support and surface of the painting is a *real,* material surface, allowing him to define this surface as transparent. Bosse's principle amounts to considering the various planes of the painting's depth as so many diaphanous surfaces through which the depicted objects and figures are seen as they are positioned at successive distances from the primary surface, which is the canvas. Bosse thereby breaks down the painting's continuous depth into discontinuous planes that are parallel to its surface. But if aerial perspective is a consequence of geometric perspective, what does it consist of? The successive planes repeat the diaphanous quality of the primary plane of the painting in such a general way that if the air between the eye and the objects is clear, pure, and sharp, then the shadowed areas should be *less brown*.

This interesting theory deserves to be analyzed more carefully, especially with regard to what is at stake in painting in general and representation in particular, for it concerns the relation between color and the space of light in paintings.

> In 1665, Bosse attacks those "Practitioners" who "make shadows and shade dark and brown, without considering the rule (which the illustrious and learned Painter, Mr. Poussin, observed rigorously in most of his later works) involving an understanding of the fact that the clearer and purer the air is, the less brown the shaded areas should be, for they are supposedly distanced from the Base of the Painting. In thinking of this air between the eye and the shadows, one should pretend to see them through a veil of very fine, white silk, or better still, through a veil of silk having the color of air"; he assures us that Raphael "did not have such a developed or perfected knowledge of how to combine or mix the color of air with other colors, in order to express the relief of bodies by means of elements that either stand out or recede, following the rule of perspectival cuts that run parallel to the plane of the Painting, in the manner of the illustrious Mr. Poussin."[7]

This is an important text for at least three reasons:

1. It implies that we must *conceptualize* (and I insist on this term) the continuity of space as a series of transparent surfaces. Continuous depth is composed of an infinite number of evanescent discrete quantities. A volume is the sum of an infinity of surfaces having no thickness—an empty, finite space that can be analyzed as the sum of an infinity of transparent surfaces that have all the thickness of clear, pure, and sharp air. This is exactly what Bosse means when he speaks of viewing objects through a series of very fine silk veils.

2. Space is a transparent thickness of air, a thickness that is "colored white"; space is theoretically and physically presented as white or "natural" light, or, in other words, as the sum of all the other colors of the spectrum. White is "the color of air."

3. The conclusion, then, is that a colored object, a green one for example, when placed behind this thickness of air colored white—or, in other words, an object *situated in space* and colored green—should be painted with a mixture of white paint, with more white being added the farther the object is from the primary surface of the painting.

This analysis gave rise to a violent debate with Le Brun concerning the so-called rule of "diminishing" or weakening colors at a distance. Is there really such a rule? And what is the meaning of the "diminishing" or "weakening" in question here?

For Bosse, aerial perspective is a geometric and linear perspective applied or extended to the universe of color. It is a matter of "observing this same perspectival rule in weakening tinted or colored brushstrokes in order thereby to make them create a *genuine* effect of depth."[8] These same laws situate the objects in the painting, as well as "their light and shadows."[9] Bosse's construction has the purity and abstraction of a theoretical model: a painting is a *realized* theoretical model. It is composed according to the laws of optics, "the Art of seeing things by means of reason and with the eyes of the Understanding."[10] In this model, light and colors—visual perception itself—are directly integrated into the utterance and into what is depicted. It is not a matter of *representing* things as the eye sees them but as the geometrical mind *conceptualizes* them.

As Teyssèdre has ably shown, Le Brun's criticism is based on perceptual experimentation focusing on the product of the visual process, sensation. His optics remains *empirical* in that it is up to experience to show whether distance attenuates colors the way it diminishes the size of objects. The painting should correspond to such perceptual phenomena by means of an "imperceptible diminishing." Here we enter into a domain that cannot be rationalized or subjected to a theoretical treatment. No optical rule governs the diminishing in question. There is merely a principle that holds that there is a *weakening in force and brightness,* the effects of which vary according to the color and density of the intervening air as well as the time of day when the object is viewed and the distance between the object and the eye of the painter/viewer. Here we have a painter's reaction to the theorist's model.

The principle of weakening is ambiguous. Although there is a sense in which it is indeed the application of geometric perspective to the domain of light and color, it relies on the autonomy of luminous and, by extension, colored phenomena, which stand independent of the abstract, geometric construction of the painting (which I have referred to as the design).

Le Brun attempts to find a happy medium. Every figure and object should get its share of luminosity and color, and *then* every figure and object will be situated in the space organized according to the laws of perspective, a space where they are *recomposed* along the axis of depth. It strikes me that this double movement echoes something we took note of in Fréart de Chambray's text. There are two eyes, the eye of light and the eye of the gaze or look, and the former is in some sense the delegate or representative of the latter. The two do not occupy the same position in the space of representation. Objects derive their luminous intensity and color from the eye of light or solar eye. The eye of the gaze composes and organizes these objects in the abstract space of geometry.

Challenging Le Brun's position, some members of the Academy inverted the order of these operations. They claimed that the definition of the object's intensity was a matter of decomposition while the definition of the represented space involved composition. Light and color depend upon the totality of the represented space, the perspectival organization of which is subordinate to color and the play of light and shadow. As a result, the representation of space and of the figures that occupy it is a matter neither of *geometric truth*, as Bosse maintained, nor of Le Brun's *experimental verisimilitude*. A painting should not be made into a *theory*. Rather, it is a *potency* or a *force*. Representation is not so much a distanced contemplation as a *potency of effect*.

## Of Black and White

The painting's potency of effect finds its technical basis in the question of black and white. Either representation is mimesis in the sense of a faithful or truthful verisimilitude with regard to the idea that articulates the very being of what is represented, in which case it is a matter of the represented object *expressing the design,* or representation is mimesis in the sense of an *effect to be imprinted* on the viewer's sensibility, an effect achieved by the painting's arrangement of forms and colors having a specific potency.

In this regard we may usefully turn to a text by Dufresnoy as interpreted by Roger de Piles and discussed by Teyssèdre. Dufresnoy, as Teyssèdre points out, articulates three "theorems": (1) "Light produces all kinds of colors and shade produces none." (2) "The more directly an object is situated opposite us and the closer it is to light, the more it is illuminated, because light weakens as it is distanced from its source." (Thus if natural light is white, this "theorem" implies that a distant object is darker.) (3) "The closer and more directly in front of the eyes an object is, the more visible it is, for sight weakens with distance."[11] In other words, not only is a distant object darker, but its contours are obscure, its outline lost.

Yet, as Teyssèdre points out, if the "theorems of light" are analytic, they are ultimately concerned with the painting's overall effect. It is not only a matter of considering what is clear and what is obscure, light and darkness together as seen in a single glance. It is primarily a matter of interpreting their relation as a means of constructing or composing the represented space, as a means of distributing objects within this space.[12]

It follows that there are two ways of understanding the relation of any given object to the *group* of objects to which it belongs. Two comparisons are helpful in clarifying this point. The image is that of a cluster of grapes, which Titian proposed as the paradigm for shadow: "[He] was committed to casting the darkest shadows 'around' the object rather than between its parts because he feared that the shadows might otherwise appear 'to penetrate it and cut them.'"[13] This paradigm was reinterpreted by Roger de Piles, who gave priority to the notion of a *group* over that of an individual, isolated object (an emphasis that we also find in Diderot, particularly with regard to the *Israelites Gathering Manna*). The first comparison concerning how to make colors stand out or withdraw involves a painter and a sculptor:

As they work the Painter and the Sculptor will have the same intention and will employ the same procedure: for just as the Sculptor fashions and sculpts with iron, the Painter uses his brush to push back objects that he

shrinks by means of a weakening of color; at the same time, he fore-
grounds and draws forward what is directly in the line of vision by using
the most colorful tints and darkest of shadows; and finally, he applies to
the naked canvas the Colors that he will borrow from Nature, Colors that
he must observe from a *single site* and at a *glance*, so that he appears to be
turning around the Figure he represents although he never moves.[14]

The second comparison involves the analogy between a painting
and a convex mirror, which I have already discussed at great length.
Here I shall focus only on Roger de Piles's interpretation of it:

> The Painter must be concerned primarily with larger shapes and with the
> effect of the Whole. The Mirror distances objects, and as a result, it re-
> veals only larger shapes, the individual parts of which are lost. In the
> evening, when night approaches, you will notice this effect all the more,
> but not as easily: for the appropriate time lasts only half an hour, whereas
> the Mirror can be used the entire day.[15]

This line of reasoning makes possible the formulation of three *theses*
concerning black and white. These theses, we shall see, bear directly
on our "reading" of Caravaggio and on the destruction of painting that
he brought about, at least in the eyes of Félibien and other academic
critics. (1) "Pure White may stand out and may also withdraw."[16] This
means that space is light and that the light in question is white, that "in
painting, light and white are the same thing."[17] (2) White "stands out
with Black and withdraws without it."[18] To put a spot of black on white
is to make the white next to the black stand out and to make the white
in the distance withdraw. (3) "There is nothing that stands out more
than pure Black."[19] Here we have a fundamental principle: "it is of
such importance, that unless it is rigorously observed, a Painting cannot make a great impression; it is easy to see at a glance whether large
objects are clearly distinguished from each other and whether depth
and distance are maintained."[20]

## Painter's Discussions

What about the idea of adding white paint when painting distant objects? Contrary to Bosse's theory, it would seem that no white should be
added since white makes objects stand out. Of course. Yet one can add
some white to the background provided that it stands in opposition to
a very dark shadow or is restrained by some very bright colors.

Just as there is "no Color closer to Air than White" there is hardly a "lighter" color, nor as a result—here de Piles goes much further than Dufresnoy—one that is more capable of withdrawing; only if one "renounces landscapes" can one afford to ignore this principle.[21]

Two ideas are being postulated here: first, the idea of a universal, *solar* light; second, that of an open space. The two are essentially and substantially interconnected. When some particular source of light, such as a torch, illuminates the scene, the light weakens in direct proportion to the object's distance from the source of light. At the same time, the space closes. Moving to the limit, we reach an absolutely black space, or, more precisely, a nonspace, a maximally dense "fullness."

Another painterly problem, the symmetrical inverse of the previous one, concerns the use of black in the foreground. "Nothing comes forward more than black"—"the most heavy, earthy, and perceptible Color."[22] Theoretically, then, black might be said to be a noncolor by virtue of its absolute proximity to the eye. What we have here is the noncolor of pure contact. But why then does "black only create holes" "in the foreground"?[23] A likely explanation is that it does so when it is not applied in large, well-blended quantities. But other painters have noticed that "light" is "what gives depth to a spherical body," making it stand out.[24] So black is the color most inclined to withdraw? No. You are confusing "contours" with "distances," black as part of the object's form, the black of "contours," with the black of "distance," black as space or rather as nonspace:

> The Brown that one mixes with the contours of the spherical body makes them recede by *obscuring* them (so to speak), by *blackening* them. And do you not see that the Reflections are an artifice used by the Painter to make the contours lighter, and that what is Blackest remains toward the center of the spherical body, as a basis for the White, and in order to trick us agreeably?[25]

Let us reformulate the "theses" on black and white. According to Dufresnoy and Roger de Piles, both are colors, or rather, *metacolors*, if we dare use such an expression.

White is the color of the air. Light is *white* light. White is *space*, the total color. Or as the Pousssinian Fréart de Chambray put it, "white . . . is a potential capable of receiving all other colors."[26] White represents daylight. It produces all other colors and is a metacolor in the sense that it is the semantic axis of complexity in the elementary structure of a "semantics" of color.

Black is a noncolor, being by definition the absence of light and space, a nonlight and nonspace. In the semantic structure of color, it is the axis of neutrality. This implies that the universe of objects is a black universe. The "insides" of things are black. To say that black is an absolute nonlight and noncolor achieved through a negation of *all the others* (and thus the negation of white, which is all the other colors combined) is to say that black is a totally determined space—not an empty space, then, but one that is full, totally dense and closed.

> Arca: 1. A chest (esp. one for keeping money in), coffer, box. b. (w. gen. or equiv.) the treasury, coffers (of a temple or association). c. financial resources, wealth, money. 2. A coffin; also, a receptacle in which bodies, esp. those of paupers, were carried to a place of burial or cremation, bier. 3. A place of confinement, cell. 4. A chest, box, cage.
>
> Arcanus, a, um:1. Kept from public knowledge, secret, private. 2. Away from public view, hidden, private, obscure. 3. (of rites) That are or must be kept secret, esoteric; (in general) mysterious, magical, mystic. 4. That keeps secrets; (masc. as sb.) a trustworthy friend, confidant. b. (poet., of night).
>
> Arceo, ere, ui (cf. *arca*) 1. To keep close, contain, hold in; (transf.) to control, govern. 2. To prevent from approaching, keep away, repulse.[27]

Black space is the space of a trunk, a coffin, or a cell. It is wholly bounded, like a tomb sealed forever. We cannot know or see what is going on inside it. We cannot know or see what it contains. What does it hold? It creates a distance. It divides and separates. "The salient feature of the school of Caravaggio is the use of a constant source of light that illuminates from above without reflections, just as this might occur in a room with only one window and with walls painted black."[28]

How, then, is it possible to tell a story?

Caravaggio's "black," "arcanian" space stands in opposition, then, to Poussin's "white" Arcadian space: "[Painting] is an imitation made on a surface with lines and colors of everything that one sees under the sun."[29]

The closed arcanian space is that of the black box. If we introduce a single light into that space, a ray of light emanating from a single source, this light has a maximum of potency and intensity. It creates a blinding effect—an effect of stupefaction.

This is the cause of a series of descriptive and normative criticisms that have been directed against Caravaggio's work. The critics complain: there is no action; he tells no story; he has no idea about how to provide an iconic representation of a series of events. And yet at the same time his paintings are a matter of representations and perfect illusions, a matter of maximal *force* and *intensity.*

In other words, Caravaggio cannot tell a story; he only knows how to paint one or two isolated figures. When he tries to tell a story, he places these figures in the foreground so that it looks as though they have been shoved forward by the density of the neutral background, that black box having an absolute density. At the same time, the expression of emotions has been reduced to the intensity of a single instantaneous impression. This reduction amounts to a kind of "Medusa-effect."

What, then, are the consequences for representation, the subject of representation, and the destruction of painting?

Light defines space in addition to the form of things; it serves as the container of objects *and* as their limits, their contours. Space, then, is not an a priori form of intuition as Kant maintained. It is not a geometric and abstract extension, an intelligible structure that is perceptually and sensorily neutral. It is not the principal attribute of substances, unknowable in itself, the geometric extension which Pascal defined *physically* as the *void.*

Space is, to speak like Zucarri, a physical substance: light, whiteness. This is the Cartesian idea of *physical* space that can be distinguished from *geometrical* space. Geometrical space is a void where *lines* are drawn. Physical space is *light,* the whiteness where objects take form. In this context, one should reread the fifth part of Descartes's *Discourse on Method,* which is devoted to questions of physics, as well as the first discourse of his *Optics,* in which light is defined as immediate physical contact at a distance and color is defined as the reflection of light on bodies. White is a straight reflection while red, yellow, and blue are reflections modified in various ways.

It follows that a body's color is nothing more than the effect on an eye that has been *touched* by light reflected by that body's surface. White light reflecting as color on the surfaces of bodies defines these surfaces for the gaze. The surprise here is that Descartes turns out to have been "Venetian."

## Caravaggio's Paradox

The paradox is a matter of presenting a "black" space to be looked at. If it is valid to equate space, light, and whiteness, a black space is a contradiction in terms, a contradiction that I "imaged" by means of the closed tomb. If the space represented in the painting's frame is a cube "open" on one side, a window on the world and a mirror reflecting the world, then we have to say that in Caravaggio's work the mirror has darkened, the window is closed, and the cube has no open side.

By generalizing and radicalizing Dufresnoy's third "theorem" ("There is nothing that stands out more than pure Black"), we reach the following conclusion: the space defined by a painting's frame is the simple and full surface of an infinitely dense black volume. As a result, a "black" painting is a represented space that *expels* the objects the painter wanted to include, forcing them outside of the painting and beyond its surface.

If a luminous beam is then projected from the space outside the frame (defined by the painting as a full and dense surface), this beam, which runs parallel to that surface, will *instantaneously extract fragments* of objects and figures from it. These fragments remain caught up in the compact texture of the surface, but they also move forward in front of it, doing so all the more strongly if the light is intense. An example is *David with the Head of Goliath* (Borghese Gallery, Rome). We can discover here a fantastic (phantasmatic?) visual "contradiction" between, on the one hand, the foreshortened arms and hand that hold Goliath's head and, on the other hand, the head itself. The lighted fragment of the head stands out from the background, which is almost entirely black, and remains caught up in the dense surface of the painting, just as the arm and hand stand out against another dense surface that is not situated on the same plane as this black background. As a result, Caravaggio obliterates the distinction between the two "blacks" in Dufresnoy's theory—namely, black as nonspace and black as the "shadow" of an illuminated volume—making this volume turn by imperceptibly confounding the place of its limit. We can imagine that Caravaggio applied an inverted version of Dufresnoy's second theorem: "White stands out with Black and withdraws without it." Putting a white spot on a black background makes this spot advance or stand out in relation to the black surface, but it does not make the black background recede. On the contrary, the black advances all the more as a result.

*Two Consequences*

A first consequence concerns narrative painting and the stories it represents. A painting's black ground is much more than a "background" or scenic space. The ground is, ultimately, the very surface of the painting. As a result, the projection of the beam of light onto the painting's plane leaves only the very edge of the surface for the arrangement of figures and objects. Only the very first line of the painting remains: the figures are constantly pushed forward; the scene on which they stand is a kind of apron or forestage. It is as though we were looking at figures in bas-relief standing out from a solid wall, the wall of an arcanian tomb. An example is *The Resurrection of Lazarus* (Museo Nazionale, Messina), which I discuss in some detail below.

To present these matters negatively, we can say that it is no longer possible to arrange figures in depth the way it was done in *The Israelites Gathering Manna*, where they were positioned on a series of terraces in the desert. It is impossible to articulate the *circumstances* that constitute the spatialization of a central represented moment, circumstances that alone allow the viewer to read or view the single represented moment as a diachronic series of narrative utterances, as a story. It is now impossible to show *a differentiated but single action* unfolding in both its syntagmatic power and its diachronic potency. Instead, representation represents but a single moment. This instant is seized the way a snapshot instantaneously captures a flash of a second. In other words the action is immobilized and made into a statue. It is *stupefied* in a Medusa-effect.

The second consequence is that the flash of light is a glance in which the gaze freezes and stupefies itself. Representation is the result of contact; vision is touch. Let us reread Descartes's comments in his *Optics:* "There is a *great difference* [my emphasis] between the stick of this blind man [which Descartes uses as an image for the *instantaneous* movement of light] and the air or the other *transparent* bodies through the medium of which we see."[30] With Caravaggio's beam of light, the glance creates an image. It creates a Cartesian image of the blind man's cane. It blinds us, for it has the "energetic" consistency of the cane. It is a poke in the eye with the cane.

By the same stroke, we realize that if the signs expressing affect serve as the letters in painting's form of narrative writing (Poussin), and if stories are told iconically by means of a recomposition of analytic expressions of emotions in a complex bodily and gestural mimicry, it follows that Caravaggio's code of gestures regresses to the single, "originary" gesture of *pointing*. This is the case because his narrations cannot transmit a message or tell a story. Instead, an emotional effect is directly imprinted through contact, capturing the instantaneous moment of its violence. In Caravaggio's work, the glance is a gesture of pointing, a wordless "this" that does away with supplementary discourses and descriptions, striking here and now. It is really true, then, that this man came into the world in order to destroy painting.

# Et in arca hoc

I shall conclude this book with some notes recording aspects of my reading of *The Resurrection of Lazarus*, a painting that can be seen as providing a kind of instantaneous snapshot image of representation itself.

What I want to demonstrate here is that, in this work, a well-ordered series of figures running parallel to the painting's plane develops and deploys a plastic and structural syntagma. This syntagma is neither narrative nor diachronic but is instead a matter of composition and distribution. The lines of force in this syntagma are illustrated in the following chart:

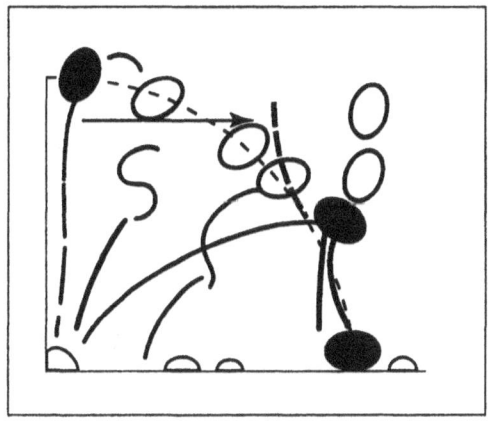

We notice, first of all, the arc of a quarter-circle, or rather an ellipse, moving from the upper middle of the left-hand side of the canvas to its lower right-hand corner. A line perpendicular to this arc, marking its left boundary as it were, is provided by Christ's figure—or, more precisely, by his body and head. The first "line" of the painting is the bottom of the frame, the ground punctuated by the feet of the standing figures. The right angle formed by the left boundary and the bottom of the frame is bisected by a line marked obliquely by rays of light and by the body of Lazarus. The elliptical arc I have defined is marked off by the figures' heads, with the rather striking exception of the head of Lazarus, which provides the last bead in an almost vertical rosary of three faces made up (proceeding downward) of Martha, Mary, and Lazarus. The result is a syntagma of composition and distribution directing the movement of my gaze as I read the painting. I necessarily obey this trajectory as I reconstruct my vision of the image. Its starting point is Christ's head in the upper part of the painting, slightly to the left, and its final point is the skull on the ground at the bottom right. Christ's head, we note, is lost in the shadows of blackness and night. The skull is struck by a flash of light. The syntagma of this "figural text" does not provide the diachronics of a narrative or the temporality of referential history.

This first schematic description is complicated by the presence of the rosary of heads on the right, situated perpendicular to the skull and between it and the head of Christ. The vertical fold of the shroud connects them all, and it, too, is violently illuminated, as if by a flash.

We may note as well, in regard to the overall figure created by these lines, that the upper "string" of the arc is traced by Christ's pointing arm and hand. His index finger touches the circumference of the arc. A tangent to the quarter-circle is provided by Lazarus's right arm and hand. His palm is open and faces the point of the index finger, which is struck by light. Although the hand faces the finger, the viewer sees it in profile.

What we see here is a *gesture of pointing and an answer to it* captured in the same moment, as if in a snapshot. Let us add Lazarus's arm to our description of the group of figures. His hand, which is open facing the viewer, is *struck by light and lets the skull drop to the ground.* This relation inscribes within the syntagma of this "figural text" the moment of pointing. This moment is a heterogeneous element because it implies no temporality in the text understood as text. Or rather, one may say that it implies a null temporality, a temporality equaling zero. Such, quite precisely, is the "story" told by the painting. At the level of the story, all of the figures in the painting are *in* the same represented moment of time. The result is what I would call a splitting of the heterotopia. In the topography of this painting's space, the first grouping develops the syntagmatic element characteristic of a figurative and representational text. The second grouping presents a snapshot of an utterance that is the act of enunciation itself, the gesture of pointing, the very moment of "conatus."

## Remarks on the Lighting

The disposition in bas-relief of the figures, their "aggregate space," is marked by a striking disjunction. That is, the flash of light that strikes Lazarus's raised hand is disjoined from the luminous plane that strikes the rest of the figures. Here the question of light and shadow involves the coherence of the distribution of luminous effects. The same issue is even more strikingly obvious, by the way, in *The Calling of Saint Matthew*, a painting in which the brush of light that comes from the upper right and strikes Matthew's face does not belong to the same source as the oblique light that also comes from the right to illuminate the scene. This disjunction of rays of light strikes me as the energetic substratum of the gesture of pointing, a kind of vector of its violence. It is as if the gesture's forcefulness were figuratively marked off from the "narrative" figures.

I also note that the horizontal line dividing the overall painting in the middle crosses Christ's outstretched arm, while the central vertical line is just a few inches to the left of Lazarus's raised hand. The diagonal lines implicitly crossing the painting from its corners cross his hand as well. Lazarus's hand, then, is positioned at the *quasi-center* of the painting.

## Remarks on the Painting's *"Quasi-geometry"*

The figures' heads are never exactly positioned on the same line or plane in the geometric construction. They are always slightly displaced away from these lines and planes. As a result, the path of the viewer's reading of the image produces other lines or planes of construction, lines or planes that are, *at the time* just as pregnant with meaning. The painting's skeleton, then, is a quasi-metric. Its topography is a topology.

## Remarks on the System of Gestures

Lazarus's hands are open: he raises one hand and drops the other, letting the skull fall. This much is clear. Caravaggio's symbolic system has an immediate effect and is "practical" if we compare it to that of Poussin, which oscillates in an undecidable way between narrative and the allegory in which the unsayable symbol is formulated. But why is the raised hand open? We may read it as the answer to Christ's pointing gesture. But what does it really mean to answer a pointing gesture, a simple indication of "this" or *hoc?* The "answer" can only be the presence of the thing itself. Pointing does not raise a question; it asserts something, or rather, it posits something while giving an order, but the order has no content. The pointing gesture does not say "do this"; rather, it says "this." The answer is "yes, this." "Hoc" *ita* "Hoc," an identity established by contact.

Lazarus's two hands constitute the "originary" enunciative gesture: the hand that is open directly to the viewer is seen by Christ in profile, and vice versa. The former is the hand of life returned or welcomed; the latter is the hand of death abandoned. The snapshot of representation is a neutral moment, or rather, a neutralization of time. It is neither life nor death. It is the unthinkable moment of resurrection, the site that cannot be occupied, the no-where of the cogito of my own death.

Once again the question of the painting's narrativity is raised. In a sense this painting is the (perfect?) realization of the narrative, iconic model I have constructed. Depth undergoes a lateral transformation. There is a double displacement of the point of view and vanishing point, which move to the central represented moment and to the beginning and end of the story. But in another sense, what is "told" in this image is the instantaneous snapshot of representation, or rather, the *instantaneity of the effect of representation.*

A phantasm to which this painting may give rise is that the skull is my representative in the painting. This would be the equivalent of the anamorphotic skull in the foreground of Holbein's *Ambassadors.*

One hypothesis that has occurred to me in regard to *The Resurrection of Lazarus* is that Christ's head and gaze are somehow neutralized by the shadows, as if they were absent. Christ is just a pointing hand, a fact that stands in contrast to the overturned skull. If the skull is overturned or inverted, then it is certainly my representative in the painting. What I imagine here is the symbolic decapitation of Lazarus. Christ, then, as a displaced and neutralized vanishing point, proves to be a gesture and forceful effect. We move from re-presentation to the effect of representation, arriving finally at the gesture of pointing, which is a moment of contact.

I imagine Lazarus's inverted face outside the arc as the skull at the endpoint of the arc's circumference, but his gaze is absent. His eyes are closed, just as Christ's gaze is missing. The entire "system" of gazes in this painting can be constructed in relation to the gap between the two poles provided by Jesus' missing gaze and Lazarus's absent one.

Lazarus's absent gaze is the atopical site of the point of view (the skull that represents me) and of the vanishing point (the missing gaze of Christ). It is the atopical site of the very painting itself. It is all the more appropriate, then, that it should be located outside the elliptical arc where the figurative-representational text articulates its syntagma.

Situated between the missing and the absent gazes is the "central" rift, the gap between Christ's pointing gesture and Lazarus's gesture of surprise. This rift is that of an instant: "adhuc"—"ecce," until now, here is. . . . Christ's pointing finger and Lazarus's astonished hand symbolize permanence in the present moment, an apostasy of the limit.

Et in arca hoc: even in the tomb, this.

Et in Arcadia ego: even in Arcadia, me.

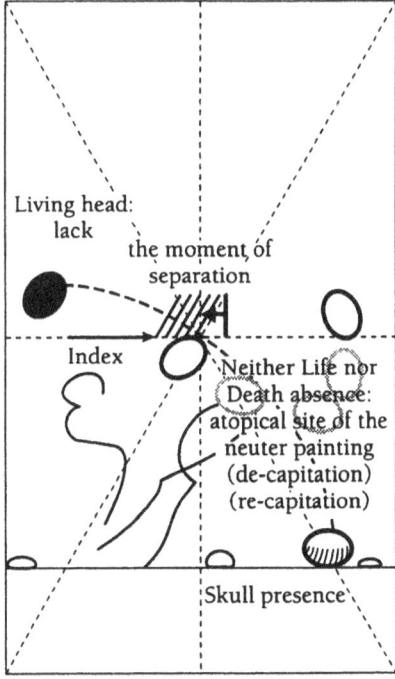

# Notes

## Postscript in the Guise of an Introduction

1. Egidio Forcellini, *Lexicon Totius Latinitatus ab Aegidio Forcellini*, 6 vols. (Patavii: Gregoriana, 1965), 4:784.

## Key Texts

1. André Félibien, "Entretien VI," in *Entretiens sur les vies et sur les ouvrages des plus excellens peintres anciens et modernes; avec la vie des architectes*, 6 vols. (Trevoux: de l'imprimerie de S.A.S., 1725), 4:194; my emphasis.
2. Ibid.
3. Ibid.
4. Nicolas Poussin, "Letter to M. de Chambray (March 1, 1665)," in *A Documentary History of Art*, ed. Elizabeth Gilmore Holt, 2 vols. (Garden City, N.Y.: Doubleday, 1957–58), 2:158.
5. Giovanni Baglione, cited in Walter Friedlaender, *Caravaggio Studies* (Princeton, N.J.: Princeton University Press, 1955), 235–36.
6. Félibien, "Entretien VI," 4:195.
7. Poussin, "Letter to M. de Chambray," 2:158.
8. Félibien, "Entretien VI," 4:191–92.
9. Ibid., 4:192.
10. Ibid., 4:193–94.
11. Ibid., 4:192.
12. Ibid.
13. Karl Van Mander, cited in Friedlaender, *Caravaggio Studies*, 260.
14. Poussin, "Letter to M. de Chambray, 2: 159.

## Allegory: The Golden Bough or the Theory of Mimesis

1. *The Aeneid of Virgil*, trans. D. Day Lewis (London: Hogarth Press, 1961), 118 (6.9–13).
2. Ibid. (6.14–19).
3. Ibid. (6.20–30).
4. Ibid., 118–19 (6.30–33).
5. Ibid., 119 (6.33–41).
6. Ibid., 120 (6.98–101).
7. Ibid., 121 (6.103–23).
8. Ibid., 121–22 (6.133–48).
9. Ibid., 122 (6.149–55).
10. Nicolas Poussin, "Letter to M. de Chambray (March 1, 1665)," in *A Docu-*

*mentary History of Art,* ed. Elizabeth Gilmore Holt, 2 vols. (Garden City, N.Y.: Doubleday, 1957–58), 2:159.

11. André Félibien, "Entretien VIII," in *Entretiens sur les vies et sur les ouvrages des plus excellens peintres anciens et modernes; avec la vie des architectes,* 6 vols. (Trevoux: de l'imprimerie de S.A.S., 1725), 4:44.

12. Virgil, *The Aeneid,* 124 (6.232–35).

## Questions, Hypotheses, Discourse

1. Émile Benveniste, "Sémiologie de la langue (2)," *Semiotica* 1, no. 2 (1969): 127–35.

2. Ibid., 133.

3. Ibid., 135.

4. Antoine Arnauld, *The Art of Thinking,* trans. James Dickoff and Patricia James (Indianapolis: Bobbs-Merrill, 1964), 29.

5. Ibid., 31.

6. Ibid., 104.

7. Ibid., 99.

8. Ibid., 101.

9. Benveniste, *Problems in General Linguistics,* trans. Mary Elizabeth Meek (Coral Gables, Fla.: University of Miami Press, 1971), 206.

10. Sigmund Freud, "Negation," in *The Standard Edition of the Complete Psychological Works of Sigmund Freud,* trans. and ed. James Strachey, 24 vols. (London: Hogarth, 1953–74), 19:238–39.

11. Marmontel, "Palémon," *Mercure de France* (June 1791); 7–8.

12. André Félibien, "Entretien VI" in *Entretiens sur les vies et sur les ouvrages des plus excellens peintres anciens et modernes; avec la vie des architectes,* 6 vols. (Trevoux: de l'imprimerie de S.A.S., 1725), 4:194.

## Readings

1. Nicolas Poussin, "Letter to Chantelou," in *A Documentary History of Art,* ed. Elizabeth Gilmore Holt, 2 vols. (Garden City, N.Y.: Doubleday, 1957–58), 2:147.

2. Poussin, cited in Anthony Blunt, *Nicolas Poussin* (New York: Bollingen, 1967), 222.

3. François Fénelon, *Dialogues des morts,* in *Oeuvres de Fénelon,* 23 vols. (Versailles: J. A. Lebel, 1820–30), 19:343.

4. Poussin, "Letter to Chantelou," 2:146.

5. From a (lost) letter from Poussin to Sublet de Noyers (1642), quoted in André Félibien, "Entretien VIII," in *Entretiens sur les vies et sur les ouvrages des plus excellens peintres anciens et modernes; avec la vie des architectes,* 6 vols. (Trevoux: de la imprimerie de S.A.S., 1725), 4:44; my emphasis. Translation is from Alain Mérot, *Nicolas Poussin* (New York: Abbeville, 1990), 311.

6. Félibien, "Entretien VIII," 4:120.

7. Ibid., 4:21; my emphasis.

8. Ibid., 4:44; this is also from Poussin's lost letter to Sublet de Noyers.

9. Poussin, conversation with Félibien, cited in Blunt, *Nicolas Poussin*, 222.

10. Félibien, "Entretien VIII," 4:123.

11. The citation is taken from an account of Le Brun's lectures. See *Conférences de l'Académie Royale de Peinture et de Sculpture pendant l'année 1667*, ed. Félibien (Paris: Fréderic Leonard, 1669), 81.

12. Ibid., 83.

13. Ibid.

14. Ibid., 81.

15. Félibien, "Entretien VIII," 4:143.

16. François Hédelin d'Aubignac, *La Pratique du théâtre* (Paris: Antoine de Sommaville, 1657), 119.

## Denegation

1. Antonio Manetti, *Vita di Filippo di Ser Brunellesco*, in *A Documentary History of Art*, ed. Elizabeth Gilmore Holt, 2 vols. (Garden City, N.Y.: Doubleday, 1957–58), 1:171–72.

2. Giulio Mancini, *Considerazioni sulla pittura*, ed. Adrianna Marucchi, 2 vols. (Rome: Accademia Nazionale dei Lincei, 1956), 1:108–9.

3. Quintilian, *The Institutio Oratoria*, trans. H. E. Butler (Cambridge, Mass.: Harvard University Press, 1979), 77–78 (10.2.6–8).

4. Giorgio Vasari, "Preface," in *The Lives of the Painters, Sculptors and Architects*, trans. A. B. Hinds (London and Toronto: J. M. Dent & Sons, 1927), 1, 3.

5. Leon Battista Alberti, *On Painting*, trans. John R. Spencer (New Haven, Conn.: Yale University Press, 1966), 64.

6. André Félibien, "Entretien VIII," in *Entretiens sur les vies et sur les ouvrages des plus excellens peintres anciens et modernes: avec la vie des architectes*, 6 vols. (Trevoux: de l'imprimerie de S.A.S., 1725), 4:138–42.

7. Nicolas Poussin, "Letter to M. de Chambray (March 1, 1665)," in *A Documentary History of Art*, 2:158; my emphasis.

8. Maurice Merleau-Ponty, *Phenomenology of Perception*, trans. Colin Smith (London: Routledge & Kegan Paul, 1962), 254–56.

9. Ibid., 256.

10. Ibid., 265–66.

11. Aristotle, *Physica*, trans. R. P. Hardie and R. K. Gaye, vol. 2 of *The Works of Aristotle Translated into English*, ed. W. D. Ross (Oxford: Clarendon, 1930), 220a.

## The Arcadian Landscape

1. André Félibien, "Entretien VIII," in *Entretiens sur les vies et sur les ouvrages des plus excellens peintres anciens et modernes; avec la vie des architectes*, 6 vols. (Trevoux: de la imprimerie de S.A.S., 1725), 4:123.

2. Ibid., 4:88.

3. Polybius, *The Histories,* trans. W. R. Paton, 6 vols. (Cambridge, Mass.: Harvard University Press, 1967), 2:349–53.

4. Félibien, "Entretien VIII," 4:88–89.

5. Immanuel Kant, "Of Beauty as the Symbol of Morality," chap. 59 of *The Critique of Judgment,* trans. J. H. Bernard (London: Hafner Press, 1951), 1198–99.

6. Anthony Blunt, *Nicolas Poussin* (New York: Bollingen, 1967), 336–53.

7. Félibien, "Entretien VIII," 4:140.

8. Leon Battista Alberti, *On Painting,* trans. John R. Spencer (New Haven: Yale University Press, 1966), 77.

9. Nicolas Poussin, "Letter to Chantelou (November 24, 1647)," in *A Documentary History of Art,* ed. Elizabeth Gilmore Holt, 2 vols. (Garden City, N.Y.: Doubleday, 1957–1958), 2:155.

10. Poussin, "Letter to Chantelou (April 28, 1639)," in *A Documentary History of Art,* 2:146–47.

## On Nominal Sentences, Fragments, Epitaphs, and Epigraphs

1. Erwin Panofsky, "*Et in Arcadia Ego:* Poussin and the Elegiac Tradition," chap. 7 of *Meaning in the Visual Arts* (New York: Anchor, 1955), 295–320.

2. Ibid., 297.

3. Ibid., 298.

4. Ibid., 304.

5. Ibid., 313.

6. See Panofsky's "Et in Arcadia Ego," in *Philosophy and History: Essays Presented to Ernst Cassirer* (Oxford: Oxford University Press, 1936), 223ff, and "Et in Arcadia Ego, et le tombeau parlant," *Gazette des Beaux-Arts* 1 (1938): 305 ff. See also Werner Weisbach, "Et in Arcadia Ego. Ein Beitrag zur Interpretation antiker Vorstellungen in der Kunst des 17. Jahrhunderts," *Die Antike* 6 (1930), and "Et in Arcadia Ego," *Gazette des Beaux-Arts* 2 (1937): 287ff. See Anthony Blunt's "Poussin's 'Et in Arcadia Ego,'" *Art Bulletin* 20 (1938): 96ff, and finally, see Jerome Klein's "An Analysis of Poussin's *Et in Arcadia Ego,*" *Art Bulletin* 19 (1937): 314ff.

7. Panofsky, "Et in Arcadia Ego: Poussin and the Elegaic Tradition," 306.

8. Ibid.

9. Antoine Arnauld, *The Art of Thinking,* trans. James Dickoff and Patricia James (Indianapolis: Bobbs-Merrill, 1964), 104.

10. Émile Benveniste, "The Nominal Sentence," chap. 13 of *Problems in General Linguistics,* trans. Mary Elizabeth Meek (Coral Gables, Fla.: University of Miami Press, 1971), 131–32.

11. Ibid., 133–37; my emphasis.

12. Ibid., 140.

13. Ibid., 142–43.

14. Virgil, *The Eclogues and Georgics of Virgil,* ed. Charles Anthon (New York: Harper and Brothers, 1852), 15.

15. Virgil, Eclogue V, trans. Paul Alpers, in Alpers, *The Singer of the Eclogues: A Study of Virgilian Pastoral* (Berkeley: University of California Press, 1979), 32.

## A Letter, a Shadow, and an Interpretive Key

1. André Felibien, "Entretien VIII," in *Entretiens sur les vies et sur les ouvrages des plus excellens peintres anciens et modernes; avec la vie des architectes,* 6 vols. (Trevoux: de la imprimerie de S.A.S., 1725), 4:86–88.

## Theoretical and Methodological Introduction

1. Michael Fried, *Three American Painters: Kenneth Noland, Jules Olitski; Frank Stello* (Meriden, Conn.: Meriden Gravure Co., 1965), 4.

2. Ibid., 5.

3. André Félibien, "Entretien VI," in *Entretiens sur les vies et sur les ouvrages des plus excellens peintres anciens et modernes; avec la vie des architectes,* 6 vols. (Trevoux: de l'imprimerie de S.A.S., 1725), 4:194.

4. Ibid., 4:193–94.

5. The Passage from Pietro Bellori's *Vite de' Pittori, Scultori, et Architetti* (Rome, 1672) appears in translation in Walter Friedlaender's *Caravaggio Studies* (Princeton, N.J.: Princeton University Press, 1955), 245, 247.

6. Francesco Scannelli, *Il Microcosmo della Pittura* (1657), ed. Guido Giubbini (Milan: Edizioni Labor, 1966), 51; my emphasis.

7. Félibien, "Entretien VI," 4:192.

8. Ibid.

9. Margot Cutter, "Caravaggio in the Seventeenth Century," *Marsyas* 1 (1941):89–115.

10. Giovanni Magno, quoted in ibid., 90.

11. Carlo Cesare Malavasia, quoted in ibid., 96.

12. Bellori, quoted in Friedlaender, *Caravaggio Studies* 241.

13. Ibid., 248–49.

14. Giovanni Baglione, cited in Friedlaender, *Caravaggio Studies,* 235–36.

15. Friedlaender, catalogue raisonné, in *Caravaggio Studies,* 157.

16. I am drawing here on Friedlaender's *Caravaggio Studies.*

17. Friedlaender, *Caravaggio Studies,* 88.

18. See Cesare Ripa, *Iconologia* (New York: Garland, 1976), 452.

19. Friedlaender, *Caravaggio Studies,* 88.

20. Ibid., 88–89.

21. Hesiod, *"Theogony" and "Works and Days,"* trans. M. L. West (Oxford: Oxford University Press, 1988), 11.

22. Ovid, *Metamorphoses,* trans. A. D. Melville (Oxford: Oxford University Press, 1986), 98 (4.793–803).

## An Analytic Strategy and a Mythical Ruse

1. Nicolas Poussin, quoted in André Félibien, "Entretien VIII," in *Entretiens sur les vie et sur les ouvrages des plus excellens peintres anciens et modernes; avec la vie des architectes,* 6 vols. (Trevoux: de l'imprimerie de S.A.S., 1725), 4:44.

2. Ovid, *Metamorphoses*, trans. A. D. Melville (Oxford: Oxford University Press, 1986), 97–98 (4.772–78).

3. Ibid., 98 (4.778–80).

4. Ibid. (4.782–83).

5. Ibid. (4.784–86).

6. Ibid. (4.786–88).

7. Marcel Détienne and Jean-Pierre Vernant, *Cunning Intelligence in Greek Culture and Society*, trans. Janet Lloyd (Sussex: Harvester, 1978).

## The Portrait in the Convex Mirror

1. Lucien Dallenbach, *The Mirror in the Text*, trans. Jeremy Whiteley with Emma Hughes (Chicago: University of Chicago Press, 1989), 11.

2. Ibid., 10.

3. Jean-François Lyotard, *Les transformateurs Duchamp* (Paris: Galilée, 1977), 27–28.

4. For an excellent discussion of the concept of *serio ludere*, see Edgar Wind, *Pagan Mysteries in the Renaissance*, new and enlarged ed. (London: Faber and Faber, 1968), esp. chap. 14, "The Concealed God."

5. Erwin Panofsky, *Perspective as Symbolic Form*, trans. Christopher S. Wood (New York: Zone, 1991).

6. Ibid., 31.

7. Ibid.

8. Ibid.

9. Ibid.

10. Ibid., 35.

11. C. A. Dufresnoy, *The Art of Painting*, 2nd ed. trans. Mr. Dryden (London: Printed for Bernard Lintott, 1716), 41, 40; my emphasis.

12. Abraham Bosse, cited in Bernard Teyssèdre, *Roger de Piles et les débats sur le coloris au siècle de Louis XIV* (Paris: Bibliothèque des Arts, 1957), 131.

13. John Pope-Hennessy, *The Portrait in the Renaissance* (New York: Bollingen, 1966), 128–30.

14. Ibid., 122.

15. Ibid., 239.

16. Walter Friedlaender, *Caravaggio Studies* (Princeton, N.J.: Princeton University Press, 1955), 203.

17. Rudolf and Margot Wittkower, *Born under Saturn: The Character and Conduct of Artists* (New York: Random House, 1963), plate 48.

18. Matteo Marangoni, cited in Jean-Claude Lebensztejn, "Au beauty parlor," *Traverses* 7 (1977):76.

19. Lebensztejn, "Au beauty parlour," 76–77.

## Psychoanalytic Interlude

1. Sigmund Freud, "Medusa's Head," in *The Standard Edition of the Complete Psychological Works of Sigmund Freud*, trans. and ed. James Strachey, 24 vols. (London: Hogarth, 1953–74), 18:273–74.

2. Freud, "Negation," in *Standard Edition*, 19:237–38.

3. Ellis Waterhouse, *Italian Baroque Painting* (London: Phaison, 1962), 31; my emphasis.

## Of Light, Shadows, and Narrative

1. Giulio Mancini, *Considerazioni sulla pittura*, ed. Adriana Marucchi, 2 vols. (Rome: Accademia Nazionale dei Lincei, 1956), 1:108–9.

2. Le Brun's "Conference" is recorded in *Conférences de l'Académie Royale de Peinture et de Sculpture pendant l'année 1667*, ed. André Félibien (Paris: F. Leonard, 1669), 85, 98–99.

3. Hubert Damisch, *Théorie du nuage: pour une histoire de la peinture* (Paris: Éditions du Seuil, 1972), 169.

4. Ibid.

5. Abraham Bosse, *Sentimens sur la Distinction des diverses Manières de Peinture*, cited in Bernard Teyssèdre, *Roger de Piles et les débats sur le coloris au siècle de Louis XIV* (Paris: La Bibliothèque des Arts, 1957), 129; my emphasis.

6. Roland Fréart de Chambray, *Idée de la Perfection de la Peinture*, cited in ibid., 129–30.

7. Teyssèdre, *Roger de Piles*, 129–30 n. 4.

8. Bosse, *Le Peintre Converty aux precises et universelles regles de son Art*, cited in ibid., 130 n. 4.

9. Bosse, *Première lettre, de Monsieur du Boccage, à l'Académie*, cited in ibid., 131.

10. Fréart de Chambray's *Idée de la Perfection de la Peinture*, cited in ibid., 130.

11. Teyssèdre is citing Roger de Piles's translation of passages from Dufresnoy's *De Arte Graphica* (*Roger de Piles*, 108).

12. Teyssèdre, *Roger de Piles*, 108.

13. Ibid., 109.

14. Teyssèdre is citing Roger de Piles's translation of this passage from Dufresnoy's *De Arte Graphica* (ibid., 109 no. 3); my emphasis.

15. Roger de Piles, *Remarques*, cited in Teyssèdre, *Roger de Piles*, 112 n. 2, 114.

16. Dufresnoy, *De Arte Graphica*, cited in ibid., 112.

17. Roger de Piles, *Remarques*, cited in ibid., 113.

18. Dufresnoy, *De Arte Graphica*, cited in ibid., 112.

19. Ibid.

20. Roger de Piles, *Remarques*, cited in ibid., 112–13.

21. Teyssèdre, *Roger de Piles*, 113.

22. Ibid., 114.

23. Roger de Piles, *Remarques*, cited in ibid.

24. Teyssèdre, *Roger de Piles*, 114.

25. Roger de Piles, *Remarques*, cited in ibid.

26. Fréart de Chambray, *Traité de la Peinture*, cited in ibid., 114 n. 3.

27. *Oxford Latin Dictionary*, ed. P. G. W. Glare (Oxford: Oxford University Press, 1992), 161–62.

28. Mancini, *Considerazioni sulla pittura*, 108.

29. Nicolas Poussin, "Letter to Roland Fréart de Chambray (Rome, March 1, 1665)," in *A Documentary History of Art*, ed. Elizabeth Gilmore Holt, 2 vols. (Garden City, N.Y.: Doubleday, 1957–58), 2:158.

30. René Descartes, *Discourse on Method, Optics, Geometry, and Meteorology*, trans. Paul J. Olscamp (Indianapolis: Bobbs-Merrill, 1965), 68–69.

# Works Cited

Alberti, Leon Battista. *On Painting*. Trans. John R. Spencer. New Haven, Conn.: Yale University Press, 1966.

Alpers, Paul. *The Singer of the Eclogues: A Study of Virgilian Pastoral*. Berkeley: University of California Press, 1979.

Arnauld, Antoine, and Pierre Nicole. *The Art of Thinking*. Trans. James Dickoff and Patricia James. Indianapolis: Bobbs-Merrill, 1964.

Aristotle. *The Works of Aristotle Translated into English*. Ed. W. D. Ross. Vols. 2 and 3. Oxford: Clarendon, 1930–31.

Benveniste, Émile. *Problems in General Linguistics*. Trans. Mary Elizabeth Meek. Coral Gables, Fla. University of Miami Press, 1971.

———. "Sémiologie de la langue (2)." *Semiotica* 1, no. 2 (1969): 127–35.

Blunt, Anthony. *Nicolas Poussin*. New York: Bollingen, 1967.

———. "Poussin's 'Et in Arcadia Ego.'" *Art Bulletin* 20 (1938): 96–100.

Chateaubriand, François Auguste René. *Génie du christianisme*, Vol. 2. Paris: Le Normant, 1823.

Cutter, Margot. "Caravaggio in the Seventeenth Century." *Marsyas* 1 (1941): 89–115.

Dallenbach, Lucien. *The Mirror in the Text*. Trans. Jeremy Whiteley with Emma Hughes. Chicago: University of Chicago Press, 1989.

Damisch, Hubert. *Théorie du nuage: Pour une histoire de la peinture*. Paris: Éditions du Seuil, 1972.

Descartes, René. *Discourse on Method, Optics, Geometry, and Meteorology*. Trans. Paul J. Olscamp. Indianapolis: Bobbs-Merrill, 1965.

Detienne, Marcel, and Jean-Pierre Vernant. *Cunning Intelligence in Greek Culture and Society*. Trans. Janet Lloyd. Sussex: Harvester, 1978.

Dufresnoy, C. A. *The Art of Painting*. 2d ed. Trans. Mr. Dryden. London: Printed for Bernard Lintott, 1716.

Félibien, André. *Entretiens sur les vies et sur les ouvrages des plus excellens peintres anciens et modernes; avec la vie des architectes*. 6 vols. Trevoux: de l'imprimerie de S.A.S., 1725.

Fénelon, François. *Dialogues des morts*. Vol. 19 of *Oeuvres de Fénelon*. Versailles: J. A. Lebel, 1820–30.

Forcellini, Egidio. *Lexicon Totius Latinitatus ab Aegidio Forcellini*. Vol. 4. Patavii: Gregoriana, 1965.

Freud, Sigmund. "Medusa's Head." In *The Standard Edition of the Complete Psychological Works of Sigmund Freud*. Trans. and ed. James Strachey. Vol. 18. London: Hogarth, 1968.

———. "Negation." In *The Standard Edition of the Complete Psychological Works of Sigmund Freud*. Trans. and ed. James Strachey. Vol. 19. London: Hogarth, 1968.

179

Fried, Michael. *Three American Painters: Kenneth Noland, Jules Olitski, Frank Stella.* Meriden, Conn.: Meriden Gravure Co., 1965.

Friedlaender, Walter. *Caravaggio Studies.* Princeton, N.J.: Princeton University Press, 1955.

Glare, P. G. W., ed. *Oxford Latin Dictionary.* Oxford: Oxford University Press, 1992.

Hesiod. *"Theogony" and"Works and Days."* Trans. M. L. West. Oxford: Oxford University Press, 1988.

Klein, Jerome. "An Analysis of Poussin's *Et in Arcadia Ego.*" *Art Bulletin* 19 (1937): 314–17.

Lebensztejn, Jean-Claude. "Au beauty parlour." *Traverses* 7 (1977).

Le Brun, Charles. "Conférence." In *Conférences de l'Académie Royale de Peinture et de Sculpture pendant l'année 1667.* Ed. André Félibien. Paris: Frédric Leonard, 1669.

Lyotard, Jean-François. *Les transformateurs Duchamp.* Paris: Galilée. 1977.

Mancini, Giulio. *Considerazioni sulla pittura.* Ed. Adriana Marucchi. Vol. 1. Rome: Accademia Nazionale dei Lincei, 1956.

Manetti, Antonio. *Vita di Filippo di Ser Brunellesco.* In *A Documentary History of Art.* Ed. Elizabeth Gilmore Holt. Vol. 1. Garden City, N.Y.: Doubleday, 1957.

Marin, Louis. "À propos d'un carton de Le Brun: Le tableau d'histoire ou la dénégation de l'énonciation." *Revue des sciences humaines* 157 (1975): 41–64.

———. *Critique du Discours, Études sur la Logique de Port-Royal and les Pensées de Pascal.* Paris: Minuit, 1975.

———. "La lecture du tableau d'après Poussin." *Cahiers de l'Association Internationale des Études Françaises* 24 (1972): 251–66.

Marmontel. "Palémon." *Mercure de France* (June 1791): 7–8.

Merleau-Ponty, Maurice. *Phenomenology of Perception.* Trans. Colin Smith. London: Routledge & Kegan Paul, 1962.

Mérot, Alain. *Nicolas Poussin.* New York: Abbeville, 1990.

Ovid. *Metamorphoses.* Trans. A. D. Melville. Oxford: Oxford University Press, 1986.

Panofsky, Erwin. "*Et in Arcadia Ego,* et le tombeau parlant." *Gazette des Beaux-Arts* 1 (1938).

———. *Meaning in the Visual Arts.* New York: Anchor, 1955.

———. *Perspective as Symbolic Form.* Trans. Christopher S. Wood. New York: Zone, 1991.

———. *Philosophy and History: Essays Presented to Ernst Cassirer.* Oxford: Oxford University Press, 1936.

Polybius. *The Histories.* Trans. W. R. Paton. 6 vols. Cambridge, Mass.: Harvard University Press, 1967.

Poussin, Nicolas. *Observations on Painting and Letters.* In *A Documentary History of Art.* Ed. Elizabeth Gilmore Holt. Vol. 2. Garden City, N.Y.: Doubleday, 1958.

Pope-Hennessy, John. *The Portrait in the Renaissance.* New York: Bollingen, 1966.

Quintilian. *The Institutio Oratoria.* Trans. H. E. Butler. Cambridge, Mass.: Harvard University Press, 1979.

Ripa, Cesare. *Iconologia.* New York: Garland, 1976.

Scannelli, Francesco. *Il Microcosmo della Pittura*. Ed. Guido Giubbini. Milan: Edizione Labor, 1966.

Teyssèdre, Bernard. *Roger de Piles et les débats sur le coloris au siècle de Louis XIV*. Paris: Bibliothèque des Arts, 1957.

Vasari, Giorgio. "Preface." In *The Lives of the Painters, Sculptors and Architects*. Trans. A. B. Hinds. London and Toronto: J. M. Dent & Sons, 1927.

Virgil. *The Aeneid*. Trans. C. Day Lewis. London: Hogarth Press, 1961.

———. *The Eclogues and Georgics of Virgil*. Ed. Charles Anthon. New York: Harper, 1852.

Waterhouse, Ellis. *Italian Baroque Painting*. London: Phaidon, 1962.

Weisbach, Werner. "Et in Arcadia Ego. Ein Beitrag zur Interpretation antiker Vorstellungen in der Kunst des 17. Jahrhunderts." *Die Antike* 6 (1930): 127–45.

Wind, Edgar. *Pagan Mysteries in the Renaissance*. New and enl. ed. London: Faber and Faber, 1968.

Wittkower, Rudolf, and Margot Wittkower. *Born under Saturn: The Character and Conduct of Artists*. New York: Random House, 1963.

# Index

Aaron, 77
Achates, 9
Acheron, 9
Aeneas, 7, 9, 11–12
Alberti, Leon Battista, 32, 53
Allori, Christofano, 134
Alphabet, 35, 39. *See also* Félibien
Androgeos, 8
*Apollo and Daphne*, 74. *See also* Poussin
Apuleius, 1
*Arcadian Shepherds, The*, 1, 15–16; and Arcadian landscape, 65–78; and denegation, 26, 45, 64; and divergent conceptions of Arcadia, 79–81; and gazes and questions, 36–39; and interpretation of "Et in Arcadia ego," 79, 81–86, 91–92; as judgment without a verb, 23; and painting as mute poetry, 35; relation to Philippe de Champaigne, 122, 124; and self-effacement of painter and viewer, 32, 40; self-interpreting nature of, 16; and self-reference, 26, 97, 115; and song, 69, 79; and spatio-temporal quasi-synthesis, 63; and structure of represented space, 56–59; as theoretical caprice, 33. *See also* Poussin
Ariadne, 8
Arnobius, 1
Athena, 113–14, 137, 145
d'Aubignac, François Hédelin, 43
Autobiography, enigma of, 40

*Bacchus*, 114, 134. *See also* Caravaggio
Baglione, Giovanni, on Caravaggio, 4, 107, 109, 111, 134
Bellori, Pietro, 81, 100–101, 103, 105–6, 109, 110–12
Benveniste, Émile, 2; and closure of representation, 26; on distinction between narrative and discourse, 24; on "I" and "thou," 119; on nominal sentences, 84–90; and Port-Royal, 25; on

semantics and metasemantics of systems of representation, 16–17; on tense, 83
Berkeley, George, 60–61
Bernini, Gian Lorenzo, 93
Berzé-la-ville, 139
Blunt, Anthony, 74, 81
Boas, G., 80
Bosse, Abraham, 130–31, 153–54, 156, 158
*Boy Bitten by a Lizard*, 114. *See also* Caravaggio
Brunellesco, Filippo, 45–48, 152

*Calling of Saint Matthew, The*, 1, 167. *See also* Caravaggio
Caprice: *The Arcadian Shepherds* as, 33; Marin's theoretical narrative as, 33
Caravaggio, Michelangelo da, 4; and criticism, 107; and the destruction of painting, 3, 6, 28–29, 110–12, 115, 150, 158, 164; and the force of color, 106; and paradox, 162; and the privileging of the surface, 108; and the production of effects of seeing, 105; and his relation to Poussin, 3–5, 28, 99, 109; school of, 48; and self-portraits, 114, 132, 134–35, 142; and simulacra, 100–102. *See also Bacchus; Boy Bitten by a Lizard; The Calling of Saint Matthew; The Conversion of Saint Paul; The Crucifixion of Saint Peter; David with the Head of Goliath; Death of the Virgin; The Decapitation of Saint John the Baptist; The Head of Medusa; Judith Beheading Holofernes; The Lute Player; The Martyrdom of Saint Matthew; The Musicians; The Resurrection of Lazarus; The Sacrifice of Isaac*
Carracci, Annibale, 137–38
Ceto, 113
Chambray, Roland Fréart de, 153, 156, 159

183